Anonymous

Ecce Clerus

The Christian Minister in Many Lights

Anonymous

Ecce Clerus
The Christian Minister in Many Lights

ISBN/EAN: 9783337027834

Printed in Europe, USA, Canada, Australia, Japan

Cover: Foto ©ninafisch / pixelio.de

More available books at **www.hansebooks.com**

ECCE CLERUS

OR

THE CHRISTIAN MINISTER IN MANY LIGHTS

BY

A STUDENT OF THE TIMES

NEW YORK: EATON & MAINS
CINCINNATI: CURTS & JENNINGS
1899

TO THE MEMBERS OF HIS HOUSEHOLD,

TO WHOM

DURING MANY YEARS OF

VARIED LITERARY AND MINISTERIAL LABOR

HE HAS BEEN INDEBTED

FOR MUCH HELP AND MANY COMFORTS,

THIS VOLUME

IS AFFECTIONATELY DEDICATED

BY THE AUTHOR.

PREFACE

THIS treatise is an attempt to deal with some pressing present-day problems having their incidence within the sphere of religion and holding peculiarly intimate relation to the ministerial calling. Fidelity to its aim in this regard makes it a more or less free and candid criticism of the spirit, status, functions, methods, and achievements of the Christian ministry, viewed in the light of the New Testament and the special requirements of the age. Some of its chapters were read as essays within recent years at meetings of evangelical associations, pastors' unions, and other ministerial gatherings held in various cities of the United States where the author has resided, exciting at the time considerable discussion, and eliciting a wide variety of opinion on the questions mooted. Such was the case with Chapters V, VI, VIII, and X, dealing respectively with "The Theme of Preaching," "The Bugbear of the Modern Evangelical Pulpit," "The Ministry and the Masses," "The Itinerant Ministry and the Settled Pastorate Compared and Contrasted."

The book is a word from the watchtower of a waning century—a century whose significance for science, philosophy, invention, for historical and critical research, for commercial expansion and industrial development, for moral, social, and penal reform, for educational, religious, and political progress, is probably greater than that of any two preceding centuries which have contributed any kind of a record to the annals of the world.

In the nature of things the retrospect and outlook obtained from the point of elevation on which the closing year of such a century places us could not but be broad, varied, and profoundly interesting. And it would be wonderful indeed if many dogmas in every department of thought did not seem different to us near its close from what they appeared to those whose mature life was lived at its beginning. With one feature only—though an immensely important one—of the general forecast thus obtained, namely, with religion in its administrative and practical aspect, is the present treatise concerned.

Though thus restricted in their scope, however, it is possible that many of the views which find expression in this volume may provoke demurrer, some on account of their novelty and strangeness, others on account of their extreme conservatism. The writer has only to say that, in either case, what he has written simply expresses his well-considered and mature convictions, and for these, as being part and parcel of his intellectual individuality, whether they be right or wrong, he can hardly be expected to apologize.

Like every other period of the world's history, only perhaps in intenser degree, the times we are passing through are transitional. A quiet but profound change has been and is taking place in opinion on many subjects, and there is a natural preference, even in departments of thought and belief not seriously influenced by such change, to have even old truths presented in the intellectual vogue and fashion of the time. The *Ewiggeist* and *Zeitgeist*—the Eternal Spirit and the Time Spirit—are not necessarily at war. They are only irreconcilable when the latter, instead of taking its cue and complexion from the former, assumes to be the dominant and determining factor. The author, while putting in a plea along with many of his contemporaries for the retention of old truths, beliefs, and institutions, earnestly desires their rehabilitation and forcible presentment in forms adapted to the needs of a busy, enterprising, inquisitive, and restless age, and he will be happy if, in any degree, his work shall prove an effective, even though nameless and impersonal, appeal of the spirit of eternity to the spirit of time. It may be that in the revolution that has for some time been proceeding in the domain of science, philosophy, historical method, and religion some opinions and doctrines of frail foundation and doubtful value have gone or are going, but the eternal facts and verities of religion—"the things which cannot be shaken"—remain. Religious doctrines and institutions emerge from times of criticism and controversy in altered shape, but the change does not reduce their value or their necessity to the spiritual life of man. And so long as it is an imperative requirement confronting those who propose by new creeds—gnostic or agnostic—to supplant Christianity in the faith and affections of mankind that they "go and get themselves crucified," there is no real ground for alarm.

CONTENTS

CHAPTER   PAGE

I. THE CHRISTIAN MINISTRY CONSIDERED AS A FACTOR IN THE CIVILIZATION OF THE WORLD.
   1. The Birth of a New Moral Force.............................. 13
   2. A New and Nobler Doctrine of Human Destiny.......... 18
   3. The Preacher's Distinctive Gift................................ 19
   4. The Secret of His Power.. 21
   5. Notable Examples.. 25
   6. Measurable Progress.. 29

II. DOMINATION OF TYPE IN THE MINISTRY.
   1. Rise of Type.. 34
   2. Its Forms Pronounced.. 35
   3. Its Rule, Rigid and Absolute.................................. 42
   4. Application of the Screw...................................... 44
   5. Neither Breadth nor Sublimity in Liberalism............ 54
   6. Manifest Destiny of the Ministry............................ 56

III. THE MINISTER IN THE MAKING.
   1. The Raw Material... 59
   2. The Molding of Environment................................ 70
   3. The Training of the Schools, which
      (1) Must adapt itself to conditions of the age.......... 75
      (2) Must not be fearful of science nor jealous of man's intellectual freedom.......................... 77
      (3) Must be varied, comprehensive, and thorough..... 80
      (4) Hence, fitted to impart the secret of power required by the times.................................... 84

IV. THE CARDINAL FUNCTIONS AND LEADING REQUISITES OF THE CHRISTIAN MINISTER.
   1. Proclaiming the Evangel...................................... 86
   2. Christ the Prince of Heralds.................................. 88
   3. Manhood is Requisite.. 90
   4. Conviction is Indispensable.................................. 93
   5. Persuasive Power.. 95
   6. Definiteness of Aim.. 98

CHAPTER	PAGE
7. A Standing Attestation of the Spirituality of the Christian Religion	99

V. THE THEME OF PREACHING.
1. The Only Saving Name 105
2. The Person of Christ 106
3. Our Great Exemplar 110
4. Teacher of His People 113
5. Pacifex Maximus 116
6. Pledge of Our Completed Manhood 121
7. "Our Most Worthy Judge Eternal" 123

VI. THE BUGBEAR OF THE PRESENT-DAY EVANGELICAL PULPIT.
1. An Important Question 126
2. Significance and Bearings of the Inquiry 128
3. Doctrine of Future Retribution, no Figment of Mediæval Fancy 129
4. No Lack of Definite Statement in the New Testament.. 130
5. The Doctrine Essential to a Complete and Well-articulated System of Christian Truth—Fourfold Apocalypse 133
6. No Theodicy in Science 135
7. Causes Operating toward Alleged Neglect:
   (1) The absence of any vivid sense of sin 137
   (2) The tendency of reason to usurp the place of faith.. 138
   (3) General theological unsettledness 139

VII. HOMILETICAL CRAFTSMANSHIP.
1. Personality of the Craftsman 146
2. Power of the Ideal in Sermon-making 148
3. Unity of Theme and Thought 151
4. Selection of Materials 153
5. Simplicity of Structure 156
6. Homeliness of Illustration 158
7. Adaptedness to the Spiritual Needs of the People... 162

VIII. THE CHRISTIAN MINISTRY AND THE MASSES.
1. Condition of the Masses 165
2. The Problem Stated 171
3. Failure of the Church to Solve the Problem 174
4. Remedies Suggested 177
5. The True Solution 183

IX. MISSIONS AND MISSIONARIES OF THE TWENTIETH CENTURY.
1. Christianity an Apocalypse 192

CHAPTER	PAGE
2. A Hundred Years of Missions	194
3. Present Outlook	198
(1) Educated heathen assume the rôle of reformer and apologist	198
(2) Adopt a policy of imitation	200
(3) Try the old experiment of persecution	201
4. Policy of Success	203
(1) There must be careful study of ethnic systems and the relation of Christianity thereto	203
(2) Such systems must be contemplated not as rehabilitated by philosophic genius, but in their stay-at-home aspect and attire, and in their practical tendencies and actual effects on the lives and morals of their votaries	205
(3) There must be adaptation of teaching to various heathen types, as affected by race, religion, historical antecedents, present political condition, degree of civilization reached, etc	209
(4) Missionaries must not lose sight of the primary object—the evangelization and salvation of heathen peoples	211
(5) Must make larger and freer concessions to the intellectual idiosyncrasies and social usages and customs of heathen communities	214

X. THE ITINERANT AND SETTLED PASTORATES COMPARED AND CONTRASTED.

1. The Itinerant Ministry not an Institution of Modern Origin	218
2. Founder of the Methodist Itinerancy	220
3. Itinerancy Defensible on the Plea of Past Utility and of High and Ancient Example	221
4. Develops a Noble Type of Character and a Fine Sense of Brotherhood	224
5. Present Practical Value, an Item Worthy of Attention	227
6. Drawbacks as Compared with the Settled Pastorate	230

XI. THE POPULAR PREACHER.

1. Popular Eloquence not the Primary Qualification of the Christian Preacher	235
2. Popularity no Infallible Sign of Public Usefulness	239
3. Antipopular Elements Inhere in the Essence of Christianity	242
4. Christianity Nevertheless a Religion for the People	248

CHAPTER	PAGE
5. Elements of Power..................................	248

XII. THE MINISTER IN AUTHORITY.
    1. No Divinely Authorized Form of Ecclesiastical Polity... 251
    2. Early Christian Leaders Indifferent as to Names, Titles, and Specific Forms of Ecclesiastical Authority....... 253
    3. The New Testament Doctrine of Authority............ 256
    4. Forms of the Embodiment of Authority in Apostolic and Subapostolic Times................................ 259
    5. Abuse of Power..................................... 263

XIII. SOME ELEMENTS AND PHASES OF MINISTERIAL LIFE AND CHARACTER.
    1. Past and Present..................................... 276
    2. Facing Initial Difficulties............................ 279
    3. The Consciousness of Worth......................... 284
    4. The Courage of Conviction.......................... 286
    5. The Sense of Humor, Pathos, and Romance........... 288

XIV. MINISTERIAL HEALTH AND HYGIENE.
    1. Importance of Attention to Hygiene.................. 296
    2. Influence of Health on Character and Temperament.... 297
    3. The Inner World of Thought and Feeling Acted on by the Outer World.................................... 298
    4. Health and Longevity Largely within the Limits of Individual Control 301
    5. Moral Value to the Minister of Sound Bodily Health.... 303
    6. Notable Instances of Early Physical Breakdown........ 304
    7. Necessity of Regular and Systematic Exercise.......... 310
    8. Benefits Secured Amply Compensate for Cost in Time .. 311
    9. Errors to be Shunned................................ 313
    10. Physical Gifts and Graces not to be Despised.......... 315

XV. THE MINISTER IN AGE, RETIREMENT, AND DEATH.
    1. Retiring to the Shadows............................. 316
    2. Premature Senility................................... 317
    3. Verdure and Sunshine on Autumn Hills............... 319
    4. The Glow of Sunset................................. 328
    5. He Being Dead yet Speaketh........................ 333

ECCE CLERUS

OR

THE CHRISTIAN MINISTER IN MANY LIGHTS

CHAPTER I

The Christian Ministry Considered as a Factor in the Civilization of the World

Christ came. The soul the most full of love, the most sacredly virtuous, the most deeply inspired by God and the future that men have yet seen on earth; Jesus. He bent over the corpse of the dead world and whispered a word of faith; over the clay that had lost all of man but the movement and the form; he uttered words until then unknown—*love, sacrifice, a heavenly origin*. And the dead arose. A new life circulated through the clay which philosophy had tried in vain to reanimate. From that corpse arose the Christian world; the world of liberty and equality. From that clay arose the true man, the image of God, the precursor of humanity.—*Joseph Mazzini*.

§. The Birth of a New Moral Force.

THE birth of Christian civilization, properly so called, was coincident with the beginning of preaching, and the leading factor in the moral and intellectual progress of mankind, since the hour when "times of refreshing" began to be given "from the presence of the Lord," has been the Christian ministry in all that wide and varied field of activity and conquest in which it has progressively unfurled the flag of occupation. The walls of the "City of God" (ἡ πόλισ ἡ ἁγία of St. John) only began to be builded when the fisherman Simon, having discovered by dint of superior prophetic insight the superhuman nature and quality of its great Corner Stone, exhorted his expatriated co-religionists, many of whom had been drawn to Jerusalem from their far-away homes for the celebration of the feasts of Passover and Pentecost, to take advantage of the favored moment that was upon them to secure a personal and experimental initiation into "the mysteries of the kingdom of God."

The special feature which was permanently to distinguish the Christian Church and the new order of things it represented, not only from the temple and synagogue and the social and religious ideas for which they stood, but also from the philosophical schools and religious cults of paganism, was the revival, rehabilitation, and wider distribution of the prophetic faculty of which in the Jewish Church there had been no trace for hundreds of years. Careful students and diligent redactors of the inspired records like Ezra had not been wanting. Distinguished scholars like Simon the Just, Hillel, Shammai, and Gamaliel had appeared. Pious patriots like the Maccabees, daring and devout enthusiasts like Bar-Cochba, saintly souls like the aged Simeon, whose attitude of prayer and earnestness of hope prepared them to perceive and welcome the earliest rays of Him who was to be at once a light lifting the veil of darkness from the nations ($\phi\tilde{\omega}\varsigma\ \varepsilon\dot{\iota}\varsigma\ \dot{\alpha}\pi o\kappa\dot{\alpha}\lambda v\psi\iota v\ \dot{\varepsilon}\vartheta v\tilde{\omega}v$) and the consolation and glory of his people Israel—of these, also, there had been many during the post-exilic ages; but there had been no soul endowed with the penetrating insight and bold utterance of the ancient seer—with that liberty and faculty of prophesying which is the first essential qualification of the Christian herald and teacher, enabling him to influence the life, thought, and motive of the individual and the community at their hidden springs. The nation in its age of decrepitude had wandered for more than four hundred years in a moral and intellectual desert, barer and drearier than that in which, according to its traditional and accepted records, it had spent forty years of its youth. During this unproductive period men had been subsisting timidly and doubtfully on the sacred *depositum* of the past—on manna grown stale and innutritive with age. The ripest wisdom of those gloomy centuries found expression in the three cautious and conservative principles attributed to the men of the *Great Assembly:* "Be discreet in judging; train up many scholars; make a hedge around the law." As Bishop Westcott remarks: "The fence was necessary because the law was not only fixed, but dying. Religion seemed capable of being defined by rule; duty had ceased to be infinite."* The sorrows and disappointments already encountered not only gave a somber color and complexion to the passing phase of national history, but also tinctured with melancholy and despair every forecast of the future.

And not alone in the dismal traditions of the Talmud, but in the apocryphal literature also, this spirit of apprehension and despondency is apparent. "Behold," says the author of the (so-called) Fourth Book of Esdras, "the days shall come that . . . the way of truth shall be hidden and the land shall be destitute of faith (*sterilis erit a fide*). . . . Then shall wit hide itself and understanding withdraw into secret chambers, and shall be sought of many and yet not found. . . . For the world hath lost his youth and the times begin to wax old."† No more was the living prophetic word spoken for the edification, guidance, comfort of the people of God. The light of inspiration was withdrawn. The seer's vision had vanished. The sacred oracle was dumb.

Beyond the pale of Judaism "outer darkness" was the phrase not inaptly applied to the moral and social condition of the nations. In the course of the seven centuries that had passed since the founding of the city, Rome had marched her legions from the Tiber to the Rhine and the Danube in the north, and had made herself mistress of the fair and fruitful regions lying between those rivers. Southward she had extended her empire as far as Mount Atlas and the

---

* *Introduction to the Study of the Gospels*, p. 61.   † *Ibid.*, p. 111.

cataracts of the Nile; west and east from the waves of the Atlantic to the banks of the Euphrates. Universal empire was her ambition, and war and conquest the means ruthlessly employed to gratify it. During the thirty years of our Lord's quiet and secluded life in Nazareth the theater of war extended over considerable portions of Asia and Africa, and the Emperor Tiberius found nothing worthier of his restless energy than holding Europe, from the Adriatic Sea to the skirts of the Black Forest, in the flames of a deadly, continuous, all-consuming strife.*

And the people who were harassed and plundered by Rome in time of war were hardly worse off than those who were ruled by her in times of peace. Romans of the patrician grade who had squandered their patrimony and private fortunes by dissipation in the city were accustomed to look to proconsulship in the provinces as a means of replenishing their exhausted treasures and retrieving their social position. Leaving Rome deeply involved in debt, they often in three years—the limit of their term of service—returned home the envied possessors of enormous wealth. They were allowed to prey upon the defenseless peoples without check or restraint, and grew rich by extortion and fraud. † When Tiberius asked Bato the Dalmatian why he made war on the Romans the brave barbarian indignantly replied,. "You affect to treat every nation as your flocks and your property, but you intrust the care of them to ravenous wolves and not to shepherds and their dogs." The masters of the world oppressed and fleeced the vanquished races over whom they exercised control, and for their temerity often had to pay dearly out of the best blood of their free citizens. "*O tempora! O mores!*" is Cicero's lament over the social and political degeneracy of

---

* See A. Ferguson, *History of the Roman Republic*, p. 444.
† See art. "The Fall of the Roman Empire," by Thomas Hodgkin, in *Contemporary Review*, January, 1898.

an age of which Sallust's Sempronia and his own relentless and unprincipled adversary, Cataline, were unexaggerated types.* "Hardly any of the elements of an unsound state of society were absent."†

Upon such a condition of affairs both within and outside the household of the chosen people there suddenly broke from the Judean wilderness the startling announcement of the herald of the New Covenant: "The time is fulfilled; the kingdom of God is at hand. Repent ye and believe the good news." The dispensation of the Christian prophet and proclaimer (κῆρυξ) had dawned. At the very outstart of his great work of "preparing the way of the Lord" the Baptist proved the genuineness of his commission quite as much by his tender reverence for the truth, purity, and beauty of the past as by his courageous and condemnatory attitude toward the sin and error of the present. He at once set suspicion at rest by assuming the integrity and continuity of God's purpose, and by exemplifying in himself the close and vital relation that subsists between the successive stages of God's work through all the world's ages. He took up the broken thread of prophecy just where it had been dropped. In his dress, diet, and chosen haunts, as well as in his teaching, he harked back to an earlier time, recalling the striking figure, the simple manner, the heroic spirit, and the divine mission of Elijah. While showing that the old prophetic word had a wider scope and a deeper import than had heretofore been thought of, he claimed for it at least a partial and provisional fulfillment in what was taking place around him. The Gospel dispensation, with its roots in the past, was the introduction of a new order of things. It inaugurated the reign of moral forces. Through its simple and unostentatious ministry it placed before the eyes of men the most exalted of ethical ideals, and subjected the popular

---

* *Oratio Prima. Contra Cat.*
† E. Hatch, D.D., *Organization of the Early Christian Churches*, p. 32.

2

mind to the direct action of the noblest and most elevating of intellectual and spiritual influences in a manner and to a degree never before possible. It was essentially a call to repentance.

2. A New and Nobler Doctrine of Human Destiny.

To mold the living character and control the present conduct of mankind by means of motives mainly drawn from a world out of sight had always been a difficult undertaking, and one which, so far as it had been tried, had never been attended with any marked success. As a matter of fact, during the Old Testament ages the experiment had seldom or never been attempted on any appreciable scale. The considerations by which poet, priest, prophet, and lawgiver had endeavored to move men to sentiments of piety and praiseworthy moral exertions were almost exclusively of a temporal nature. The strain of exhortation invariably ran as in the extremely beautiful words of Eliphaz the Temanite in the Book of Job: "Acquaint now thyself with him, and be at peace: thereby good shall come unto thee [mark what kind of good]. Receive, I pray thee, the law from his mouth, and lay up his words in thine heart. If thou return to the Almighty, thou shalt be built up, thou shalt put away iniquity far from thy tabernacles. Then shalt thou lay up gold as dust, and the gold of Ophir as the stones of the brooks. Yea, the Almighty shall be thy defense, and thou shalt have plenty of silver. For then shalt thou have thy delight in the Almighty, and shalt lift up thy face unto God. Thou shalt make thy prayer unto him, and he shall answer thee, and thou shalt pay thy vows. Thou shalt also decree a thing, and it shall be established unto thee: and the light shall shine upon thy ways."*

---

* Job xxii, 21-30. To whatever period in the development of the Old Testament literature this noblest of ancient poems may be assigned, it still remains a typical expression of the ethical spirit of the Hebrew people during the whole of their eventful history.

Rare were the souls who were capable of discerning the inner beauty and intrinsic blessedness of the divine service, of perceiving the limitless scope it offers for the growth and development of man's higher nature, and of choosing it for its own sake, regardless of its apparent temporal disadvantages, on the one hand, or its obvious present recompense, on the other. But the capability of appreciating this loftier plea of faith—the argument drawn exclusively from the nature, needs, dignity, and unmeasured capacity of the soul—and of building on the higher ground is to be the rule rather than the exception under the *régime* of him who has "brought life and immortality to light through his Gospel." Those who habitually think and act in presence of the eternal future, and in lively anticipation of its promised good, are to have, by virtue of their spiritual insight and elevation, the greatest power to influence and control the present. The princes of the spiritual empire are they who steadily subordinate the visible to the invisible, the essentially provisional to the essentially permanent. The wisest and noblest are ordained to reign. The meek are to inherit the earth ; the saints are to judge the world.

3. The Preacher's Distinctive Gift.

The preacher's significance and value, therefore, for his particular age—his power to mold its life and thought—lies in the fact that as one possessing prophetic and interpretive insight, he is authorized boldly to proclaim the mind and will of God. He discerns in the interminable and apparently aimless conflict in which generation after generation eagerly expends its thought and energy, the working of eternal principles which make for righteousness, and is able to forecast and foretell the general issue with absolute certainty. He looks far behind him for hints of action and clews of guidance, and far before him for his goal. He sees, as it were, the dark veil that persistently clings to the face of things partially removed, so that the grand motives and issues of life stand disclosed in their eternal nature. For him spiritual truth, moral beauty, enduring blessedness, though concealed, yet essentially exist beneath the suffering, sorrow, sin, and disorder which are spread over the world within and the world without—over man and over nature. In the incarnate Son of God he sees the great Prophet of all time. In his spotless and perfect humanity he sees the glorious possibility which lies back of all the degradation, ignorance, and misery of the race. He discerns in him who "lighteth every man coming into the world" the true moral dignity and completeness of man's nature, and is encouraged to hope for his restoration to personal holiness and to perfect harmony with God. Studying carefully the great moral conflict going on around him, he perceives, with increasing vividness, the spirits of men, their motives and aims, the springs of individual and national life, till all the relations of time no longer exist in his vision, till all passing strife is referred to the final conflict of good and evil, foreshadowed in the great judgments of the world, and all hope is centered in the triumph of Christ and in the completion and fullness of his kingdom. He thus draws hope and inspiration from the certainties of the future in fighting the seemingly doubtful battle of the present. He appeals "from Philip drunk to Philip sober;" from the delusive dream and specious appearance of the moment to the eternal reality; meanwhile resting confidently in the grand conviction of

> One God, one law, one element,
> And one far-off divine event
> To which the whole creation moves.

4. The Secret of His Power.

And precisely in proportion to the closeness and fidelity with which the influence of the preacher on the intellectual problems and social and political life of his time has conformed to the type of Christ it has been deep, all-pervasive, fruitful, and enduring.

Offering himself freely for service or sacrifice, as the bond-slave (ὁ δοῦλος) * of his Master, he has been, in proportion to the completeness of his self-subjugation and self-surrender, the salt of society and the salvation and enrichment of the world. He has won an empire whose scepter has not dropped from his grasp with the dissolution of his earthly being. His influence for good, as one who has worthily occupied a place, however lowly and obscure, in "the glorious company of the prophets," abides. Like the morning star, his modest fame does not go down

> Behind the darkened west,
> Nor hide obscure amid the tempests of the sky,
> But melts away into the light of heaven.

He ascends to join the "choir invisible" and take rank with

> Those immortal dead who live again
> In minds made better by their presence; live
> In pulses stirred to generosity,
> In deeds of daring rectitude; in scorn
> Of miserable aims that end with self;
> In thoughts sublime that pierce the night like stars,
> And with their mild persistence urge men's minds
> To vaster issues.

His allotted sphere has been now narrow and circumscribed, confined to the care of a handful of souls; now indefinitely extended so as to be ecumenical, including "all people that on earth do dwell," like the wisest and the noblest of the popes of Rome. He has spoken for the instruction of mankind from within the walls of a prison, like St. Paul from the traditional Mamertine, or Bunyan from the overcrowded and insalubrious dungeon that once stood on the piers of the old Ouse bridge at Bedford, or St. Cyran, encouraging, counseling, directing, the Port Royalists from

---

* This is the significant and deliberately chosen term used by the apostles to express their personal relation to Christ. Christianity dignified service. A word which signified the lowest degradation among men became, under its teaching, a term of highest honor in the kingdom of God.

his captivity at Vincennes. He has found his chosen empire in some dismal cave, like St. Jerome's retreat at Bethlehem, or in some lonesome haunt of the forest, like that of Peter the Hermit near mediæval Amiens. He has been hunted into exile like Cyprian, Athanasius, and Chrysostom. He has voluntarily immured himself within the walls of a monastery, self-bound thereto by ascetic vow, or romantic sentiment, or religious love of solitude stronger than chains or bars or doors of iron, like the earlier and later founders of the Benedictine rule, like the Bernards of Clairvaux and Cluny and the lofty souls that made Port Royal famous, such as Arnauld and Pascal. He has found the weapon of his spiritual warfare in the gift of tongues or the translator's pen, like the author of the Vulgate, the Gothic Bishop Ulphilas, Wyclif, Tyndale, Luther, and the learned and devout De Saci, who toiled for years at his incomparable French version amid the gloom of the Bastile. He has constructed systems of theology which have tinctured the faith, colored the creeds, and controlled the thought of Christendom for centuries, like Augustine, Aquinas, Anselm, and Calvin. He has contributed to the growing light and freedom of the world from the pulpit, like the "Golden-mouth" of Antioch and Byzantium, like Basil, Savonarola, Knox, Whitefield, and Chalmers; or from the bishop's throne, like Leo I, Gregory I, and Gregory VII; or from the professor's chair, like Melanchthon at Wittenburg, with two thousand of the noblest youth of Europe at his feet, and Arminius at Leyden, elaborating, amid the fierce fires of enmity and intemperate controversy, a reasonable and credible doctrine of God and of redemption for the religious mind of our time, and Schleiermacher in Berlin recalling the attention of his countrymen to the heart and essence of religion in his *Reden über die Religion*, thus reviving for a moment the dying faith of the Fatherland, and Neander in the same university resisting the onslaught of Tübingen criticism with its own chosen weapons. He has relieved the cares and sorrows of the hearthstone and brought a ray of heavenly light to the bedside of the sick and dying, like Richard Baxter, Samuel Rutherford, and Jonathan Edwards, and a thousand other faithful pastors who have played the part of "sons of consolation" to their people. He has organized world-embracing crusades for the salvation of the neglected masses of the people, like General Booth ; or started an evangelizing impulse which remains unspent after the lapse of a hundred and fifty years, like John Wesley. He has made the world better and brighter for the songs he has sung, like George Herbert, Isaac Watts, John Newton, Bishop Ken, John Keble, and Charles Wesley, whose hymns have helped to enrich the religious life and experience of thousands. By the force of his character as a spiritual man, by the depth and strength of his convictions as a diligent student of God's word, by the loftiness of his calling as the spokesman of heaven, by the intimate relation between his official duties and the most vital concerns of those who have confided in him as their spiritual counselor and guide, he has been able to mold individual character, to influence public sentiment, and to largely shape the destiny of nations. He has been the steadfast friend of popular enlightenment, freedom, and reform, and the foe alike of private wickedness and public wrong. He has enriched the world's literature with books of lasting fame and value, has averted social and political disaster, crowned and discrowned kings,* arrested the triumphant march of conquerors,† and made powerful tyrants

---

* Apart from the subjugation of Henry IV by Hildebrand, "a king of England consented to hold his kingdom as a fief from the pontiff's hand . . . a king of Aragon resigned his realms to the apostle Peter, and Naples beheld her throne conferred by the same all-commanding power on a family wholly foreign to her soil."—Ranke's *History of the Popes*, vol. i, p. 23.

† "Already Attila had reduced Aquileia to a heap of ruins and driven her people to seek shelter for themselves in the lagoons of the Adriatic, where they founded the famous city of Venice. He now resolved to force his way over the Apennines . . . and pass in vengeful triumph up the sacred way which had seen the imperial people trample for so many centuries upon the necks of barbaric kings. Rome, however, deemed it best to anticipate Attila's arrival, and sent an embassy to deprecate the victor's wrath,

turn pale and tremble at his words.* He has not talked about new heavens and a new earth "wherein dwelleth righteousness" without putting forth strenuous personal efforts to realize the golden dream, nor gone about with preoccupied air, ultra-solemn mood and mien, cold, narrow, self-absorbed, supramundane, intolerant of the erring, impatient of the weak, indifferent to the anxieties and sorrows of the poor, contemptuous of the sins and follies of the proud and powerful, as if he were something far

> too wise or good
> For human nature's daily food.†

There have been occasionally prominent in the ministry and service of the Church, it is true, men of earthly and alien spirit, swayed by the love of power and public fame, fond of the tinsel and glitter of material wealth, of social prestige and distinction, preferring "fleshly wisdom" to the "simplicity of Christ," and willing, in despite of that apostolic touchstone, "As many as are led by the Spirit of God they are the sons of God," to employ the dubious arts of intrigue, diplomacy, and double dealing. There have been shepherds of crime and blood and violence like Alexander Borgia, Julius II, Clement VII, and Innocent III, who offered thanks publicly to heaven for the massacre of the Huguenots; and successors of St. Peter steeped in low, sensual pleasures like Leo X—men who have brought dis-

---

the principal place in which was occupied by the venerable pontiff Leo I, canonized by the Church of Rome with the name of 'Great.' Leo was a man of rare ability, eloquence, firmness, and knowledge of the times. In the curious taste of his day he was styled the Cicero of Catholic rhetoric, the Homer of theology," etc.—Sheppard's *Fall of Rome*, p. 207.

* Lorenzo de' Medici entreating Savonarola to moderate the tone of his denunciations is a case in point.

† A stenographic report of a speech delivered in Wilmington, Del., by a recent candidate for the presidency of the United States makes him to use the following language of "some ministers of the Gospel:" "Tell them the people are hungry and starving, and that men out of work are driven into crime, and they cannot understand why everybody is not as well off as they are. . . . The common people were never aided in their struggle upward by those who were so far beyond them that they could not feel their needs and sympathize with their distress." The character here alluded to has always existed, especially in prosperous and luxurious times, but everything is against his ever becoming a prevailing type.

credit on their profession and reproach and scandal to the
Church. There have been those who, while publicly and
professionally magnifying divine truths and exalting spiritual virtues as worthy always of an immediate and prime
consideration, have personally treated them as of less than
second-rate consequence, thus producing irritation, resentment, and confusion in men's minds, or bringing about the
still worse result of swelling the ranks of the already large
army of cynics, infidels, and atheists, and giving pertinence
to the words addressed by Ophelia to her brother Laertes,
when he sought with some excellent counsels to fortify her
virtue and womanhood against possible temptation:

> I shall the effect of this good lesson keep,
> As watchman to my heart. But, good my brother,
> Do not, as some ungracious pastors do,
> Show me the steep and thorny way to heaven;
> Whiles like a puffed and reckless libertine,
> Himself the primrose path of dalliance treads,
> And recks not his own rede.

Of these hirelings of the fold it may be affirmed that they
entered not by the door of the sheep, but climbed up some
other way. Their claim to a recognized place in the great
brotherhood of believers is disputed, and an impartial yet
exacting posterity offers to their memory nothing but the
doubtful tribute of a sincere regret that, sharing the honor
of the loftiest calling and the stimulus of the greatest possibilities, they despised their day of opportunity and played
the part of the unworthy.

5. Notable Examples.

That the force and effectiveness of the Christian religion
as a civilizing factor has ever been proportioned to the
fidelity of its ministry and discipleship to its central idea—
its one imperative requirement—a severe and self-restrain-
ing yet self-oblivious and cheerful purity of heart and life,
history bears ample and indisputable witness. Herein has

lain the simple and sure solution of every problem—social, industrial, ethical, religious—that has seriously engaged the attention and thought of mankind. The quiet and unostentatious martyrdom or witness-bearing of noble natures such as Wesley, Spurgeon, Finney, Müller, has given men within the limits of a human lifetime a deeper and truer estimate of the practical value of truth and righteousness than science, philosophy, and theology combined, supported by all the aids and arts of eloquence and the powerful prestige and sanction of the schools, have imparted in the course of centuries. The world owes, to-day, a deeper debt of gratitude to the man who, clad in the coarse garb of the desert and sustained by its homely fare, said, at the cost of his head, to a licentious despot, "It is not lawful for thee to have her," than to the man who stood in holy places, wore sacred vestments, was the recipient of great public veneration as the high-priestly head of the Jewish Church, and saw the authority of the "ten holy words" trampled in the dust without a syllable of protest. And while among the most precious of the world's literary treasures, sacred or profane, none has a higher value than the writings of the man who esteemed himself "less than the least of all saints," the world has been willing to forget the very name of the magnate to whom unwittingly, in a moment of noble indignation, he said, "God shall smite thee, thou whited wall." * The royal science of religious thought, not less than the present spiritual condition of Christendom, is more indebted to Athanasius, harassed, persecuted, impoverished, evil-spoken of, three times banished from his attached people and from the work he loved so well, than to the tall, handsome, eloquent presbyter † whose

---

* Acts xxiii, 3.
† By orthodox writers of this day Arius is described as tall of stature, with a downcast look, and "a figure composed like that of a subtle serpent to deceive the guileless by his crafty exterior." Epiphanius speaks of him as simple in his attire, with an address "soft and smooth, calculated to persuade and attract, so that he had drawn

praises were sung in the streets, in serio-comic strains of his own composing, by the women and children of Alexandria.* As far as a fragrant memory and an enduring fame are concerned, there are few persons who would not prefer the fate of the devout, labor-loving, narrow-minded Cyprian, obliged on account of the Decian and later persecutions to supervise his diocese from a place of concealment,† and ultimately condemned to a martyr's death as an enemy to the gods of Rome and her religious laws (*inimicus Diis Romanis et sacris legibus*),‡ to the easy and luxurious life of the affable, diplomatic, liberal-minded Eusebius of Nicomedia, or of him of Cæsarea, basking in the smiles of Constantine, and betraying "the faith once delivered to the saints" and the interests of the "kingdom" which is "not of this world" into the hands of the emperor and the ladies of the imperial court. We are richer at this hour for the life, toil, and hardship of Jerome, with his hermitlike instincts, his unremitting ardor in the pursuit of sacred lore, his fondness for study and retirement, than for the violence, cruelty, intrigue, and restless ambition of Cyril of Alexandria, whose name Milman felt obliged to brand with infamy,§ and whose stern spirit and stormy methods Charles Kingsley has so vividly depicted in *Hypatia*. For all the higher interests of morality and religion, Bishop Latimer, sending a New Testament to his concupiscent and crafty sovereign,

---

away seven hundred virgins from the Church to his party." We may accept the facts of course, without the sinister hint they are employed to convey.

*Athanasius complained of Arius's degradation of sacred themes in his *Thalia*. See *Orations of Athanasius against the Arians*, edited by Dr. William Bright, Regius Professor of Ecclesiastical History, Oxford.

†Neander's *History of the Christian Religion and Church*. Fifth edition, p. 78.

‡Pontus, in *Vita Cypriani*, p. 13. Roman jurists distinguished three kinds of law—*jus sacrum*, religious law ; *jus publicum*, common law, and *jus privatum*, law determining private rights. So the celebrated rhetorician and pleader Quintilian says " (*legum*) *genera sunt tria ; sacri, publici, privati juris*."

§ Toward Jews, pagans, and heretics, or what he considered such, Cyril showed no mercy. Dean Milman thus characterizes him: "He may be a hero or even a saint to those who esteem the stern and uncompromising assertion of certain tenets the one paramount Christian virtue, but while ambition, intrigue, arrogance, rapacity, and violence are prescribed as unchristian means; barbarity, persecution, bloodshed as unholy and unevangelical wickedness, posterity will condemn the orthodox Cyril as one of the worst of heretics against the spread of the Gospel."—*Latin Christianity*, vol. i, p. 145.

Henry VIII, with the leaf turned down and the page marked at the words "Marriage is honorable in all, and the bed undefiled; but whoremongers and adulterers God will judge," has a significance and a value that a thousand courtly Wolseys, humoring their imperious and headstrong master in his whims and caprices and condoning his darkest crimes, could never pretend to; while the triumphant martyrdom of the faithful bishop was the most fitting antithesis to the final shipwreck and shame of the diplomatic and aspiring cardinal. And the clerical satellites of that most dissolute of kings, Charles II, learned, witty, and brilliant as many of them were, will never be named with the same veneration and respect by posterity as the gifted and saintly author of *A Good Man the Living Temple of God*, who left the far more exemplary court of Cromwell and its lucrative chaplaincy because of the unendurable coarseness of its manners and the insalubrity of its moral atmosphere, or Bunyan, who during the same reign spent twelve of the best years of his life in a cell of the county jail, though ranking high among the best writers, ablest preachers, and most law-abiding citizens of his age.*

The names of the great preachers, philanthropists, ecclesiastical rulers, and reformers of history are not recalled by monuments in bronze or marble. Their true memorial is the work they have done and the world they have bequeathed to the generations succeeding them, enriched and ennobled by their thought, their example, and their labors. They built their souls into their work. They stamped their personality on their age and live again in minds made better by the high standard they personally honored and strove to establish. And the brief but expressive eulogy to Sir Christopher Wren, which the visitor

---

* Froude's attempt to justify the legal forms under which Bunyan was deprived of his liberty is lame and inadequate. See *Life of Bunyan*, in English Men of Letters Series.

to St. Paul's Cathedral in London, the noblest of the many monuments of his exhaustless and versatile genius, reads over the north door of the choir, beneath which rest his remains: "*Lector ... si monumentum requiris circumspice,*"* may be justly applied to these makers of the world's best ages.

> We crave not a memorial stone
> For those who fell at Marathon.
> Their fame with every breeze is blent;
> The mountains are their monument,
> And the low plaining of the sea
> Their everlasting threnody.†

6. Measurable Progress.

To seize two widely distant points of history and survey the ground between them which has been traveled over, and note the progress that has been made and the factors that have figured most prominently in the transition stages and epochal scenes of the period, will often give a striking view of the potent influence exerted on the civilization of the world by the Christian religion and the men who have expounded and defended its truths, controlled its councils, and directed its beneficent energies. "Two of the most satisfactory hours I ever spent were far apart in time and place," says Bishop Mallalieu, of the Methodist Episcopal Church. "The one was in Arkansas, in an uncouth board shed, where two hundred people were crowded together to listen to the preaching of the Gospel. Though the structure was rude and uninviting, in fact, almost comfortless, yet it witnessed the revelation of the power of God in the outpouring of the Spirit until the place seemed as really filled with the divine presence as did the upper chamber on the day of Pentecost. Believers were greatly strengthened and encouraged, and nearly a score of penitent men and women bowed before God on the rough,

---

* "Reader ... if you seek his memorial, look around."
† *The Three Fountains*, p. 100.

carpetless floor to seek salvation in the pardon of their sins. The other hour of sacred, precious memories was spent in York Minster. It was the close of day—a bright English summer day. The setting sun poured a wealth of light and glory through the magnificent stained-glass windows of that wonderful temple. It was an hour full of glorious thoughts. The saintly men and women that for many centuries had walked beneath that superb roof, among the shapely pillars, and had mingled their prayers and songs in those dim aisles, seemed once again to throng the place; and as the twilight gloom filled the sanctuary, pure, sweet, holy communings with all the good and with God filled the heart and soul."

But perhaps the most significant feature of this striking contrast is that the original church—erected for the baptism of Edwin, King of Northumbria, by Bishop Paulinus, first bishop of the province, in 627—which stood on the ground now occupied by the Minster—was precisely the rude wooden shed of the Arkansas worshipers. The present Metropolitical Church of the city of York took nearly a thousand years to build. Its structure exhibits, as it stands, half a dozen distinct styles of architecture. While the unity of design has been remarkably preserved, many hands and many ages have contributed to its completeness.* It therefore marks the consummation of a glorious history—is, in fact, the culmination of more than a millennium of Christian civilization. Many years ago it was the frequent privilege of the present writer, during a prolonged stay in York, to worship in the magnificent fane which to-day adorns the city in which the great Constantine assumed the imperial purple, and where for a long time it was fondly believed by the citizens and by the English people generally he had his nativity,† a city famous as the headquarters of the distin-

---

* See Rain's *History of York*.

† When, in *Panegyrici Veteres*, it is said that Constantine gave additional historic luster to the old city—*illic oriendo*—the reference probably is, as Gibbon suggests, to his assumption within its walls of the place and power of an Augustus of the empire,

guished Roman Imperator Agricola, as the residence for a short time of Hadrian and Severus, as the last resting place of more than one of the masters of empire, and in later centuries as the place of assembly for many generations of the mediæval British Parliament, and the home of several of England's greatest kings and their courts. His youthful ears were often charmed there with the most exquisite cathedral music to be found in England or elsewhere, not excepting that of St. Paul's, of Westminster, of Canterbury, and other English cathedral churches, to which he has also listened. He has seen the stately processions of Church magnates within its walls, as at the great Church Congress of 1869, when Archbishop Longley, of Canterbury, and Archbishop Thomson, of the Northern Province—preceded by the civic dignitaries and mace-bearer and clad in canonical attire—and the bishops and clergy of both provinces, and of many colonial dioceses, moved slowly along its historic aisles into the choir; and he has witnessed the pompous display of great dignitaries of the law of the solemn-faced English type, with their ermine flowing yards behind them, and grave-mannered barristers on circuit with their silken robes and wigs faultlessly neat and prim, as at Assize times. In the intellectual, social, and religious life of that city of churches and charities, of schools and scholarly men, one sees, as one does in many other present-day centers of intellectual and religious activity, the high-water mark of Christian culture and refinement. Since those days the author has worshiped in congregations varying in size from the smallest to the largest; now with less than a dozen in a village church, now with several thousands—as in Spurgeon's Tabernacle, London, and in Talmage's large church, Brooklyn city, both of them since burned down; now in churches ornate and costly to an extravagant degree, and

---

and his going forth thence to write his splendid record as an *imperator* and ruler in the annals of Roman story. There can be no doubt that his real nativity was Nissa, in Upper Moesia, February, 274 A. D.

now in churches puritanically bare, and plain enough to satisfy the scruples of George Fox himself. And everywhere he has been compelled to acknowledge the unique and sovereign power of Christianity and of the Christian pulpit in the mighty strides of progress upward and forward which are registered in the displacement of the wooden shed of Paulinus by such metropolitical churches as those of Canterbury, and York, and Cologne, and St. John's Lateran, and the Roman St. Peter's. And he is constrained to adopt the language of Cardinal Newman as more true of the typical Christian minister in the wide field of history, and as a master craftsman employed on the stately fabric of the universal City of God, than of the occupant of the chair of St. Peter, to whom the cardinal exclusively applied them: "He is no recluse, no solitary student, no dreamer about the past, no doter upon the dead and gone, no projector of the visionary. He for eighteen hundred years has lived in the world; he has seen all fortunes, he has encountered all adversaries, he has shaped himself for all emergencies.... From the first he has looked through the wide world of which he has the burden; and, according to the need of the day and the inspirations of his Lord, he has set himself now to one thing, now to another; but to all in season and to nothing in vain. He came first upon an age of refinement and luxury like our own, and in spite of the persecutor —fertile in the resources of his cruelty—he soon gathered, out of all classes of society, the slave, the soldier, the highborn lady and the sophist, materials enough to form a people to his Master's honor. The savage hordes came down in torrents from the north, and [he] went out to meet them and by his very eye he sobered them and backed them in their full career. They turned aside and flooded the whole earth, but only to be more surely civilized by him and to be made ten times more his children even than the older populations which they had overwhelmed. Lawless kings arose, sagacious as the Roman, passionate as the Hun, yet in him they found their match and were shattered, and he lived on. The gates of the earth were opened to the east and the west, and men poured out to take possession, but he went with them as a missionary to China, to India, to Mexico, to Africa, to the great Republic of North America, and the islands of the South Pacific Ocean—carried along by zeal and charity as far as those children of men were led by enterprise, covetousness, or ambition. . . . Has he failed to meet and to minister to the deepest and most essential needs of the human soul up to this hour? What gray hairs are on the head of Judah, whose youth is renewed like the eagle's, whose feet are like the feet of harts, and underneath the Everlasting Arms?"*

---

*Newman's *Idea of a University Defined and Illustrated*, pp. 13, 14. The author has taken the liberty to adapt the latter part of this beautiful passage.

CHAPTER II

Domination of Type in the Ministry

The Heavenly City, in its wanderings on earth, summons its citizens from all nations, . . . being itself indifferent to whatever differences there may be in the customs, laws, and institutions by which earthly peace is sought or preserved, not rescinding or destroying any of them, but rather keeping and following after them as different means adopted by different races for obtaining the one common end of eternal peace, provided only they are no obstacle to the religion by which men are taught the worship of the one supreme and true God.—*St. Augustine*, "De Civitate Dei," xix, 17.

Be sure that whenever the religion of Christ appears small or forbidding, or narrow, or inhuman, you are not dealing with the whole—which is a matchless moral symmetry; nor even with an arch or column—for every detail is perfect —but with some cold stone removed from its place and suggesting nothing of the glorious structure from which it came.—*Henry Drummond*.

> Enough—and too much—of the sect and the name;
> What matters our label, so truth be our aim?
> The creed may be strange, but the life may be true;
> And hearts beat the same under drab coats or blue.
> —*Whittier*.

1. Rise of Type.

THE Renaissance liberated thought from the hierarchal tutelage of centuries, and Protestanism, having assisted in the breaking of the spell, sought to consecrate the new freedom and enlist its potent and restless energies in the interests of religion and morality. The result of the intellectual emancipation of Europe, however, was precisely what a deeper insight into human nature would have taught its promoters to anticipate, namely, the assertion of an unrestricted right of private judgment in religion, the rise and growth of sectionalism, and the production, within the narrow domain of each religious coterie, of teachers and leaders with a peculiar mental squint and a marked denominational accent. From the period of the Reformation downward Protestant unity has been continually breaking up and crumbling into fragments, and there has been a steady multiplication of ecclesiastical shibboleths side by side with a growing sense, in later times, on the part of a thoughtful few, in all communions of the evils of a rigid, oversensitive, and arrogant sectarianism. The condition of the Christian world at the present moment, with its bewildering diversity of sects, creeds, customs, and forms of ecclesiastical organization and government, is making it difficult even for men of the thoroughest culture and widest catholicity of spirit not to "cramp their hearts" nor "take half views of men and things;" and a full-orbed spiritual manhood, not to speak of a broad-sympathied Christian cosmopolitanism, is almost entirely out of the question. Every denomination has its own ideal ministry, its own standard of clerical character and qualification—usually a collection of social, moral, and intellectual attributes and religious prejudices combined, in varying proportions, according to an unwritten prescription, and answering more or less perfectly to the indefinable traditional pattern recognized and required within the body.*

2. Its Forms Pronounced.

This conformity to type, though possibly a necessity in the present condition of things, and probably not an unmixed evil, can yet hardly be regarded with complete satisfaction in view of its obvious tendency to defeat the prime object of the Christian religion, which is avowedly to confer on the world, in and through its varied ministry, the

---

* An able and scholarly man, who has had much to do for many years with the training of young ministers in a theological school of one of the largest and most influential denominations in England, thus writes: "The Methodist ministry has developed a type of its own remarkable for two things. First, for the persistence with which it has dwelt on the central truths of saving religion; and, secondly, for the fervor it has thrown into the preaching of those truths. It should be frankly conceded that in one sense its range of topics has been comparatively narrow. Those topics, indeed, have included the central verities of redemption, and have implied a great deal more. A similar limitation applies to other Churches and ministries. Human knowledge can only cover one side of God's truth....The Methodist ministry has made certain parts of the Gospel its own.... *We are extremely anxious that Methodism should be true to the type of preaching which is its own creation.* It is a type worth preserving."—*Professor J. S. Banks, in Methodist Times,* August 8, 1895.

noblest, the most evenly-balanced, and most perfect type of manhood. "He gave some to be apostles; and some, prophets; and some, evangelists; and some, pastors and teachers; for the perfecting of the saints, unto the work of ministering, unto the building up of the body of Christ: till we all attain unto the unity of the faith, and of the knowledge of the Son of God, unto a full-grown man (εἰς ἄνδρα τέλειον), unto the measure of the stature of the fullness of Christ" (Eph. iv, 11-13).

Peculiarities of doctrinal belief, or of Church polity and usage, though formerly held with more zeal and tenacity than at present, when, indeed, there is a growing tendency to regard them as a vogue of the past, have left their impress deep and broad on most present-day Churches, giving to the whole expression of their religious life that distinctive tone and color which a stranger instantly detects. Even the culture which has been defined as "the complete spiritual development of the individual," and again, as "the compensation of bias," does not enable the representatives of sectional Christianity to entirely escape the denominational lisp or conceal the denominational livery. Men who stand among their brethren like Saul among the men of Benjamin, head and shoulders above them all, get to some extent warped and twisted in their intellectual growth and moral sympathies by the limits, restrictions, and omissions of a creed and a polity which are necessarily narrower and shallower than the whole Christian teaching and discipline —the precious *depositum* of Him who said, "The words that I spake unto you are spirit and are life;" and, "Ye shall know the truth, and the truth shall make you free." "You congratulate me upon being the Vicar of Leeds," wrote Dr. Hook, the learned author of *The Lives of the Archbishops of Canterbury*, to a friend, soon after entering on his labors in a field in which he achieved a signal success; "but I am only vicar in name; the real vicar is a

Methodist preacher called John Rattenbury; I am come to alter that."*

This evil result was inevitable. For the use of creed, often a necessity and a help at the outstart of new religious movements, has uniformly degenerated into a mischievous restraint upon intellectual and spiritual freedom. While the construction, spirit, and purpose of almost every doctrinal symbol from the time of the Council of Nicæa downward have been mainly negative, and have been intended more to safeguard subscribers against the invasion of error than to give theological information, it has been held and employed in the most positive manner, as if it contained the most complete and most authoritative declaration of all that is to be believed. † It has been forgotten that all dogmatic postulates must necessarily be inadequate expressions of Christian faith in consequence of their polemical and negative character. For example, Trinitarianism, as often formulated, on the one side, and Unitarianism, as mostly held, on the other, are half truths standing over against each other in unreconciled antithesis.‡ The unique mystery of revealed religion lies between these negatives without positive solution, perhaps incapable of it in human terms. § But this negative character of the creed has been entirely lost sight of, with the result of making the life and faith, both of the ministry and membership of denominational Churches, narrow, fettered, fearful of fresh truths, and

---

* John Rattenbury was a regular circuit minister of the Wesleyan denomination in Leeds, England. At the time of Dr. Hook's advent he was very popular in that large manufacturing town as a preacher and revivalist.

† *Vide* Rev. Charles Gore's, *Incarnation of the Son of God*, p. 177.

‡ "Because I believe in the Father, the Son, the Holy Spirit—Three in One, One in Three—I claim to be a Unitarian. Unity is harmonized and cooperative complexity. Unity is not loneliness. They who deny the Deity of the Saviour are not Unitarians, they are Solitarians. They know not the music, the peace, the rapture of unity."— *Dr. Joseph Parker*, Sermon before the Free Church Congress, Nottingham, England, 1895.

§ 1 Tim. iii, 16. The reading of ὅς in place of Θεός, adopted by Lachman, Tischendorf, Tregelles, and the Revisers, in no way diminishes the importance of the apostolic statement, as to the mystery (τὸ μυστήριον), which is "confessedly great" (ὁμολογουμένως μέγα).

even of old truths in new aspects; incapable of comprehending and afraid to claim its whole glorious inheritance in Christ. It has been forgotten that "Christianity is not a logical or mathematical problem, and cannot be reduced to the limitations of a human system. It is above any particular system, and comprehends the truths of all systems. It is above logic, yet not illogical; as revelation is above reason, yet not against reason."

Before the rise of the great philanthropies and missionary agencies of modern Christendom, and especially of the recent widespread interest in social and industrial questions, affecting the well-being of millions of the people, the religious world presented the aspect of a series of water-tight compartments, and the piety of the individual Christian was estimated according to the fidelity and exclusiveness with which he confined himself and his active sympathy, beneficence, and prayers to his own tank. The Rev. John Owen, one of the founders of the British and Foreign Bible Society, and one of its first secretaries, says, "Christians had been taught to regard each other with a kind of pious estrangement, or rather with *consecrated hostility*." And he remarks that the scene in the convention "which formed the society seemed strange" to him, and "indicated the dawn of a new era in Christendom."* "I can introduce you as a gentleman, but not as a minister," said a High Anglican clergyman to his Nonconformist brother of the cloth in a large social gathering in London. "And I can speak of you as a minister, but not as a gentleman," retorted the dissenter. The one groundless "dogma of the Apostolic Succession," says Hugh Price Hughes, "has done more to produce division, discord, bitterness, and misery than any other vain imagination of the mind of man. At this moment, in spite of all the humanizing influences of

---

* Address of Dr. A. S. Hunt, Corresponding Secretary American Bible Society, before World's Congress of Missions, at Chicago, September 29, 1893.

Christianity and civilization, it is carrying strife and wretchedness into thousands of English homes."

It is a curious illustration of the way in which "wheat and tares grow together until the harvest" that the very age which voices its catholic sentiment in the words of Oliver Wendell Holmes: "I never saw a church door so narrow I couldn't go in through it, nor one so wide that all the Creator's goodness and glory could enter it "*—an age which can smile in patronizing and commiserating mood at the zealous orthodoxy of St. John, leaving the public baths at Ephesus because Cerinthus was there, or the childish illiberality of Polycarp, repelling Marcion in the streets of Rome as "the firstborn of Satan"—should be obliged to recognize the same untamed and inhospitable disposition in a favorite poet whom it regards as registering the high-water mark of cultured sainthood, the happiest blending of Christian piety and classic lore in our time. The amiable and saintly author of the *Christian Year* did not hesitate to brand his dissenting fellow-Christians as heretics. His distribution of mankind religiously is as follows: "Christians properly so-called—that is, Catholics; Jews, Mohammedans, and heretics; heathens and unbelievers." In rural England, where the Established Church assumes the right to dominate, a clergyman has been heard to say publicly, "Dissenters' prayers may reach the throne of God only to be hurled back as infamous blasphemy;" while another has been known to truculently claim control of both the amenities of earth and the mercies of heaven, in the following language, spoken to a poor woman: "If you allow these dissenters to pray with your husband, I will not administer the sacrament to you, and that will mean *damnation*." As a specimen of the uncompromising animus and arrogant attitude of high ecclesiasticism toward less pretentious forms of piety and polity the following, taken from Gace's Cate-

---
* *Over the Teacups.*

chism, circulated by thousands in rural and municipal England, may fairly challenge comparison with anything to be found in the darkest ages of Christian history:

"We have amongst us various sects and denominations who go by the general name of dissenters. In what light are we to regard them?" "As heretics."

"Is, then, their worship a laudable service?" "No; because they worship God according to their own evil and corrupt imaginations and not according to his revealed will; and therefore their worship is idolatrous."

Christianity, however, being characteristically and essentially a religion of peace and good will, can never hope, even in its most degenerate forms, to excel in malediction; and the rarest examples of recorded anathema are not Christian, but Jewish and Mohammedan. When Renan unveiled the statue of Spinoza at The Hague, about twenty years ago, he claimed for that philosopher the grandest of all possible distinctions. "From this point," he said, alluding to the later home of Spinoza, on the Pavilioen Gracht, "God was the nearest seen." His Hebrew co-religionists, however, took a very different view of the deep and daring speculations of the author of the *Ethics*. "By the sentence of the angels, by the decree of the saints," ran the fierce and blistering strain of their imprecation, "we anathematize, cut off, curse, and execrate Baruch Spinoza, in the presence of these sacred books with the six hundred and thirteen precepts written therein, with the anathema wherewith Joshua anathematized Jericho; with the cursing wherewith Elisha cursed the children, and with all the cursings which are written in the Book of the Law. Cursed be he by day and cursed by night; cursed when he lieth down and cursed when he riseth up; cursed when he goeth out and cursed when he cometh in; the Lord pardon him never; the wrath and fury of the Lord burn upon this man, and bring upon him all the curses which are written in the

Book of the Law. The Lord blot out his name under heaven. The Lord set him apart for destruction from all the tribes of Israel, with curses of the firmament which are written in the Book of the Law. . . . There shall no man speak to him, no man write to him, no man show him any kindness, no man stay under the same roof with him, no man come nigh him."

"With these amenities, the current compliments of theological parting," remarks Matthew Arnold, "the Jews of the Portuguese Synagogue at Amsterdam took, in 1656, . . . their leave of their erring brother, Baruch, or Benedict, Spinoza. They remained children of Israel, and he became a child of modern Europe."*

"From Moses to Moses [that is, Maimonides] no one has risen like Moses," wrote the liberal-minded admirers of the great Jewish scholar and philosopher on his tombstone. "Here lies Moses, the anathematized heretic," wrote his enemies.

Denominationalism doubtless has some advantages, but when all the good to which it can fairly lay claim is weighed against the evils for which it is directly responsible the latter so largely preponderates that few will hesitate to nod assent to the words of Bunyan, with which he answered the bigots of his day and denomination—words which the present writer heard Dean Stanley, in a lecture on "The Names of the Early Christians," indorse with that impressive solemnity of tone and manner which is only born of deep conviction: "And since you would know by what name I would be distinguished from others, I tell you I would be, and hope I am, *a Christian;* and choose, if God should count me worthy, to be called a Christian, a believer, or other such name which is approved by the Holy Ghost. And as for those factious titles of Anabaptists, Independents, Presbyterians, or the like, I conclude that they came neither from Jerusalem nor Antioch, but rather from hell and Babylon;

---

* Arnold's *Essays in Criticism*. First series. Boston, 1865, p. 237.

for they naturally tend to divisions. 'You may know them by their fruits.'"* "It is quite a mistake," says Mr. C. F. Aked, the popular Baptist minister of Liverpool, "to suppose that we are Baptists because we baptize. We baptize because we are Baptists. Our position never grew out of our views and practices of baptism. Our views and practices grew out of our position as Baptists." †

3. **Its Rule, Rigid and Absolute.**

The narrowing and withering spirit of creed and ecclesiastical particularism has held its own, in some quarters, from Bunyan's day till now, and at this hour "the fruitful bough by a well," whose branches happen to "run over" the denominational "wall," has no more opportunity for quiet growth and expansion than the favorite son of Jacob, who thousands of years ago excited the envy and anger of "the archers" that "sorely grieved him and shot at him and hated him." There is something infinitely pathetic in the plaint of a gifted thinker and devoted Congregational pastor in London, well known, both as an author and preacher, on both sides of the Atlantic, when he says:

"The deepest trouble of the true preacher's soul is this, that men and life conspire to make it easy for him to do his worst, and difficult, or well-nigh impossible, for him to do his best. The solid phalanx of good, hard-working, unthinking people that fill the ranks of most Christian and unchristian societies are blissfully tolerant of their minister as long as he will not think. Let him work on the lines of the accepted creed; let him engage in ingenious defenses of its several articles; let him assume a foundation and build what he pleases thereon, and they are well content. That is what they mean by truth, or rather, as they prefer to call it, with a fine but very necessary distinction,

---

* *Peaceable Principles and True.* Bunyan's Works, Hansard Knolly's Society edition, p. 648.
† Sermon on the Place of Baptists in the Making of England.

the truth. But suppose, just because his life is consecrated to study and thought and prayer, and he is committed to the venture of finding what really is true, he is driven, as true men have in all ages been driven, to distinguish between those parts of the foundation which are solid rock, and other parts which are the idle concrete of tradition, what will be his fate? The solid phalanx closes against him, this uncomfortable disturber of the accepted positions. *Quieta non movere* is the watchword. Suspicion, misrepresentation, flouts, and scorns are his portion. The young are solemnly warned to keep away from so dangerous an influence. Assailed by foes whom he cannot possibly distinguish or discover, he may find his work arrested and his life made a burden. Pity does not dwell in the fiery heart of orthodoxy. Torquemada is simply the blazing sixteenth-century representative of an eternal phenomenon. Should you turn round seriously to inquire how great the deviation of this proscribed heretic is from the accepted faith, you might be puzzled to find any deviation at all. Should you honestly inquire whether the deviation, such as it is, is, after all, right, you might be forced to confess that it is—truth clear, self-evident, irrefragable. But your strength is that you do not inquire. Your power over your victim is that he feels bound to inquire; to be candid; not to believe a lie. You are conscious of no such necessity. Your function is to defend your traditional creed at all costs. Your victory is won when foes, good and bad, are driven outside the lines."*

So absolute is the rule of the type and the domination of the "standards" that when a minister develops original features of character—assumes the rôle of a fearless reformer of obvious abuses, or becomes an earnest and conscientious investigator and student, or presents and emphasizes some new or neglected phase of an old truth, or brushes aside some superannuated and useless ecclesiastical

---

* Rev. R. F. Horton, in *Methodist Times* for February, 1894.

tradition, custom, or usage—his daring individualism and departure from the accepted type is usually punished, either with the slow torture of social martyrdom, like Frederic W. Robertson, of Brighton, or with the much milder penalty of expulsion from the clan, as in the case of Spinoza and of Dr. William Robertson Smith, late Adams Professor of Arabic in the University of Cambridge, who, in 1881, after years of controversy in the press and in the courts of the Church, was finally removed, without trial, from his chair as Professor of Hebrew and Old Testament Exegesis in the Free Church College of Aberdeen. It is this kind of fate which gives such profound pathos to the words of Arminius in his letter to Uitenbogaert at the moment when Francis Gomar and his following were hounding the great Leyden theologian to death; showing how much deeper and nobler is the holy passion for truth than the persecutor's melodramatic frenzy for orthodoxy. "Truth, even theological truth," he says, "has been sunk in a deep well, whence it cannot be drawn without much effort." "I should be foolish were I to concede to anyone so much of right in me as that he should be able to disturb me as often as he pleased. Be this my brazen wall—a conscience void of offense. Forward let me still go in search after truth, and therein let me die with the good God on my side, even if I must needs incur the hatred and ill-will of the whole world."

4. Application of the Screw.

The vain effort after conformity to a false and impossible *human* ideal has led not only to forgetfulness of the vital law of "diversity of operations by the selfsame spirit," by which alone the *divine* ideal can ever become a certified reality, but with a not unusual fatefulness it has brought about, almost uniformly, the substitution of a greater error for a less, namely, the sacrifice of love and pity—which are the life and essence of religion—in the supposed interests of faith, which is only its partial and precarious intellectual expression. The vaunted motto of Catholic Christianity, *semper eadem*, has been powerless to arrest the deep currents of earnest thought and conviction which bear men's minds forward in every age, but it has often led to an indolent contentedness with truth's impalpable shadow in place of its enduring substance, and has disfigured the page of the Church's history with its darkest stain, the unreasoning and ruthless despotism of authority. Nothing more strikingly illustrates the utter incapability of even the wisest and best of men to understand and appreciate the manifold operations of the All-knowing Spirit of God in the infinitely diversified thought and life of men, and their consequent unfitness to exercise authority in a sphere where they are so hopelessly at sea, than the attitude of the Roman Church toward various religious movements, within and outside her pale, through which Providence has conferred unmeasured blessing on millions of the race. The faintest ripple on her broad and stagnant waters has been regarded as the signal for alarm, and the Malchus of the Catholic household only escapes the swift and sure stroke of Peter's sword by yielding an unmurmuring submission and obedience to the Apostolic Chair. Dominic is encouraged because he is a faithful and affectionate son of his mother—the Church—and is willing to blend a watchful regard for the prerogatives of authority with his mission of salvation and enlightenment; * but the German monk, bent on bringing about the resurrection of a long-buried truth, and the release of the soul of religion from a worse than Babylonian captivity, is an object, first, of amused curiosity, then of suspicion and anxiety, then of alarm, then of baffled intrigue and violence. Loyola may preach chastity and poverty, however alien these venerable

---

* When Pope Honorius III confirmed the statutes and established the Order of St. Dominic he gave it, as its symbol, a dog with a torch in his mouth—the dog to watch and the torch to illumine the Church.

and rare attributes may be from the habitual disposition and practice of the princes of the Church, if only he will enforce along with them the more sovereign and more serviceable virtue of obedience. Purity and self-denial, though of the very essence of godliness, are by no means indispensable to the stability of authority. Obedience, however, is its corner stone—the rock on which the whole fabric of ecclesiastical power must ever rest, and against which the gates of hell shall not prevail. Nor can the liberty allowed to Loyola and Lainez—the apostles of obedience—be accorded to the deep-souled St. Cyran and his studious and scholarly friend Jansenius, fathers of worthy spiritual children—teachers of loftiest and most luminous souls like Arnauld, Pascal, Nicole, Le Maitre, De Saci, and Mère Angelique and her sister Agnes. It was only from within the gloomy shadows of his prison at Vincennes, to which his early friend and quondam flatterer, Cardinal Richelieu,* had consigned him, that the Abbot of St. Cyran was permitted to speak to the hearts that loved and trusted him, and that preferred his solemn admonitions to the lighter and more dulcet strains of the hirelings of the fold. It was from his dismal cell in the Bastile that De Saci sent the clear and kindly ray of the word of the " Eternal " into thousands of French homes. It was in the face of the frown of papal authority that the *Augustinus* of Jansenius was given to the world and became " the signal of a contest which for nearly seventy years agitated the Sorbonne and Versailles, fired the enthusiasm of the ladies and the divines of France, and gave to her historians and her wits a theme, used with fatal success, to swell the tide of hatred and of ridicule—which has finally swept away the temporal greatness, and which silenced, for a while, the spiritual ministrations of the Gallican Church." †

* "' Gentlemen, I introduce to you the most learned man in Europe,' was the flattering phrase by which Cardinal Richelieu made known the friend of his youth to the courtiers who thronged his levée."—*Stephen, Critical and Miscellaneous Essays,* p. 100.

† Stephen, *Critical and Miscellaneous Essays*, p. 102.

But if Rome is hard upon the irrepressible inquiries and aspirations of her own children, how strangely considerate and tender she can be toward those who, weary of the perils and responsibilities of intellectual freedom, seek rest from their wanderings and surer steps for their feet by returning to her fold! Who can fail to be struck with the kindly tone and consummate policy of Cardinal Wiseman's letter on "Catholic Unity," published when the famous Oxford controversy was at its height? "Are we," he asks, "who sit in the full light, to see our friends feeling their way toward us through the gloom that surrounds them, and faltering for want of an outstretched hand, or turning astray for want of a directing voice, and to sit on, and keep silent, amusing ourselves at their painful efforts, or perhaps allow them to hear, from time to time, only the suppressed laugh of one who triumphs over their distress? God forbid! If one must err—if, in the mere tribute of humanity, one must needs make a false step—one's fall will be more easy when on the side of two theological virtues than when on the cold, bare earth of human prudence. If I shall, in my dealings, have been too hopeful in my motives or too charitable in my dealings, I will take my chance of smiles at my simplicity, both on earth and in heaven. Those of the latter, at least, are never scornful."

But not against Rome alone does impartial history prefer the charge of seeking to secure theological uniformity and the dominance of type by the ruinous policy of suppression. Passing by cases where envy, obstinacy, infidelity, hypercriticism, disappointed ambition, or mere love of notoriety may have led to schism and secession, let us confine ourselves to the men of marked ability, of high and original character, of conscientious convictions—often sustained by indisputable learning and argument—for whom the narrowness and inelasticity of Protestant sects have found no place. One of the most distinguished examples of nonconformity to any prevailing type of ecclesiasticism is Richard Baxter. In love for his fellow-beings, in pity for their sins and sorrows, in labors for their enlightenment and happiness, he has probably never been surpassed. Even the man who wished himself "accursed from Christ for his brethren's sake, his kinsmen according to the flesh," did not devote himself more unreservedly and unremittingly to the highest known form of benevolence—the spiritual salvation of men. By his unwearied toils he transformed the Kidderminster of his day, and yet fell short of his own lofty ideal of pastoral fidelity. "I confess," he says, "to my own shame, that I remember no one sin that my conscience doth so much accuse and judge me for as for doing so little for the salvation of men's souls and dealing no more earnestly and fervently with them for their conversion. . . . My conscience telleth me that I should follow them with all possible earnestness night and day, and take no denial till they turn to God." But though the leading features of Baxter's character and the motives of his life were simplicity itself, his intellectual and spiritual grandeur, his unruffled serenity and studied moderation, his charity, which never failed, made him an insoluble enigma to the factions of his day—which quarreled with each other, about the holiest things, in a manner the most unholy and discreditable. In spite of his Episcopal antecedents and training he became a Presbyterian, and, while he loved both the persons and the principles of the Puritans, he had no objection to a modified form of episcopacy, though he himself declined the offer of the bishopric of Hereford.

Roger Williams was a man of a different type. While Baxter was irenical and tolerant of differences, the militant and aggressive temper of his more vigorous and equally remarkable contemporary led to agitation and unsettlement and made a much deeper impression on the ecclesiastical movements of his time. Williams kept the Church and civil courts of colonial New England busy, and filled the friends of a State religion with constant anxiety and alarm lest connivance at or toleration of his views as to the relation of Church and State should lead the authorities of the home government to withdraw the charter of the colony. He might have said, in the words of another, "Lay on my coffin a sword, for I was a brave soldier in the Liberation War of Humanity." Two hundred years and more in advance of his age, he was not so intelligible to his own times as he is to ours. He is, first, a clergyman of the Established Church of England. Subsequently his passion for freedom has transformed him into an extreme New England Puritan. Later still he is an exile and a martyr for conscience' sake. And though, finally, he is the founder of the great and prosperous Baptist denomination on this side the ocean, he appears, on the whole, to have found the specific limitations of his last resort in the Church militant quite as restrictive and distasteful as any of the earlier. And it is certain that, if he had been a narrow-minded sectarian, after the model of his age, he could never have merited the eulogy of Milton, who spoke of him as "that noble confessor of religious liberty." Nor could he, as an ordinary denominationalist, have excited to the extent he did the odium of such men as Dr. Cotton Mather, to whom Rhode Island, on his account, was "the Gerizim of New England, the common receptacle of the convicts of Jerusalem and the outcasts of the land." The island itself, as a portion of God's creation, Dr. Mather was willing to think worthy of all praise. He seems to have felt regarding it as Bishop Heber felt in regard to Ceylon when he wrote his well-known Missionary Hymn—esteeming it a place

> Where every prospect pleases,
> And only man is vile.

"The island is, indeed, for the fertility of its soil, the temperateness of its air, etc., the best garden of all the colony, and were it free from *serpents*, I would call it the paradise of New England." As things were, however, the good old Puritan could only say, with a regret from which one would be glad to believe malice was absent, "*Bona terra, mala gens.*" He evidently fancied that the serpent was not a native of the original home of human innocence, or else his special affection for Williams and his colony led him to wish for them an exemption from exposures which God had not thought essential to the safety and happiness of the first human pair. The vagaries and fantasies of freedom, its excesses, outrages, and crimes, are something fearful to contemplate; but freedom is, has been, and must ever continue to be the essential condition of human power and excellence. It has ever been the madness of such men as Cotton Mather and those who thought and acted with him two hundred years ago—madness that could not claim the poor excuse of method—to think of cutting down the tree of liberty and still hope to retain the advantage of its shade.

Seventy years ago no one was the innocent occasion of a greater sensation in ecclesiastical circles than the tall, stately, eloquent Scotchman who was pastor of Regent's Square Presbyterian Church, London. For two years (1819–21) Edward Irving had been the assistant of Dr. Thomas Chalmers in St. John's Church, Glasgow, and was little known. When subsequently he went to London, and the fine Regent's Square structure was built to accommodate the increasing crowd of wealthy and aristocratic people attending his powerful and attractive ministry, his popularity grew apace. With his advancing fame, however, came some extravagance of speech and doctrine leading to criticism, charges of heresy, ecclesiastical litigation, and, finally, expulsion from the ministry. As Dr. Fairbairn, Principal of Mansfield College, Oxford, said to the writer: "The fate of the noble fellow—great in mind as in stature—was ultimately determined by the ministers of a small rural presby-

tery in Annan, whose collective brain force was not equal
to that of the man they deposed from the ministry of the
Church." An incident recorded in Dean Ramsay's *Reminiscences of Scottish Life and Character* faithfully mirrors the
prevailing opinion of Irving's orthodox fellow-countrymen.
He had been lecturing in Dumfries, and one of his clerical
admirers in the town, of the name of Watty Dunlop, who
had not been fortunate enough to hear the lecture, met next
day on the street a fellow-citizen who had the reputation of
being something of a wag. " Weel, Willie, man," said Dunlop to his friend, " and what do ye think of Mr. Irving?"
" O," said the critic, contemptuously, " the man's cracked!"
To which the quiet but pertinent reply was, " Willie, ye'll
often see a licht peeping through a crack!"*

For his rare organizing genius, masterly power of command, and restless evangelical activity John Wesley found
no place within the pale of the Church to which he clung,
even to the last, with that same romantic tenacity which
characterized all his purposes, and stood out in marked relief in the transcendently noble and beautiful example he
has bequeathed to his followers. He violated, as the pressing exigencies of the work successively required, not only
his own personal prejudices, but almost every portion of the
Episcopal rubrics, and, with a beautifully unconscious inconsistency, died with the comforting conviction that he
had been all his life a loyal and dutiful son of the Anglican
Church. High Churchmen in England have written volume
after volume to demonstrate his High Church principles and
practice.† The Low Church, or evangelical section, with
whose representatives he was closely allied during his whole

---

* The greater portion of Irving's Church in London remained true to him in all his troubles, and he is regarded as the founder of what is known as " The Catholic and Apostolic Church " in England, though in reality he had very little to do with its organization. See Mrs. Oliphant's *Life of Irving*.

† The chief of these are *John Wesley and Modern Methodism*, by Rev. F. Hockin; Urlin's *Wesley's Place in Church History*, and his *Churchman's Life of Wesley;* Overton's *Life of Wesley*. Among books taking an opposite view is Dr. Rigg's *Living Wesley*.

life, has claimed him as its corypheus and chieftain. But, as far as Wesley's catholic-spiritedness and theological liberalism were concerned, he was the broadest of Broad Churchmen, and in this, at any rate, his position was fairly reflected in the late Dean Stanley, as the following entry in his Journal under date of August 20, 1789—only two years before his death—clearly evinces: "I met the society (at Redruth) and explained at large the rise and nature of Methodism, and still aver I have never read or heard of, either in ancient or modern history, any other Church which builds on so broad a foundation as the Methodists do, which requires of its members *no conformity either in opinions or modes of worship, but barely the one thing,* 'to fear God and work righteousness.'" Clearly "this broad foundation," if accepted by the English Episcopal Church, to which Wesley thought he continued to belong, would have made it just what Matthew Arnold wanted it to be, "a national society for the promotion of goodness," and what Dean Stanley wished to make Westminster Abbey, "the embodiment of his idea of a comprehensive national Church."* Equally obvious is it that if British and American Methodism had avowedly built on Wesley's "broad foundation," and been content to impose on its ministry and membership no heavier theological burden than "barely the one thing," it must have worn a very different character and aspect from what it does to-day. Since Wesley's time ministers have been tried for heresy, condemned and expelled, whom it is certain Wesley himself would never have disturbed. He fought Calvinism more as a practical hindrance to evangelistic enthusiasm and success than as a theological system, though the work of the eloquent and highly dramatic Calvinist, Whitefield, was even more fruitful of conversions than his own. Himself a learned and acute theologian, he never dreamed of asking anyone else to indorse his per-

---

* See art. "Dean Stanley," in *Blackwood's Magazine,* February, 1894.

sonal and peculiar views; still less, of imposing on his preachers and people the voluminous and vague standard of faith—consisting of a considerable portion of his works —which is now tacitly accepted by Methodists of all denominations.*

In the Church life of the century, however, perhaps nothing is more suggestive of the inadequacy of the denominational type of ministry to meet the ever-varying needs of the world, while at the same time perpetuating and multiplying its own peculiar evils, than the genesis and growth of that remarkable religious movement—the Salvation Army. William Booth, its founder and autocratic chief, was an ordained clergyman of the Methodist New Connection—one of the smallest, least enthusiastic, and least progressive of the many sections of English Methodism—but on account of the nonconformability of his evangelistic methods to the rules of the denomination he was driven outside the lines to become, under the guidance of divine Providence, along with his devoted and talented wife, the agent in founding a religious community whose operations have extended into many lands, and whose membership has grown, in less than a generation, to be more than ten times that of the denomination that expelled him. The irresistible enthusiasm and absolute freedom from conventional restraint which characterize this ever-onward-moving wave of evangelism are sufficiently indicated in General Booth's reply to one who asked why his army succeeded where everything else had failed: "You see," said he, "we have no reputation to lose; we are not obliged to stop and consider what any-

---

* The portion of Wesley's sermons which, together with his *Notes on the New Testament*, constitutes the theological standard of British Methodism has never been authoritatively defined. Though the subject has been mooted in the English Conference in recent years, its discussion has been significantly deprecated by the conservative theologians of the denomination as inopportune and dangerous. The doctrinal basis of American Methodism is still more vague and uncertain, the articles of the Methodist Episcopal Discipline being for the most part of a negative and controversial character. Heresy in the few rare instances where it exists is comparatively innocuous because it is allowed to pass unnoticed.

body will say; everybody has settled it that we are fools, if not a great deal worse; and, therefore, we can go into a town and do exactly what we think best without taking the least notice of what anybody may say or wish. We have only to please God and get the people saved, and that is easily done."*

5. Neither Breadth nor Sublimity in Liberalism.

It is quite natural to suppose that the conditions of a symmetrical Christian culture, and a powerful and effective spiritual manhood and ministry, which orthodoxy apparently has failed to supply on any extensive scale, would be found in liberal Churches; but as regards the freedom which great religious souls most care for—freedom to believe and preach God's inexhaustible word unmarred by authoritative human interpretation, and exemplify and enforce a thoroughgoing Christian righteousness after the type of the Sermon on the Mount, which all admire, but few practically adopt—the sects that are the most ostentatiously liberal are, as a rule, the nearest approximation to a prison of the spirit. For by refusing to believe in a human divinity they have necessarily excluded faith in a divine humanity. By denying the endless retribution, which is the natural and inevitable consequence of eternal sin ($αἰώνιον\ ἁμάρτημα$, Mark iii, 29) they have broken the scepter of the divine moral government and have exposed the majesty of law to contempt. By reducing the object of faith to bring it within the grasp of reason they have expatriated infiniteness, mystery, moral grandeur, and spiritual joy from religion, which is their true and only fatherland and home. In the interests of a narrow and arid rationalism they would repress such aspirations as that of the distinguished musician, Samuel Sebastian Wesley, when, betraying in his last moments one of the deepest instincts of the soul, he said, "Draw aside the curtain and

---
* *Beneath Two Flags*, p. 30.

let me see the sky." The awe-inspired inspiration of catholic Christianity which in preachers like Chrysostom and Savonarola and Massillon and Bossuet, in painters like Fra Angelico, Da Vinci, and Raphael, in sculptors like Lorenzo Ghiberti, Brunelleschi, Donatello, and Michael Angelo, in poets like Dante, Milton, Tennyson, and Whittier, and in musicians like Handel, Haydn, Bach, and Mozart, has consecrated eloquence, harmony, art, and beauty to the loftiest ends and made moral and intellectual nobility something more than a vague dream or a bare possibility—this greatest power of the soul liberalism has maimed, and left like a broken-winged eagle sprawling on the plain gazing piteously toward the sky, into which it has no power to soar. Heterodoxy is not necessarily the synonym of spiritual liberty, any more than orthodoxy, whatever that may really be, necessarily means intellectual bondage.* Very close neighbor to the danger of narrowness and bigotry is the much subtler peril of a "cheaply won character for toleration, which does not mean charity at all, but carelessness for the souls of others and the absence of belief in oneself."

As to the "liberty of prophesying," it is often more restricted in so-called liberal communions than in the more broad-based and conservative Churches; and he who ventures to display the courage of his convictions even among the professed champions of breadth and freedom, and aspires to be a knight-errant of the truth, must be content with a diadem of thorns, as that gifted young Unitarian whose dust sleeps in the fair city of Florence found to his cost when, at the high altar of liberalism in the city of

---

* "Christianity cannot tolerate mental indolence. It is important to notice this because of the popular delusion that to be evangelical in doctrine is to be feeble or outworn in mind. It is supposed that heresy alone is modern, original, progressive. . . . Taken as an intellectual conception, nothing can be sublimer than the evangelical faith. Its God, its Trinity, its views of sin, its cross, its mystery and glory of blood, its spiritual revelation, its spirit of righteousness and consolation, its day of judgment, its eternal life, its everlasting punishment, and its final dominion over the total universe are not ideas that can be grasped by incompetence or lassitude of mind."—*Dr. Parker's Sermon at the Nottingham Free Church Congress.*

Boston, he dared in his famous ordination sermon,* fifty years ago, to challenge the dogmatic postulates of the Unitarianism of his day, and subsequently, in the teeth of the prevailing sentiment of his denominational associates, claim for the Negro, in chains, the inalienable rights and immunities of manhood.

6. Manifest Destiny of the Ministry.

But though, even in this advanced age, we are far from realizing, from any point of view, the manifest destiny of the Christian ministry, and do not feel any deep dissatisfaction with a state of things which so often obliges us to give to a sect what was meant for humanity, we are not absolutely without signs of the coming of a better day. There is a wider and fuller recognition of the fact that the prime aim of religion is a right condition of the heart and an exemplary rectitude of life rather than correct methods of thinking or subscription to any particular creed. And the growing power of this new ideal is showing itself in an increased interdenominational comity, in a large and free interdenominational cooperation and fellowship like that of the Young People's Society of Christian Endeavor, in mutual annual greetings, in frequent pulpit exchanges, in frank and friendly discussion of differences, in a general implicit condemnation—and in an increasing number of instances definite disavowal—of the tendency "to raise matters trifling and indifferent to the level of matters essential, practically creating new societies for the purpose of giving to such matters an importance which could never be conceded to them in the larger body of Christians." There is an increasingly clear and distinct perception of the fact that the true orthodoxy—the orthodoxy of Jesus and of Paul—is not so much a faultless logic as a perfect Christian love.

---

* *The Transient and the Permanent in Christianity* and *Discourses of Matters Pertaining to Religion*, Theodore Parker's Works, edited by Francis Power Cobbe, London.

As Dr. Boyd Carpenter, Bishop of Ripon, pertinently remarks, in a letter on the advantages of conference written to the Grindelwald Reunion of Churches, "More to be desired than any approach to identity of opinion, or any hollow profession of spurious agreement, is *the bettering of the spirit in which we hold our views.* Deepened sympathy and loftier elevation may be given to those who yet agree to differ. It may be an open question, indeed, whether federation of variety is not more advantageous than pale, perhaps insincere, uniformity of thought. But, however that may be, conference gives men the opportunity of understanding one another's language. . . . The removal of apprehensions . . . is like the lifting of the white mists which gather round the mountains and valleys and obscure the beauty of the landscape. Such gains may be ours by conference, without in the least seeking anything by unworthy compromise of our intellectual integrity. But, chiefest and best of all, we may be led to realize how much wider is God's truth than man's interpretation of it, and how much greater is the spirit of Christ than all controversy."

Similar is the strain of another distinguished ecclesiastical leader of the time, the Rev. Charles Gore, Principal of Pusey House, Oxford : "We, in our time," he says, "have learned to give great prominence to the virtue of considerateness. The rough and summary classifications of men in groups, the equally rough and summary condemnations of them, the inconsiderate treatment of heretics and even of speculators, these facts in Church history strike us as painful and unworthy. Considerateness, we say, is a Christian virtue. ' Let your considerateness be known unto all men.' We look back to our Lord and are astonished that any can have failed to see his intense respect for individuality, his freedom from fanaticism—in a word, his considerateness. Certainly it is there. Only, lest we should be arrogant, we need to remember that other ages and other races have caught more readily in Him what we ignore—his antagonism to pride or to the selfish assertion of property—and that the whole is not yet told. Only all together, all ages, all races, both sexes, can we grow up in one body 'unto the perfect man;' only a really catholic society can be 'the fullness of him that filleth all in all.' Thus we doubt not that, when the day comes which shall see the existence of really national Churches in India and China and Japan, the tranquillity and inwardness of the Hindu, the pertinacity and patience of the Chinaman, the brightness and amiability of the Japanese, will each in turn receive their fresh consecration in Christ and bring out new and unsuspected aspects of the Christian life; finding fresh resources in him in whom is neither Jew nor Greek, neither male nor female, barbarian, Scythian, bond nor free, but Christ all in all." *

---

* *The Incarnation of the Son of God*, being the Bampton Lectures for 1891, p. 184.

CHAPTER III
The Minister in the Making

And he who is of David and yet before him, the Word of God, despising the lyre and harp, which are but lifeless instruments, and having tuned by the Holy Spirit the universe and especially man—who, composed of body and soul, is a universe in miniature—makes melody to God ont his instrument of many tones; and to this instrument—I mean to man—he sings accordant: "For thou art my harp and pipe and temple"—a harp for harmony, a pipe by reason of the spirit, a temple by reason of the word; so that the first may sound, the second breathe, the third contain the Lord.—*Clemens Alexandrinus*, "The Exhortation to the Heathen."

1. The Raw Material.

WITH a beautiful fitness the Christian ministry has, from the first, drawn its raw material and recruited its ranks from every social and intellectual stratum and from every kind of employment, profession, and pursuit. Claiming, as it does, a divine origin and guarantee, perfect catholicity of scope, and unbroken perpetuity of function, it is of all institutions under the most solemn bond and obligation not "to give to a party what was meant for mankind." There can never legitimately exist any principle of discrimination in the selection of its candidates except a purely moral and religious one. The only strictly absolute condition of admission to the sacred service is the experience and exemplification of the spiritual life—"the new man, which is in course of being renewed unto knowledge after the image of Him that created him." Apart from this supreme and sole insistence, which has often been ignored, but never with impunity, every requirement is a matter of prudence and expediency. Prince and peasant, pauper and millionaire, the handsome and the homely, men of the highest erudition and most brilliant gifts and men of average powers and meagerly furnished minds, have been equally impelled, by the divine energy within them, to put their hands "to the plow." While, on the one hand, the ripest learning and capacity of the world have been consecrated to the labors of a field in which a few fishermen and others of like social grade were the honored pioneers, on the other hand, a lowly birth, an obscure pedigree, an empty wallet, or the want of culture has never been permitted to discredit the vessels of God's election or handicap admission to "the goodly fellowship of the prophets."

In receiving to-day some of the most eloquent of her spokesmen and the ablest of her leaders and administrators from antecedently unlikely quarters, the Christian Church is not only in harmony with the best traditions of the past, but also secures for herself the additional advantage of keeping in vital and effective touch with the masses to whom her message of mercy is specifically addressed. Whenever she is most alive to her great opportunity in the world and most loyal to her exalted Head, who himself sprang from unfavored and unpromising soil, she feels instinctively that her true hope is in the people; and that if the people are to believe in the divinity of her mission, to be molded by her ideals and edified and helped by her instructions, she must approach them in a form that is truly representative of their social status, and speak to them in tones expressive of an intelligent and thorough sympathy with their peculiar sorrows, anxieties, and cares. "O my Lord, wherewith shall I save Israel? behold, my family is poor in Manasseh, and I am the least in my father's house" (Judg. vi, 15), was the modest disclaimer of the youth whom God called from the severe and exacting toil of his father's threshing-floor, in a time of national anxiety and panic, to deliver his people, driven by the myriad hosts of Midian and Amalek to hide in "dens, and caves, and strongholds" of the mountains, and left by the periodic raids of their ruthless foes with neither "increase of the earth," nor "sheep, nor ox, nor ass." And the man who accomplished so much with so little—confounding and scattering the multitudinous host of the invader by the simple device of lights concealed, amid the darkness, in earthen pitchers—suggested to the apostle Paul the method and motive of God's procedure in the selection of his agents. "We have this treasure in earthen vessels that the transcendent greatness of the power ($\dot{\eta}\ \dot{\upsilon}\pi\varepsilon\rho\beta o\lambda\dot{\eta}\ \tau\tilde{\eta}\varsigma\ \delta\upsilon\nu\dot{\alpha}\mu\varepsilon\omega\varsigma$) may be of God, and not of us" (2 Cor. iv, 7).

"For my descent, then," says Bunyan, with characteristic open-heartedness and simplicity, "it was, as is well known by many, of a low and inconsiderable generation; my father's house being of that rank that is meanest and most despised of all the families of the land. Wherefore, I have not here, as others, to boast of noble blood, and of an high-born state according to the flesh, though, all things considered, I magnify the heavenly Majesty for that by this door he brought me into the world to partake of the grace and life that is in Christ by the Gospel."* And yet, when that most dissolute and despicable of English kings—Charles II —expressed his astonishment to Dr. John Owen that a man of his erudition should go to hear a tinker preach, Owen, so far from dissembling his deep admiration for the greatest preacher and best known popular writer of his age, replied, "May it please your majesty, if I could have that tinker's talent for preaching, I would gladly give in exchange all my learning."

Some of the greatest of the Christian fathers were the children of poverty. Such certainly was Chrysostom— golden-mouthed—the Demosthenes of Greek Christianity, whose eloquent and heart-searching expositions of the Gospel doctrine attracted the attention of heathen, heretic, Jew, and Christian alike, and of whose homilies on the

---

* *Grace Abounding to the Chief of Sinners*, p. 1.

Gospel of Matthew, Aquinas, the most famous of the schoolmen, declared that to him they were "worth more than the whole city of Paris." Such was Athanasius, whose consummate courage and matchless dialectic skill enabled him at twenty-five to control the theological decisions of the Nicene Council and, with faultless discrimination in the meaning of vertebral theological terms, elaborate the most carefully and subtly worded creed of early Christendom.* Such was Augustine, whose writings, steeped in religious emotion, dominated the thought and molded the theology of the Western Church for more than a thousand years; and though rapidly yielding to a nobler, humaner, and more reasonable interpretation of Christ's teachings, can hardly be said to have entirely lost their savor even to-day.† Such were the Irish missionaries who followed Columba to the southwest of Scotland in the early part of the sixth century. From the bleak and barren gneiss-rock which they had selected as their home amid the outer Hebrides the monks of Iona, and later those of its offshoot—Lindisfarne—on the east coast, bore the torch of saving truth through a large portion of western Europe in the seventh and eighth centuries—a period notorious for its intellectual gloom, sanguinary strifes, and social disintegration. In the heart of the English Midlands, where, as the historian remarks, "heathendom fought desperately for life," Lichfield Cathedral stands, to-day, a beautiful and enduring memorial of one of them—Ceadda—the St. Chad to whom it is still dedicated. "So simple and lowly in temper" was he "that he traveled on foot, on his long mission journeys, till Archbishop Theodore with his own hands lifted him on horseback." And where now rise the stately and ivy-crowned ruins of Melrose Abbey in the Scotch lowlands—the region

---

* With the Athanasian Creed, so-called, the thrice-banished bishop of Alexandria had nothing to do, it being the production of a much later age.

† Patricius, father of Augustine, was of noble birth, but, like many noble Romans of his day, of slender and precarious fortune.

of "Cheviot and Lammermoor, Ettrick and Teviotdale, Yarrow and Annan-water," which are still "musical with old ballads and border minstrelsy," is the scene of the labors of another—the Apostle of the Lowlands—Cuthbert. His favorite haunts were the "remoter mountain villages"—groups of "straw-thatched log huts in the midst of untilled solitudes"—from whose roughness and poverty other teachers turned aside. "His patience, his humorous good sense, the sweetness of his look, told for him, and not less the stout, vigorous frame which fitted the peasant-preacher for the hard life he had chosen. 'Never did man die of hunger who served God faithfully,' he would say to his companions when nightfall found them supperless in the waste. 'Look at the eagle overhead! God can feed us through him if he will'—and once, at least, he owed his meal to a fish that the scared bird let fall. A snowstorm drove his boat on the coast of Fife. 'The snow closes the road along the shore' mourned his comrades; 'the storm bars our way over sea.' 'There is still the way of heaven that lies open,' said Cuthbert."* Such noble souls show how, amid the sorrows and anxieties of a life of material want, toil, and hardship, may be cultivated a true wealth of heart, contentment of mind, and majesty of character.

How poor would have seemed the boasted intellectual splendor of the Renaissance, or the still grander moral and spiritual triumphs of the Reformation, without the name of the little German boy who sang, barefooted and bareheaded, in the streets of Eisenach for his daily bread! The man who made Erfurth and Wittenberg household words, whose magnificent personality still haunts the narrow streets of Worms—most hoary and most venerable of German cities—and the grim old castle of the Wartburg, was emphatically the child of penury and indigence, whose father earned a precarious livelihood, as a lead miner, amid the barren moun-

---

* Green's *History of the English People*, vol. 1, p. 54.

tains of Saxony. Hooker, whose place even to-day is that of a prince among English thinkers and theologians, and whose name stands easily first as a master of stately Elizabethan prose, was a poor, fatherless and friendless boy when the discerning Bishop Jewell discovered in him "a diamond in the rough," and resolved to give him, at his own expense, the coveted advantage of an Oxford training. Calvin's fine genius and precocious gravity made him a tonsured ecclesiastic and brought him Church preferment as a boy of twelve, in his native diocese of Noyon, and won him the favor of his noble and wealthy neighbors the Montmors, with whom he mostly lived and by whose generous munificence he received the best education his age could afford—under such Latinists as Corderius, such Hellenists as Melchior Wolmar, and such jurists as Pierre de l'Etoile and Andreas Alciati—the latter being reputed the ablest law professor in Europe. But the eminent Dutch divine Arminius, whose doctrine of redemption, after centuries of unbroken conflict with Calvinism, has now everywhere vanquished the older system and brought about the liberalization and expansion of religious thought,* was less fortunate in his birth and early circumstances, being left fatherless in infancy, and fitted for the place he adorned in the new University of Leyden in a disputatious and stormy age, first by the aid of generous friends, and then at the cost of the Merchants' Guild of Amsterdam by recommendation of the burgomasters. Peter Bertius notes that "his widowed mother, who as long as she survived led a life of piety, was

---

* Dr. Jortin, in his *Dissertations*, says: "In England, at the time of the Synod of Dort, we also were much divided in our religious opinions concerning the controverted articles (five articles of the Remonstrants), but our divines having taken the liberty to think and judge for themselves, and the civil government not interposing, it hath come to pass that from that time to this almost all persons here of any note for learning and abilities have bid adieu to Calvinism, have sided with the Remonstrants, and have left the Fatalists to follow their own opinions and to rejoice (since they can rejoice) in a religious system consisting of human creatures without liberty, doctrines without sense, faith without reason, and a God without mercy."

"His sermons, lectures, and orations," says the famous Anglicized Frenchman, John Fletcher, speaking of Arminius, "made many ashamed of absolute reprobation, and the *bad-principled* God who was before quietly worshiped all over Holland."

The Minister in the Making 65

called to the exercise of the utmost frugality in the maintenance of herself and her three fatherless children."*

The exemplary, almost ideal, domestic life of the parents of the Wesleys was one constant battle with straitened circumstances—an unremittent strain of anxiety and effort to educate their children and keep the proverbial wolf from the door. No two persons, probably, ever gave so much to the world in their gifted offspring and received so little from it in return as Samuel and Susanna Wesley.† Their most distinguished son, John, was probably never worth $200, in his own right, during the whole of his long, laborious, and singularly useful life, and yet if he had adopted as his motto the apostolic words, ὡς πτωχοί πολλοὺς δὲ πλουτίζοντες,‡ nothing could have been more felicitously appropriate. § In 1790—the year before his death—he ceased his lifelong practice of noting down the details of his personal expenditure. "I will not attempt it any longer," he says, "being satisfied with the continual conviction that I save all I can and give all I can—that is, all I have." ‖ When he died, at the ripe age of eighty-eight, he had little more to dispose of by will, apart from the revenue from his writings, than the six sovereigns which he bequeathed to six poor men who carried him to his grave, and a bunch of skeleton keys, which, though handed over annually with

---

* Funeral oration.

† For three successive generations, as Mr. Augustine Birrell points out in his lecture on John Wesley, the Wesleys had been harassed and kept poor by various legal difficulties.

‡ 2 Cor. vi, 10, As poor, while yet enriching many.

§ In the *Odyssey*, πτωχοί (beggarmen), like ξένοι (guests), are regarded as sharing in a special manner the divine pity and protection. It is not too much to suppose that in the apostle's use of the word there is a subtle reference to this interesting parallel between the Christian and the pagan πτωχός. It is the manner of Paul half-playfully to mark these coincidences. At Athens he noted in this semi-humorous strain how members of different philosophic sects in the city sneered at him contemptuously as a σπερμολόγος (*a picker-up of seeds*)—a hungry bird of passage snatching a hasty mouthful from the busy street where he happened to alight. Students of the Life of St. Francis of Assisi know how large a place this ancient sentiment, that the poor are the special *protégés* of heaven, fills in the practical life of that noblest and sweetest of Italian saints, and in that of the early Franciscans. See *Life*, by Paul Sabatier.

‖ Telford's *Life of Wesley*, p. 345.

dramatic solemnity—together with a Bible he used—to each succeeding president of the Wesleyan Conference by his predecessor in office, no one has ever yet discovered the use of, and probably no one ever will. His eloquent co-adjutor, Whitefield, earned his living in his boyhood by drawing foaming jugs of ale for his widowed mother's customers, and blacking the boots of gentlemen who visited her inn in the old city of Gloucester. The other original members of the Oxford Club lived in well-feathered nests and died in them, and their names are now almost forgotten.*

The leading ministers of the early Methodist Church, though men of scholarly habits and attainments, and mostly eloquent and successful preachers, were all poor men, and leaned by force of natural sympathy toward their social kindred in the lowlier ranks of life. "Their voices were heard in the wildest and most barbarous corners of the land, in the dens of London, or in the long galleries where in the pauses of his labor the Cornish miner listens to the sobbing of the sea." When that justly celebrated orientalist and commentator—Dr. Adam Clarke—arrived, as a youth, at Kingswood School, near Bristol, the earliest of Wesleyan educational institutions, where he hoped to spend a short period in better preparing himself for the Methodist ministry, he did not have the equivalent of more than three cents in his purse;† and this almost pathetic impecuniosity, so far from being singular, only established an additional point of conformity between him and the great majority of his fellow-evangelists. No one can doubt that the early intimate fellowship of the renowned Father Taylor with illiteracy, poverty, and scantily remunerated toil, as a common sailor before the mast and in various later efforts to earn

---

* This is the case, in spite of Tyerman's labored effort to confer immortality upon them in his *Oxford Methodists*.
† Etheridge's *Life of Dr. A. Clarke*, p. 64.

a livelihood, largely accounts for the intuitive and intense sympathy with the sorrows, cares, and aspirations of the people which so greatly contributed to his remarkable success, in the city of Boston, as a preacher to poor seamen for more than forty years. "No American citizen—Webster, Clay, Everett, Lincoln, Choate"—says Dr. Bartol, "has a reputation more impressive and unique. In the hall of memory his spiritual statue will have forever its own niche. . . . He stands for the sea; the greatest delegate the ocean has sent upon the stage of any purely intellectual calling, at least in this part of the world.* Even Spurgeon, equally eminent as a pastor, preacher, commentator, author, educator, and philanthropist, was obliged to forego the advantage of a university training because his parents had no money to pay for it; and the vivid remembrance of difficulties encountered and conquered in his youth inspired the unfaltering hope and courage with which he labored to rescue the victims of sin and temptation around him from the wreck of fortune, health, and character, and from the social submergence and chronic heartache and hopelessness which are otherwise their almost certain fate.

It is impossible not to see the immense advantage to the Christian Church of this intimate personal acquaintance of her ministry, in its nobler and more efficient types, with the wholesome, though unwelcome, discipline of poverty. On the one hand, it offers some guarantee for the continued applicability and force of that very important item in her Founder's program which, deeply considered, is really a summary of the whole: "The poor have the Gospel preached to them." On the other, it serves to shield a class which, in spite of certain economic theories and socialistic dreams of the age, will always comprise the great majority of mankind—namely, the industrial and meritorious poor—from the false feeling forced upon them by the classes above

---

* *Father Taylor, the Sailor Preacher*, p. 425. Haven and Russell.

them, and by those among themselves, who have an ax to grind, that intellectual refinement, social worth, and moral self-respect and dignity are impossible without money. This impression, as maleficent and insidious as it is difficult to destroy, needs to be wiped clean out of the heart and thought of the people before the teachings of Jesus can reach, inspire, and elevate them to any appreciable extent; and nothing is better fitted to demonstrate its unreality and emptiness than the cheerful advent among them of that messenger of peace whose "feet are beautiful upon the mountains," even though he come with "neither purse, nor scrip, nor shoes."

The fact has a significance of its own, that the sanction and indorsement of piety in its lowlier forms on the part of the ministers of Jesus, by their personal acceptance of its material anxieties and cares, has been a principal feature of every genuine revival of a pure and uncorrupted Christianity. It was remarkably prominent in the age of its genesis and juvenility, and though often buried deep for centuries together, it has been regularly resurrected with every serious and really successful effort to recover the simplicity and power of the Gospel, to recall men's minds to its incomparably lofty ethical standard and redeem the fallen fortunes and declining prestige of the Church. No mission to the heathen ever succeeds without it—that is, if we gauge and estimate success according to the intensely spiritual standard which the genius and spirit of the Gospel itself supplies. It was, in great part, the secret of Xavier's great work in India and Japan, of John Eliot's power over the red men of colonial Massachusetts; of Brainerd's over the tribes of the Delaware and Susquehanna; of the triumphs of the early Moravian missionaries in such diverse and widely distant latitudes as Greenland and the West Indies, and it explains, in the opinion of a shrewd observer,[*] the growing

---

[*] Hon. W. S. Caine, *Letters from India.*

popularity of the Salvation Army to-day among the polyglotal peoples of India. Brahmanism, Buddhism, and Mohammedanism—the three great religions which have successively striven for supremacy, and have deeply influenced, and are to-day deeply influencing, the destinies of millions of mankind—have alike consecrated poverty as Christ did, and though the devotees of these religions have no idea of the motive that ennobles and exalts it in its Christian form, they cannot easily understand any religion that eliminates and ignores it. More than sixty years ago Edward Irving, that most majestic of Scotch orators—if we except, perhaps, his friend Chalmers—greatly offended the managers and friends of the London Missionary Society when, accepting their urgent invitation to preach their annual missionary sermon, he selected for his text the words of the divine commission : " Go your ways : behold, I send you forth as lambs among wolves. Carry neither purse, nor scrip, nor shoes ; " and powerfully urged the applicability of the apostolic principle of self-support to modern missionary enterprise. And yet to the present writer nothing seems more impotent and unpromising than the attempt to evangelize the diversely-habited, diversely-mannered, many-traditioned, and many-tongued heathen world, with its prehistoric and hoary civilizations, by simply sending them first-class specimens of the modern educated gentleman, often wholly unschooled in the systems of thought which confront him on the threshold of his work, and heavily handicapped from the outset with the prejudices, mannerisms, and sense of superiority which are the peculiar vices of a civilization which in itself, as compared with other and earlier types, has no intrinsic and peculiar moral value whatever; vices which serve only to emphasize painfully and invidiously the contrast between the social and religious system he represents, and the social and religious institutions he hopes to reform. As long as the Augustinian,

Benedictine, Dominican, Franciscan, Cistercian, Carmelite, and Moravian communities were brotherhoods of poverty they were brotherhoods of moral and spiritual power. Their intense sympathy with the people, even when it assumed grotesque and repulsive forms, was electrical, and made their simple exhortations irresistible to peasant and prince alike. There was something indescribably sublime in the enthusiam, kept constantly at a white heat, of men who the more they scorned the ordinary privileges and pleasures of life the more firmly they seemed to grasp the secret of all inner and essential joys. And the voluntary assumption of a condition which seemed to rob them of the smallest crumb of earthly comfort, while it reserved to them the richest and rarest music of the heart—the strange union of a poverty-stricken exterior with an incalculable store of inward wealth—found, for all men of spiritual insight, a sufficient explanation in the characteristic avowal of St. Francis of Assisi to his boon companions at the outstart of the Grand Renunciation, that he had resolved to marry a lovely lady who for more than a thousand years had mourned her widowhood in seclusion and silence—the Lady Poverty; or, in the saying of the Calabrian, Gioacchino Di Fiore, "*Qui vere monachus est nihil reputat esse suum nisi citharam*" (He who is a monk in truth considers nothing to be his except his harp).

2. The Molding of Environment.

But if the Christian religion has found the exponents of its primary and essential verities, the exemplars of its loftiest virtues, and the ablest champions of its beliefs, doctrines, and invigorating moral discipline not among the wordly wise, the wealthy, or the nobly born ($ζύγενεῖς$),[*] it cannot be said that in summoning men to the work of the Gospel ministry the "Searcher of hearts" does not discriminate, and

---

[*] 1 Cor. i, 26.

seek the gifted "heralds of salvation" where, to his all-seeing eye, they are the likeliest to be found. It was not because Amos was a poor, hard-working herdsman of Tekoa that he was called to exercise the prophetic office and unveil those great principles of God's moral government of the world, which he saw working in his own day secretly and silently toward more vivid disclosure and fuller vindication in a future age. Nor, on the other hand, were the seraphic devotion, the brilliant gifts, and the exemplary patriotism of Isaiah passed by because he chanced to be of princely birth and breeding. The bare fact that Simon was poor, and caught fish for a living, did not specially qualify him for the apostolate or commend him to Jesus as the fittest to be first among the twelve. Nor was the Tarsian academician, the accomplished graduate of Asia's most famous school of learning and distinguished pupil of Gamaliel—prince of Palestinian rabbis of his day—discredited on account of his aristocratic descent,* or debarred by his learning and logical acuteness from being a preacher to the illiterate multitude; God's chosen vessel to bear among the Gentiles the fragrance of the only "name under heaven given among men, whereby we must be saved."

The great preachers and doctors of Christendom, in every age, have been men who enjoyed in their birth, childhood, and youth morally wholesome and auspicious surroundings. And if there is any atom of truth in the old saying, "The rockers of the cradle are the rulers of the world," it probably finds its first and highest application here. The incidence of the divine choice seems to be largely determined by two factors which have always been present and prominent in the history of human development, namely, heredity and environment. These two factors "are the master influences of the organic world. These have made all of us what we are. These forces are still ceaselessly playing

---

* Phil. iii, 5.

upon all our lives. And he who truly understands these influences; he who has decided how much to allow to each; he who can regulate new forces as they arise and adjust them to the old, so directing them as at one moment to make them cooperate, at another to counteract one another, understands the rationale of personal development. To seize continuously the opportunity of more and more perfect adjustment to better and higher conditions, to balance some inward evil with some purer influence, acting from without—in a word, to make our environment at the same time that it is making us—these are the secrets of a well-ordered and successful life." *

The influence of home and of early association and environment on some of the most notable actors on the stage of ecclesiastical history is strongly marked and easily traceable. The devout and gentle spirit of his mother, Anthusa, left its own deep and indelible impression on Chrysostom, as he himself informs us, and to her maternal oversight and mastery of the noblest of all the arts, the art of molding character, we are largely indebted for one of the grandest figures on the historical horizon of the early Church. Athanasius, the distinguished expositor and apologist of the Nicene Christology, breathed from earliest childhood the wholesome atmosphere of earnest religious thought and practical philanthropy, being bred in the home of the primate of Alexandria, and allowed frequently to visit in his boyhood the retired haunts of St. Anthony, the hermit of the Nile. Of Monica, mother of Augustine, Neander says: "Whatever treasures of virtue and worth the life of faith, even of a soul not trained by scientific culture, can bestow were set before him in the example of his pious mother;" and that great light of the Latin Church and episcopate has more than once embalmed, in his writings, the memory of his mother in the expression of his gratitude for her tender-

---

* Drummond's *Natural Law in the Spiritual World*, p. 183.

ness and solicitude.* Anselm, deservedly designated the chief of mediæval theologians (*scholasticorum doctorum princeps*) by his admiring disciple and inseparable companion, Eadmer, of Canterbury, and certainly one of the brightest lights vouchsafed by divine Providence to a dark and dismal age, owed everything to the pious care and attentions of his mother, Ermenberga,† and his boyish heart bitterly bewailed her loss when she died, and felt like a ship that had slipped its anchor—almost entirely overwhelmed amid the tossing billows of the world.‡

The mother of Luther was a woman of tender heart and noble mind, *exemplar virtutum* (a pattern of the virtues), as Melanchthon calls her, and her love served to mitigate the unwarrantably severe disciplinary *régime* of the father. Melanchthon, on the other hand—so named by his erudite kinsman Reuchlin, prince of Hebrew scholars as Melanchthon was of Greek—was from infancy a child of too much love and too many favors. With the gentleness and amiability of a woman, he would hardly have weathered the tempests of the Reformation had he not been sheltered and strengthened by association with rougher and more strenuous natures. Calvin—peculiarly fortunate in his home and friends, his schools, and teachers—was from the first marked for supremacy, and yet it was not the "still small voice" of the home, or the school, or the temple that discovered the depth and strength and nobleness of his nature, but the storm and earthquake of conflict and the fierce fires of controversy,

---

* *Confessiones*, Book ix, 33. From the *De Vita Beata* Dr. Pusey translates the following beautiful tribute addressed by St. Angustine to his mother, "You through whose prayers I undoubtedly believe and affirm that God gave me that mind that I should prefer nothing to the discovery of truth; wish, think of, love naught besides." In *De Dono Perseverantiæ* he says, "To the faithful and daily tears of my mother it was granted that I should not perish."

† Hugo Læmmer, in the Preface to his edition of the *Cur Deus Homo?* p. 3, says, "*Pater quidem Gundulfus rerum familiarum incuriosus nec tam largus quam prodigus præ negotiis secularibus instituendum neglexit filium, mater autem Ermenberga officiis domesticis probe functa inde a prima pueritia illius pectus pietate studuit imbuere.*"

‡ "*Navis cordis eius, quasi anchora perdita, in fluctus sæculi pæne tota dilapsa est.*" Praef. edition, p. 4.

thus illustrating the sentiment of Goethe, that "talent forms itself in solitude, character in the stream of life."* He has himself told us, in the Preface to his Commentary on the Psalms, how the stern mandate of his lifelong friend Farel, enforced by a still sterner malediction, compelled him to arm for the fight and set his face toward the foe. He was passing through Geneva, August 5, 1536, intending to leave next day, but Farel, with an insight and sagacity almost prophetic, solemnly threatened him with the curse of heaven if he preferred his studies to the work of God, that now required his prompt assistance. "These words," says Calvin, "terrified and shook me as if God from on high had stretched out his hand to stop me, so that I renounced the journey I had undertaken." † Arminius had been so well cared for by his friends and widowed mother as to draw from Beza, whose lectures he attended at Geneva, a eulogium addressed to the clergy and magistrates of Amsterdam, of which any youth might well be proud.‡ Even Wesley's truly wonderful work ceases altogether to appear miraculous when we remember the intellectual nobleness and moral grandeur of his parents, notably of his mother, and the care with which she attended to his early education and religious training.

---

* "*Es bildet ein Talent sich in der stille*
Sich ein Charakter in dem Strom der Welt."

† Calvin, like all great souls, was a many-sided man, but one aspect of his character, and a very important one, seems to be entirely lost sight of in the estimate of the present age. With strong and deep convictions, and a logical acuteness amply competent to defend them, he blended great tenderness of feeling and a large capacity for friendship. As Dr. Schaff remarks, "Men, by a blessed inconsistency, are often kinder than their creeds."

‡ "From the period when Arminius returned from Basle to us at Geneva both his acquirements in learning and his manner of life have been so approved by us that we form the highest hopes respecting him, if he proceed in the same course as that which he is now pursuing. . . . For the Lord has conferred on him, among other endowments, a happy genius for clearly perceiving the nature of things and for forming a correct judgment upon them, which, if it be hereafter brought under the governance of piety, of which he shows himself most studious, will undoubtedly cause his powerful genius, after it has been matured by years and confirmed by his acquaintance with things, to produce a rich and most abundant harvest. These are our sentiments concerning Arminius, a young man, as far as we have been able to form a judgment of him, in no respect unworthy of your benevolence and liberality."—*Letter of Beza to Rev. Martin Lydius*, Works of James Arminius, Nichols's edition, vol. i, p. 25.

Not always does the mantle of the sire fall fittingly on the shoulders of the son, but the two greatest preachers of the last five decades were sons of the manse. Spurgeon went to London a beardless boy of nineteen years from a home proud of the preaching traditions of three generations. He went to leave in its busy but sad life deeper traces of his personality and work than the charioteers of Pompeii have left in the worn pavement of the streets they once enlivened by their presence, and both his sons are to-day adorning the ministerial profession and maintaining the high ancestral reputation for ability and eloquence. And no one who has read the *Life of Dr. Lyman Beecher*, by his son Charles, will wonder that, from a hearthstone which had often been the landing place of mercies because the starting place of prayer and lofty purpose, so many preaching Beechers should have come—one of them *facile princeps* of the American pulpit, if not of that of the world, in his day.

3. The Training of the Schools.

But there yet remains to be considered the training of the schools, which

1. *Must adapt itself to conditions of the age.*

So long as the Christian Church aspires, as the visible representative of the "Kingdom of God" on earth, to universal dominion over the human mind she must qualify her ministers to be the real, if not the acknowledged, leaders and teachers of their times. With this in view she must not hesitate to demand from them conformity to the highest known standard of moral and spiritual life and submission to a thorough and comprehensive intellectual discipline. The vision of the "watchman" on the walls of Zion needs to be clear, strong, and sustained to-day to a degree never required before, for his range of prospect has greatly expanded during the eventful century now drawing to a close, and problems—moral, social, intellectual, industrial, personal, and national—challenge his faculty of analysis and discrimination to-day, of which the men of a generation or two ago never dreamed. And while the field of his responsibility has widened, some of the resources on which he might have safely counted in the past are hardly to be reckoned on now. The only weapon that can be effectively used in the warfare of our time is that finely tempered sword of sanctified Christian culture—the light of truth. Mere acceptance of denominational shibboleths and "isms" avails no more. The prestige of theological systems and the dynasty of the system-builders as such have appreciably declined. The decrees of ecclesiastical councils are no more than mere echoes of the past—either dead or dying. The dawn of Christian reason is with us, and the era of authority has closed. The emancipation of individual judgment, with all its undoubted perils, is already an accomplished fact. The present century has canonized sober, reverent, labor-loving criticism, welcomed its presence in our halls of learning, science, and historical research, and in many notable instances has politely asked it to "take a chair"—and stay. Amid the growing light the empire of creeds that conclude with damnatory clauses is being rapidly dissolved. Men are beginning to discern the deep meaning of the Lord's prophetic word, "Ye shall know the truth, and the truth shall make you free," and are being attracted by the force and beauty of his prayer, "Sanctify them through thy truth." To-day every noble thought finds friends and every real power is welcomed. Both hands are extended to hail the man who sees, beyond old sunsets, the light of a new dawn for mankind. And while everywhere the yoke of *false* authority is being unceremoniously broken, it is only that men may bend their necks the more willingly to the *true* dictation. The theological school must, therefore, get nearer the pulse of current thought, mark the change and revise its curriculum; and, adapting its instructions to the new conditions, make men who shall be competent to meet the reasonable requirements of the age.

2. *Must not be fearful of science or jealous of man's intellectual freedom.*

As a matter of fact, Christianity, justly interpreted, is not fearful of science, jealous of man's intellectual freedom, or anxious to fasten padlocks on his thoughts. Its fundamental verities, which constitute the assured anchorage of faith, grasp firmly the rock of Eternal Being, and are confirmed and vindicated, not imperiled or obscured, by inquiry. There are music and majesty—both—in the words of Hooker: " Dangerous it were for the feeble brain of man to wade far into the doings of the Almighty, whom, although to know be life, and joy to make mention of his name, yet our soundest knowledge is to know that we know him not as indeed he is, neither can know him, and our safest eloquence concerning him is our silence when we confess without confession that his glory is inexplicable, his greatness above our capacity and reach."* But, admitting the sublimity and beauty of the sentiment, is the risk against which we are admonished a real one ? Where is the danger of wading too far into the doings of the Almighty, whether in the realm of science, of history, of philosophy, or theological thought ? Is not our chief peril of a totally opposite kind ? Is not that research urged upon us as the very pith and marrow of our strength and blessedness ? "One thing have I desired of the Lord, that will I seek after ; that I may dwell in the house of the Lord all the days of my life, to behold the beauty of the Lord, and to inquire in his temple." Is not the secret of the Lord with them that fear him ? And did not the prophet Amos, while deprecating formalism and enslavement to ceremonial routine,

---
* *Laws of Ecclesiastical Polity*, book i.

entreat his fellow-countrymen to "seek" not Bethel, nor Gilgal, nor Beer-sheba, but to "seek Jahveh" and live? "Seek him that maketh the seven stars and Orion, and turneth the shadow of death into the morning, and maketh the day dark with night: that calleth for the waters of the sea, and poureth them out upon the face of the earth: Jahveh is his name." Could modern science and philosophy covet nobler charter than this?

Nothing, in truth, so stimulates to free, wholesome, manly, independent thinking as the great truths and doctrines of revealed religion, and nothing offers so complete a solution of all the great problems of life and of thought. And to the few men who have followed the inward light, and wandered, and been ostracized and persecuted, in their time, for their deviation from the narrow sheep track of so-called orthodoxy, the world owes to-day a larger debt of gratitude than to the many who, forgetful that God has still "more light and truth to break forth from his word," have been satisfied with what they inherited, and have quietly stayed at home, thus incurring the reproach of their worthier brethren: Why abode ye "among the sheepfolds, to hear the bleatings of the flocks?" No consideration avails to restrain the truth-loving mind from seeking to enrich and ennoble faith and widen the skirts of light. The most thoroughly trained disciple of Palestinian rabbinism and rising hope of a decadent faith suddenly changed front, when new conviction came, and became the champion of Christian freedom and "the apostle of the Gentiles." From one of the oldest and most venerable monastic orders of the Catholic Church sprang the man who gave Protestantism to history. The most promising pupil of Dr. Reynolds—the zealous exponent and advocate of Puritanism and the Presbyterian polity, in Oxford, in the latter half of the sixteenth century—was Hooker, whose *Ecclesiastical Polity* is still regarded as the greatest argument for an episcopalian *régime*. The world would probably never have heard of Arminius or Arminianism if the ardent young theologue of Amsterdam had accepted without criticism or question the Calvinism of Beza, whose lectures on the Epistle to the Romans he attended at Geneva and greatly admired. The most pronounced and most distinguished High Churchman of the eighteenth century is claimed as the founder of Methodism, which is perhaps the most anti-ritualistic and most anti-sacerdotal of Protestant denominations. William Ellery Channing, the corypheus of New England Unitarianism, was educated as a Calvinist; and for a time was pastor of a Calvinistic church in Federal Street, Boston, Mass. Cardinal Newman frankly acknowledged his indebtedness for the beginnings of the spiritual life to the preaching of the commentator Thomas Scott, whose anti-Romish sentiments were peculiarly strong.* The most zealous and successful propagandist of the Roman Catholic Church in England since the era of the Reformation was the late Cardinal Manning, who was a graduate of Oxford. And Spurgeon, though he never would acknowledge his spiritual paternity, bowed beneath the weight of religious conviction under a sermon preached by a decided Arminian, one wet Sunday morning, in the old military town of Colchester, England.† Religious belief is neither a thing of heredity nor the creation of the schools. It is as the lightning, which "cometh out of the *east* and shineth even unto the *west*." In this, as in many other things,

God fulfills himself in many ways,
Lest one good custom should corrupt the world.

Though men have assumed the sanction of Christianity for all manner of narrowness, shallowness, and bigotry, it is

---

* *Apologia Pro Vita Sua*, p. 56.

† The Rev. Robert Eaglen, the man who preached in the little Primitive Methodist church on the day young Spurgeon wandered into it a perfect stranger to everyone, and the only man in England who ever claimed to be, humanly speaking, the means of Spurgeon's conversion, was personally though not intimately known to the author. He was a man of frail health and feeble constitution, and was early obliged to retire

noteworthy that it is within the Christian literature, and not otherwhere, that the noblest exhortations to the cultivation of intellectual sanity, sagacity, breadth, and penetration —" the spirit of power, and of love, and of a sound mind "— are found. " Be ye not unwise, but understanding what the will of the Lord is ; " " Howbeit in malice be ye children, but in good sense be ye full-grown men " (τέλειοι).

It is, then, not only agreeable to the genius of Christianity, but absolutely required by the condition of the age, that the Christian Church, having selected the candidates for its ministry from the best available material, should seek in its university and seminary instruction to preserve, direct, and develop their individuality and independence of thought with a view to their adequate equipment for the keen and interminable conflict with the prevailing unbelief and apathy in which they are destined to be engaged.

3. *Must be varied, comprehensive, and thorough.*

Equally needful is it that such preparatory drill should be as varied in character and as comprehensive in range and scope as possible, so as to impart to the student " the versatility of intellect, the command over his own powers, the instinctive just estimate of things as they pass before him, which sometimes, indeed, is a natural gift, but commonly is not gained without much effort and the exercise of years."* It is safe to say that nowhere has a thoroughly disciplined and well-balanced judgment a greater value or a larger opportunity than in the ministerial profession, and nowhere is the conspicuous want of it attended with more disastrous results. By judgment, however, we do not mean merely that familiar and homely quality of mind which

---

from active service. He was characterized by a singular devoutness of spirit, deep theological convictions, great simplicity of character, and an unassuming manner. He once contrived to meet Mr. Spurgeon, and endeavored by a full and detailed description of the church, congregation, and other attendant circumstances to bring his convert to an acknowledgment of him as the agent in God's hands of opening to him "the door of faith," but though Spurgeon admitted the accuracy of his account, he peremptorily refused to recognize him as the preacher of the occasion.

* Cardinal Newman's *Idea of a University*, p. 174.

withholds a person from the commission of mistakes to the injury of his fortunes or his reputation, but "that master-principle of business, literature, talent, which gives him strength in any subject he chooses to grapple with, and enables him to seize the strong point in it."* The great leaders, teachers, and orators of the Christian Church have all been willing to purchase this inestimable gift at the cost of years of varied and unremitting mental toil and application. In their view, versatility—an immense advantage in any profession—was entitled to take rank among the cardinal virtues in a minister of Christ, inasmuch as it seemed to realize the *divine* ministerial ideal—"wise as serpents, and harmless as doves." It was to this many-sided intellectual development the apostle of the Gentiles owed the facility and freedom with which he became "all things to all men" that he "might by all means save some." Whether he addresses his own infuriated fellow-countrymen, in their vernacular Syriac, from the steps of the Tower of Antonia, in Jerusalem, or quotes to fastidious Athenians on Mars' Hill lines pregnant with Christian truths from their own approved poets, or expounds to the Greek-speaking Jews of the Dispersion (δι Ἑλληνιϛτάι) in Rome the divine truths available to them in the Septuagint Scriptures, or seeks to kindle the spark of faith in the minds of the fickle Galatians, or pleads for an exclusive loyalty to God among the more enlightened and reliable men of the Asian metropolis —the home of the great goddess Diana—his various knowledge and versatile gift of speech are a never-failing resource, everywhere securing respectful attention to the truths he wishes to declare. It was an immense advantage to early Christianity that its great apologists, Justin Martyr, Origen, Clemens Alexandrinus, Athanasius, were as familiar with Greek philosophy as their opponents. Augustine's thorough acquaintance with Plato's subtle and sublime rea-

---

* *Idea of a University*, p. 174.

sonings was no small part of his fitness for the place he has filled in the history of Western religious thought. Chrysostom and Basil both studied Roman law, thus setting an example followed by many of the most eminent of the Latin fathers. No de' Medici that ever walked the streets of Florence was the equal of Savonarola even as a statesman. Wyclif was scarcely more skillful in translating and interpreting the word of God than in the art of negotiation and diplomacy. Melanchthon was an expert in law, medicine, and philosophy, and lectured to the youths of Germany and the adjacent countries on the poetry of Homer and the epistles of St. Paul in the same course, making the former contribute to the elucidation of the latter, and seeking, like Solomon, "Tyrian brass and gems for the adornment of God's temple." Calvin and Beza both attained distinction as students of jurisprudence in the University of Orleans, as Luther had done before them at Erfurth. Hooker's association with the benchers of the Inns of Court, as Master of the Temple, brought many sharp thorns to his pillow, and occasioned him great mental disquietude, but its value was simply incalculable in preparing him to write the greatest treatise on law known to the English tongue. Bunyan's brief boyish experience among the heroes of Fairfax's army was no small part of the moral and intellectual preparation which enabled him to describe the exalted character of "Greatheart," and without his personal participation in the siege of Leicester we could hardly have had the stirring scenes of the siege of Mansoul in the *Holy War*. William Carey was equally at home on the cobbler's stool, in the pulpit, and in the professor's chair. Charles G. Finney's training as a lawyer not only gave him an influence over the legal mind no one else ever possessed, but contributed no small element of his power as a preacher of the Gospel.* Isaac Barrow was none the less a distin-

---

* Speaking of Finney's evangelistic labors in Rochester, N. Y., his biographer, Dr.

guished pulpit orator because he was the leading mathematician of his age and preceptor of Isaac Newton—the greatest mathematical genius known to history. The fame of Thomas Chalmers as a preacher began with the publication of his "Astronomical Discourses"—a not surprising fact when it is remembered that his first love as a student was not evangelical theology, but the exactest of the sciences.

The minister's education is only adequate when it enables him not only to be in sympathy with all the dominant educational, scientific, and literary interests of his time, but also with all the main departments of art and handicraft and professional activity. Such only is the mental discipline which is fitted to give a man, in the words of one eminent alike as a preacher, author, educator, and ecclesiastic, "a clear, conscious view of his own opinions and judgments, a truth in developing them, an eloquence in expressing them, and a force in urging them. It teaches him to see things as they are, to go right to the point, to disentangle a skein of thought, to detect what is sophistical, and to discard what is irrelevant. It prepares him to fill any post with credit and to master any subject with facility. It shows him how to accommodate himself to others, how to throw himself into their state of mind, how to bring before them his own, how to influence them, how to come to an understanding with them, how to bear with them. He is at home in any society, he has common ground with every class; he knows when to speak and when to be silent; he is able to converse, he is able to listen; he can ask a question pertinently and gain a lesson seasonably when he has nothing to impart himself; he is ever ready, yet never in the way; he is a

---

Wright, says: "Finney's audiences were composed of the most intelligent portions of the people, including the lawyers, who invited him almost in a body. As he proceeded from night to night with his lectures, addressed especially to them, the interest increased and finally culminated, without any call on Finney's part, in a spontaneous movement, in which the lawyers, almost *en masse*, arose one evening and expressed their determination henceforth to live Christian lives and to acknowledge God before the world."
—*Life of Finney*, p. 102.

pleasant companion and a comrade you can depend upon; he knows when to be serious and when to trifle, and he has a sure tact which enables him to trifle with gracefulness and to be serious with effect. He has the repose of a mind which lives in itself while it lives in the world, and which has resources for its happiness at home when it cannot go abroad. He has a gift which serves him in public and supports him in retirement, without which good fortune is but vulgar, and with which failure and disappointment have a charm. The art which tends to make a man all this is in the object which it pursues as useful as the art of wealth or the art of health, though it is less susceptible of method and less tangible, less certain, less complete in its result."*

4. *Hence fitted to impart the secret of power required by the times.*

Not for its own sake, however, is the comprehensive and complete development of the preacher's moral and intellectual personality to be sought, but for the sake of the greatly augmented power for service which it imparts. Standing as we do in the early dawn of an epoch when all authority, power, predominance, leadership, come only by manhood, by capacity, by broad intelligence and intense moral insight, by close conformity to the mind of Christ, this is an important consideration. This century, now old with many sorrows and labors, and unique in the number and character of its triumphs and achievements, is mainly distinguished for its having seen the inauguration and acknowledgment of the empire of moral ideas. For some little time longer, probably, mankind will consent to be plagued in religion, as in politics and social life, with the man of superficial smartness, the master of tact and diplomacy, but there are unmistakable signs of the cultivation of a keener popular judgment and discrimination. Even where the crudities of the charlatan and the legerdemain of the empiricist linger the

---

* Newman's *Idea of a University*, p. 176.

longest men of light are becoming more and more the men of leading. With the force of an indisputable moral axiom the truth commends itself to men that a clear and comprehensive spiritual insight is the only sure basis of authority and power; that he alone who knows how to *serve* his fellow-men with "thoughts that breathe and words that burn" can have any just claim or real competency to *rule* them. Ultimately the world will consent to be governed only by divinely inspired ideals, and he who gives men these will have no need of crozier, crown, tiara, sword, or scepter—the baubles of a barbarous bygone time—to assert or symbolize his power. Like the ideal theocratic ruler, he will govern his sheep by feeding them; he will be the watcher of his own fold—not leave it to an hireling. "He will feed his flock like a shepherd."

CHAPTER IV
The Cardinal Function and Leading Requisites of the Christian Minister

Johannes was in the waste, washing and preaching the washing of amends-deeds on sin's forgiveness. And to him went forth all the Judeisc realm and all the Hierusalem-men and were by him washed in Jordan's flood, naming their sins. And Johannes was clad with camel's hair and a felt girdle was round his loins; and he ate grass-steppers and wood-honey. And he preached, and said, "A stranger cometh after me of whom I am not worthy that I, bowing down, should unknit his shoon's thong. I wash you in water! he washeth you in Holy Ghost."— *Wyclif*, "The Good-News after Marcus's Telling."

He should employ himself, as the one business of his discourse, to bring home to others and to leave deep within them what he has before he began to speak to them brought home to himself. What he feels himself and feels deeply he has to make others feel deeply; and in proportion as he comprehends this he will rise above the temptation of introducing collateral matters, and will have no taste, no heart, for going aside after flowers of oratory, fine figures, tuneful periods, which are worth nothing unless they come to him spontaneously and are spoken "out of the abundance of the heart."—*John Henry Cardinal Newman.*

Prædicatorem esse ministrum Dei per quem verbum Dei à spiritûs fonte ducitur ad fidelium animas irrigendas.—St. Charles.

1. Proclaiming the Evangel.

FROM the moment of the first appearance of the Baptizer in the Judean wilderness one set of terms of clear and decisive import is constantly employed to express the cardinal idea and leading function of the evangelical ministry. These words not only have a well-defined and familiar signification, but are almost ubiquitous in their range and scope. They are used by all the principal writers of the New Testament, with one remarkable exception. And even their conspicuous absence from the fourth gospel and from the epistles and Apocalypse of St. John only adds emphasis to the frequency with which they occur in the Synoptic gospels, in the Acts, and in the epistles of St. Peter and St. Paul.*

Christianity in its inception, and for perhaps the first twenty-five or thirty years of its existence, was nothing more than a simple oral proclamation (κήρυγμα), whose subject-matter was a peace-imparting evangel (εὐαγγέλιον)—an item of gracious tidings, forecasting and hastening the universal reign of heaven (ἡ βασιλεία τῶν οὐρανῶν) upon earth. And the function of the proclaimer (κῆρυξ) was evidently intended to be the primary and essential, though not exclusive, feature of the new economy to the end of time. Statesman, prince, philosopher, rhetorician, and poet in pagan lands; lawgiver, priest, prophet, and ruler among the chosen people, had each had his day; now had dawned the hour of the Christian herald—the dispensation of the evangel of human redemption. In this evangel lay the power of God for the salvation of those who believe. Of course, like all the nobler institutions of history, the office of the Christian *Ceryx* has seriously suffered from perversion and neglect. For centuries together its very idea has been almost lost, with consequences the most disastrous to the moral and spiritual welfare of mankind, but the words invariably used in the evangelic and apostolic records clearly indicate what was its original form and was meant to be its continuous and abiding character. The office, under various names, was one of eminence and honor in all Eastern and classic lands. The dignity and authority of its occupant arose from his representative character and the power that lay behind him. He spoke the mind and declared the purpose of kings, courts, senates; and princes and their powerful armies paid attention to his word; as when the Roman legate C. Popilius Lænas, the herald of the Senate, met the army of Antiochus Epiphanes in the Egyptian desert, in sight of Alexandria, and making a circle in the sand with his staff around the

---
*See Appendix to chap. iv.

haughty scion of the Seleucidæ, who sought to stave off his demand by an evasive answer, declared that to step beyond that line before a satisfactory reply had been given would be to incur the wrath of the Roman people.

2. Christ the Prince of Heralds.

It is hardly matter for marvel that the Christian Church, which ultimately consented to receive as its distinctive designation a name originally imposed by the satirical wits of a depraved Syrian city, hesitated just as little to borrow some of the most prominent features of its administrative machinery and some of the most honored of its official titles from the civil governments under which it grew.* In the present instance it found in the office of the *Ceryx* an institution adapted for its purpose ready to hand, and adopted it with no further modification than that of devoting it to the nobler function of proclaiming everywhere in the name of heaven, "Peace on earth among men of good disposition." Correctly and comprehensively defined, the Christian evangel is Christ. It is the transcript of his nature, the product of his mind, the outcome of his acts and doctrines and life and death combined; and its one grand object is to secure the fulfillment of his purpose in the salvation of mankind. Christ is the proclamation and proclaimer—both—of the "kingdom of God." He is "the Faithful and True Witness" of everlasting facts and truths—"the beginning (ἡ ἀρχή) of the creation of God.† He is born to be King of Truth and of true souls, and to demonstrate truth's illumining and liberating power. He is Master (ἐπιστάτης), Teacher (διδάσκαλος), Leader (κα Ὁηγητής), Lord (οἰκοδεσπότης), Healer (ἰατρός), Saviour (Σωτήρ), Ruler (κύριος), and Shepherd (ποιμήν) of his people. He is the outshining of

---

Vide Hatch's *Organisation of the Early Christian Churches*, lectures ii and iii; also Bishop Lightfoot's *Epistles of St. Paul* (Philippians), p. 95.
† Rev. iii, 14.

God's glory (ἀπαύγασμα τῆς δόξης) and the perfect impress of his substance (χαρακτὴρ τῆς ὑποστάσεως)* He is the Firstborn (πρωτότοκος) of the physical and moral universe, the Creator and Consummator of the ages.† He is the Apostle and High Priest of his people,‡ and the Paschal Lamb (ὁ ἀμνός), slain from the foundation of the world for their sin and their salvation.§ He is the Captain of deliverance to believers,‖ the Arbiter of destiny to all men, holding in his power the keys of Hades and Death.¶ He is the Living One,** and the Dispenser of life,†† having a name that is above every name,‡‡ and inheriting the endless worship of men and angels. For "when he again shall have brought in the firstborn into the world (εἰς τὴν οἰκουμένην) he saith, And let all the angels of God worship him.§§

All this he is, and more. But he is first and last and chiefly the herald of eternal things—of God, his love, his Fatherhood, and coming universal reign. Hints and glimpses of all this there had been before, but greatly obscured by partial and imperfect presentation. Jesus purged the gold from all alloy, restamped it with his own image and superscription, and made it current coin. He spoke the universal language of the soul, and men knew his voice. "The sources of religion lie hid from us," says a great authority in jurisprudence.‖‖ "All that we know is that now and again in the course of ages some one sets to music the tune which is haunting millions of ears. It is caught up here and there, and repeated, till the chorus is thundered out by a body of singers able to drown all discords and to force the unmusical mass to listen to them." "I follow Christ," says another, with equal force and beauty, "because I have heard him speak a natural language, and because I have heard beating in his heart the heart of all. Therefore

---

* Heb. i, 3.   † Col. i, 15; Rom. viii, 29.   ‡ Heb. iii, 1.
§ Rev. xiii, 8.   ‖ Heb. ii, 10.   ¶ Rev. i, 18.
** Rev. i, 18.   †† John x, 28.   ‡‡ Phil. ii, 9.   §§ Heb. i, 6.
‖‖ Sir James Fitzjames Stephen's *Liberty, Equality, Fraternity.*

he is not for me a person who was and is no more, but the eternal contemporary of us all, the symbol of a spirit which rests with us always. *The visible truths of the human and divine Evangel* rise every morning, on my horizon, like new luminaries. I salute and adore them with the same admiration as if I were seeing them for the first time. Miracles, dogmas, strangeness of forms, which worried me at first, worry me no longer. Across them all I see only one thing —' Man in search of God, God in search of man.' " Thus has the great Proclaimer awakened and elicited the latent divinity that lay paralyzed and dumb in human souls.

3. Manhood is Requisite.

And as the Prince of heralds was his own proclamation— himself the Door by which men were to enter the fold— himself the Bread of heaven in the strength of which they were to live, so those whom he now summons to proclaim his message to the world must themselves be the noblest moral product of their age and the best part of the message they endeavor to declare. It is not abstract but concrete truth that tells. The real power of any argument is not simply fidelity to facts and to logical *formulæ*, but the force and fire of the soul that forges the links of the chain. It is not so much the sermon as the man behind the sermon that constitutes the true dynamic of the pulpit. Not for science, or philosophy, or theological dogma, nor yet for the products of art, the triumphs of eloquence, the marvels of inventive genius, or the lore of scholarly study and research, is the world's hunger keenest and most constant, but for manhood and womanhood. More of the former it never had than it has to-day, and yet its heart was never hungrier, more feverish, more restless, than it is now. The vision for which " the whole creation groaneth and travaileth in pain together until now " is the lingering advent and apocalypse of a redeemed and ideal humanity. As a recent writer has forcibly observed, "All arts, inventions, philanthropies, religions, are but *tentaculæ* put forth searching for the means to make the man of the future, who shall be what all who have the vision and faculty divine have always prophesied he would yet be —a microcosm, the mirror of the universe. We, in our little corner, doing our work well-nigh unnoted by the world at large, are helping by our small increments of power to create this complete human being—the goal of all desire and hope. The coral zoophyte builds not more surely on the unseen reef that which yet shall rise in gleaming beauty above the deep sea's level blue than we are building for universal and perfected human nature. Nothing less is in our thought, and nothing else; for by ideals we live, and this ideal has been upon our consciousness from the beginning." In everything fidelity to the ideal is the one grand secret of effectiveness. Milton contemplating the composition of his great epic, the *Paradise Lost*, has told us how this conviction awed him. "He who would be a true poet," he says in his *Apology for Smectymnuus*, "or who would speak in laudable things, ought himself to be a true poem—that is, a composition and pattern of the best and most honorable; not presuming to sing high praises of what is worthy unless he have in himself the experience, and the practice, and all that is praiseworthy." No preacher can proclaim higher things than he knows, or present a mightier and more exalted Christ than has been realized in his own experience and embodied in his own personality. Unless constantly sustained and inspired by the Perfect Ideal, his theme will ever be beyond his grasp, and discerning persons will see the hopeless struggle after the unattained and unattainable with pain and pity. It is the Shekinah that makes the temple a holy place, and in the experience of the preacher, as in that of Christ himself, there must be an incarnation before there can be an exaltation. Assuming that as the soul of the preacher is so will the soul of his sermon be, the

Church is justified in insisting that men of small moral stature are no more competent to preach than an African bushranger is competent to interpret the music of Handel, Beethoven, or Wagner. "Such preachers," says a master of the craft, "show their hearers a dingy ceiling instead of an open sky; make them paddle on a pond when they might be scudding across an ocean. They are retail hucksters of the higgling class. They dispense the little truth they are capable of assimilating in small packets, tied with feeble thread, and stamped with the impress of their own Lilliputian qualities. It is these exiguous, pettifogging dealers in sacred things that have helped so much to produce for us the small God, the small Bible, the small life, the small past and present and future, that in many religious circles one can hardly move without treading upon something. On the other hand, the sermon of a man of finely statured qualities, a man of height and breadth, a man of magnitude and magnanimity, a man whose soul is a continent and not the churchyard of a country parish, will as inevitably partake of his greatness as in the ancient mythologies the children of the gods inherited the divinity of their parents."

The public proclamation, in the person of the proclaimer himself, of a richer and nobler manhood constituted and conserved by the abiding fullness ($\pi\lambda\acute{\eta}\rho\omega\mu\alpha$) of the Spirit would insure the perpetual recurrence of the Pentecost; thus fulfilling the intention of Christ, inducing a widespread, radical, and thorough repentance ($\mu\epsilon\tau\acute{a}\nu o\iota a$), or change of mind, and meeting the one obvious and crying need of the age. "I expect," says the author of the *Tongue of Fire*, "to see cities swept from end to end, their manners elevated, their commerce purified, their politics Christianized, their criminal population reformed, their poor made to feel that they dwell amongst brethren—righteousness in the streets, peace in the homes, an altar at every fireside—because I believe in the Holy Ghost."

4. Conviction is Indispensable.

Nor is it difficult to explain the source (humanly speaking) of this power of consecrated spiritual manhood in the ministry; for the essential element in all noble personality is conviction, and conviction is commanding and contagious. The really great souls of the world have been the great believers of the world. And this is true whether the believer be a Syrian like the reformed polytheist Abraham, a Hebrew like the sublime Jahvist, Moses; an Arabian like Mohammed, a Hindu like Sakya Mûni, the Buddha; an Iranian like the noble Zarathustra, the founder of the Perso-Iranian national religion; a Chinaman like Kong-fu-tse, or a Jew like the founder of the one absolute eternal, all-conquering religion, Jesus of Nazareth. Everywhere and in all time the word that stirs men, influencing their judgments and supplying sufficient motive power to their wills, is the speech of the man who says, "I believe, and therefore have I spoken." Men do not find fault with dogma if it be a true δόκει μοί *—a living personal conviction. They only object to it when it is dead, as they would object to any other unburied corpse. Even a hard and cold skepticism is overawed and carried captive by the eloquence and majesty of faith. The philosophical deist Bolingbroke and the suave but insincere Chesterfield were charmed with the whole-souled appeals of George Whitefield. The most honest and ablest of present-day secularists, George Jacob Holyoake, makes no secret of his liking for the preaching, to which he occasionally listens, of the distinguished English Methodist, Hugh Price Hughes. "I have listened to Mr. Spurgeon," says that cultured Unitarian, Moncure Conway, "and borne away an impression that strong men may be unconscious of the genius that o'ermasters them. I heard him preach on the text, 'Lead us not into temptation.' Now, thought I,

---

* The word *dogma* simply means personal opinion earnestly held, being probably derived from the common Greek phrase δόκει μοί—"it seems to me."

we shall hear a good, old-fashioned account of election and reprobation and a clear exposition of the mystery of iniquity. Nothing of the kind, or at least very little of the kind; a small theologic 'grace before meat,' preceded a sermon full of pathos and power, dealing with the actual trials and temptations of this great city. We saw the poor youth in many a strait, striving to conquer the seductions of evil; we saw the thin, shivering seamstress going to her comfortless home with the pittance gained by her weary toil, as the finery of vice flaunts by her and the tempter whispers in her ear. It was vivid as a scene from 'Faust;' it started tears to the eyes, and I soon perceived that when that sermon was prepared Calvin was bowed into a corner, and the stern face of London held the preacher with its glittering eye."

It was an overmastering sense of the truth he proclaimed that explains the power of the Baptizer over the degraded Idumean prince who "did many things and heard him gladly;" of a Chrysostom confronting the heresy and heathenism of Antioch, or the self-conceited sophists of Byzantium; of an Ambrose humbling the imperious but guilty spirit of Theodosius, against whom, stained with the blood of thousands of massacred men, women, and children, he closed the door of the church at Milan until his crime was atoned for by a genuine repentance; of a Leo arresting the menacing advance of the barbarian Attila; of a St. Bernard over popes like Honorius II, Innocent II, and Eugenius III, and princes like Lothaire, and brilliant philosophic heretics like Abelard, and crowded councils like that of Sens and that of Vezelay; of a Savonarola demanding at the couch of the dying Lorenzo de' Medici fruits meet for repentance as a condition of absolution; of the sick and prostrate Wyclif resisting the emissaries of Rome who had crept into his bedchamber at Lutterworth to receive his dying recantation; of Latimer over the greatest and most headstrong of the Tudor kings;

of Cranmer over his relentless enemies and his own instinctive shrinking from the tortures of martyrdom; of William Farel over Calvin; of John Howe over Cromwell; of Massillon over Louis XIV; of Chalmers over Carlyle; of Frederick William Robertson over the honest doubters of Brighton; of Lyman Beecher over the brilliant young Wendell Phillips; of Charles G. Finney over the hard-headed lawyers of Rochester, N. Y.; of Peter Akers and Thomas H. Stockton over the honest Springfield laywer whom a wise Providence had foredoomed to conduct a great nation safely through the furnace of affliction for four eventful years.

This same loyalty to conviction made Calvin prince of Geneva and pope of the Reformed Churches, gave John Knox an almost undisputed control over the religious life and thought of Scotland in the latter half of the sixteenth century, enabled Baxter, though physically frail, to hallow all the hearthstones of Kidderminster by his prayers and pastoral visits, and as a fire in the bones of Bunyan drew more than a thousand people to welcome his words in the early dawn of a week-day winter's morning on his occasional visits to London. It made Francis d'Assisi a sweet and amiable saint; St. Dominic, an irresistible propagandist; Xavier, Brainerd Carey, and Martyn, great missionaries; St. Augustine, Beza, and Arminius, princes in the great domain of theology. It led John Wesley to see, after a careful perusal of Jeremy Taylor's *Holy Living and Dying*, that all he had or was or might become by diligent use of his powers, place, and opportunities "must either be a sacrifice to God or to himself," and to act accordingly without a moment's intermission or truancy for more than fifty laborious and fruitful years.

5. Persuasive Power.

A natural outcome of conviction is persuasive power, giving the Christian orator a control over the intellectual and ethical nature of man such as no other speaker can possess in an equal degree. Even that which seems to approach it in point of effectiveness, in parliamentary or forensic effort, owes all its real force to the same strong sense of moral right and responsibility. When Lord Chatham succeeded for a time in crippling the efforts of Lord North's government to oppress the American colonies it was that great statesman's firm belief in the supremacy of moral principles that gave effect to his memorable protest: "You cannot conquer America. If I were an American, as I am an Englishman, while a foreign troop was landed in my country, I never would lay down my arms—*never!* NEVER! NEVER!" To the same sublime confidence in truth and justice is to be attributed the success as advocates of freedom and equity of such men as Patrick Henry in Virginia and James Otis in Massachusetts, of William Wilberforce contending for the emancipation of the slaves in the British West Indies, of Richard Cobden and John Bright urging on Sir Robert Peel and his government the reversal of the Corn Law policy, of Wendell Phillips defending against overwhelming odds the character and conduct of the ill-fated Elijah Lovejoy in Faneuil Hall, of Mr. Gladstone pleading before the English people the cause of the massacred Bulgarians against the Turk and the criminal apathy of a Tory government.

But the platform, the senate, and the bar cannot be expected to inspire the highest style of eloquence to the same extent as the Christian pulpit. With the lecturer, the legislator, and the advocate the case is always more or less complicated and the issue doubtful. The burden of the preacher, on the other hand, is not so much a burden of proof (*onus probandi*) as it is the effective announcement of the message of God's love and the free offer of reconciliation to men self-condemned, consciously lost, and hopeless and eternally wretched without divine mercy. "Knowing, therefore, the fear of the Lord, we persuade men." It is the strength and clearness of God's case in the interminable controversy with man that makes the simplest presentation of the leading verities of the Gospel by the thoroughly convinced and consecrated preacher "the power of God unto salvation." The present writer has seen more than two thousand people in Spurgeon's Tabernacle overmastered by the emotions with which they struggled, pocket handkerchief in hand, while the preacher, who had just returned from his winter asylum in the Riviera, still partly lame with gout and evidently suffering, leaned heavily on the rail of his platform, and with a pathos of tone and manner impossible to describe besought the six thousand people before him to "stagger not at the promise of God through unbelief, but to be strong in faith, giving glory to God."* John Wesley's Journals are full of such scenes, and Whitefield lived and even died in the midst of them. "O God! is it a man or an angel," reverently exclaimed Robert Hall, himself known as the "prince of preachers," instinctively rising to his feet as Richard Watson, tall, thin, and pale, but handsome, described to a large congregation the security, blessedness, and honor of those who have safely consummated their earthly pilgrimage and reached the world out of sight. "For about half an hour," says an eyewitness, describing a remarkable scene when Bishop Simpson once preached in the Congregational Memorial Hall, London, "he spoke quietly, without gesticulation or uplifting of his voice; then, picturing the Son of God bearing our sins in his own body to the tree, he stooped, as if laden with an immeasurable burden, and rising to his full height, he seemed to throw it from him, crying: 'How far? As far as east is distant from the west, so far hath he removed our transgressions from us.' The whole assembly, as if moved by an irresistible impulse, rose, remained standing for a second or two, then sank back

---

* The preacher's text was Rom. iv, 20.

into their seats. A professor of elocution was there. A friend who observed him . . . asked him when the service was over, 'Well, what do you think of the bishop's elocution?' 'Elocution!' was the reply, 'that man doesn't want elocution; he's got the Holy Ghost.'"

6. Definiteness of Aim.

But even the highest order of manhood and the intensest personal convictions conjoined with power to move men's wills and lead them to decision require a point of concentration—need to be complemented and crowned by a definite and sustained purpose to bless. It can never be justly alleged that the Gospel has failed until it has been fairly tried. And it cannot be said to have been fairly tried until its preachers become thoroughly inoculated with its self-abnegating and aggressive genius, with that infinite and insatiable desire for the salvation of men which the author of *Ecce Homo* happily designates the "enthusiasm of humanity." "If God did not give me souls, I think I should die," exclaimed Whitefield. "I would think it greater happiness for myself," wrote that most popular and most practical of commentators, Matthew Henry, "to gain even one soul to Christ than mountains of gold and silver." And Brainerd, as he waited in the evening of his bright but too brief day for the "chariot" to appear, murmured, reminiscentially and thankfully, "I cared not where or how I lived, or what hardships I passed through, so that I could but gain souls to Christ. While I was asleep I dreamed of such things, and when I waked the first thing I thought of was this of winning souls to Christ." Like many noble young minds who are to-day being disciplined by apparent failure in the first years of their ministry for greater spiritual achievements in the days to come, John Chrysostom mourned the fruitlessness of his preaching while crowds hung unweariedly upon his lips. One night he seemed in a vision to be preaching in the Cathedral Church of Antioch, and amid the attentive multitude he saw "One like unto the Son of man," listening with an intent yet grieved look upon his kingly brow. The Lord was waiting, and apparently in vain, for some word which he might apply to dying souls who had gathered from the dim streets of the city to hear "the Gospel of the grace of God." From that day the preaching of Chrysostom was changed, and anxious souls were gathered into the kingdom of God. It is in this voluntary returning of men to the love and service of their Creator that the true glory of Christianity lies; and yet, notwithstanding its learning, its eloquence, its earnestness, and its exalted moral character, perhaps nothing is more painfully characteristic of the ministry of the times than the want of clear, continuous insight into the supreme aim and purpose of the great dispensation of mercy and deliverance under which it is our privilege to live.

7. A Standing Attestation of the Spirituality of the Christian Religion.

But if the preaching function of the ministry, as above explained, be the central and dominant one, it is also the one abiding attestation and guarantee of the spirituality and inwardness of Christianity. "Faith cometh by hearing, and hearing by the word of Christ. But how shall they believe in him whom they have not heard? And how shall they hear without a proclaimer? And how shall they proclaim except they be sent, even as it is written, How beautiful are the feet of them that bring glad tidings of good things!"

The triumph of the preacher is the victory of faith; his suppression or enfeeblement is its sure decline and death. The status of the preacher, and not this or that element of doctrine, is the true *articulus stantis aut cadentis ecclesiæ*— the test of a growing or declining Church. To no fact does history bear a clearer or more unequivocal witness than to this. From the time of Cyprian the tendency to substitute the priest for the proclaimer; to emphasize the eucharistic sacrifice as a spectacle addressed to the eye, to the neglect of the living message spoken to the understanding, the conscience, and the heart, steadily grew, with now and then a feeble and feverish spasm of revolt, until the light of the glorious Gospel of Christ feebly glimmered on the verge of absolute extinction amid the far-extending gloom and superstition of the early Middle Ages. A great spiritual force which requires its living agent to be morally and intellectually at his best was supplanted almost universally by a sacramental celebration, which, however significant, beautiful, and necessary, makes no imperious demand on the ethical and intellectual nature of the celebrant. The whole nature and drift of the Christian ministry suffered from the change, and the service of God was performed with feelings and motives worthy only of a heathen fetich. It was, as contemplated in this degraded form—when he saw the vulgar peddler of a huckstering Church offering for sale the mercies of heaven in the street, and promising the people release of their relatives and friends from purgatorial pains on payment of a coin—that it aroused the moral indignation of Luther, as it had before provoked the courageous criticism of Wyclif in England, of Hus in Bohemia, and of Wessel and Wesel and other pre-Reformation reformers in Germany and Italy.

For many successive centuries Christianity as a spiritual religion lost its hold on the intellect of Europe, and the philosophy of Aristotle usurped the place of the Sermon on the Mount and the teachings of St. Paul. Philosophers, heretics, eremites, monks, idle or aspiring ecclesiastics of various grades and orders abounded,

> Thick as autumnal leaves in Vallombrosa,

but preachers were few or none; and sincere faith and

godly living almost vanished from a Church whose chief shepherd—and he not the worst of his order—blushed not to insinuate to his fellow-hirelings of the desecrated fold, "The Christian fable has been very useful to us."

In times of spontaneous popular awakening, like that led by St. Francis d'Assisi and his Brothers Minor in Italy, or in moments of peril to the hierarchical authority, as at the time of the Reformation, when, as Ranke points out, the reigning pope, Clement VII, dreaded to accept the suggestion of the emperor, Charles V, and submit the affairs of the Church to the consideration of a general council, liberty has been given to the *preacher* to restore the confidence which the *priest* had forfeited, and revive the waste places which the priest had made desolate and barren.* But, though by the preaching of such men as Francis and Dominic, and Bernard of Clairvaux, in the eleventh and twelfth centuries, and by that of Savonarola in the closing years of the fifteenth, and of Xavier and Lainez in the sixteenth, a powerful preaching impulse was given, for a time, to a portion of the regular clergy such reforms were so completely out of harmony with the interests and traditions of the Catholic hierarchy that they were doomed irrevocably to a speedy death. Every such movement has had, like that of St. Francis, its Ugolino, and has had to yield ultimately to ecclesiastical pressure, intrigue, diplomacy, or violence. The Church which exalts the mass has no normal place for the preacher who points the eager eye of men to a risen and triumphant Christ, just as the ceremonial and priestly system of the temple had no place for the prophet with his

---

* "The word 'priest' has two different senses. In the one it is a synonym for presbyter or elder, and designates the minister who presides over and instructs a Christian congregation; in the other it is equivalent to the Latin *sacerdos*, the Greek ἱερεύς, or the Hebrew כֹּהֵן (*the offerer of sacrifices*), who also performs other mediatorial offices between God and man. How the confusion between these two meanings has affected the history and theology of the Church it will be instructive to consider."—*Lightfoot*, "St. Paul's Epistles," p. 186. It is needless to say that the word "priest" is used in the text in the latter and more common of these two senses.

sublime moral teachings. Where the error of this great perversion is persisted in, as is the case to-day over two thirds of Christendom, the priest stands forever at the altar, looking back through the dismal shadows of the past and saying to a sinful and despairing world, of Him who is the only source of hope, "He is dead! He is dead!" Where, on the other hand, a nobler and truer faith is held and proclaimed, the preacher is a prophet, and goes forth with his face illumined with the light of the "good time coming," proclaiming the welcome and exultant news, "He is risen, and is become the first fruits of them that slept." The priest gloomily concentrates the attention of faith on a cross from which the mangled and bleeding form of the Redeemer has never been taken down ; the preacher directs the eye to the empty sepulcher illumined with the radiance of angelic visitants, and from whose dark and cold interior the Lord has ascended to heaven.

APPENDIX TO CHAPTER IV

The verb κηρύσσειν (*to proclaim*) occurs 61 times in the New Testament; 40 of these are found in the Synoptists, 19 in the epistles of St. Paul, and 2 elsewhere. Κήρυγμα occurs 16 times—in Matthew 8, in Luke 2, in St. Paul's epistles 6. Εὐαγγελίζεσθαι is met with 55 times, Luke employing it, in his gospel and in the Acts, 25 times ; St. Paul 24, and other New Testament writers 6. Καταγγέλλειν occurs in 18 places; 11 of these are in the Acts and the rest in Paul's epistles. Εὐαγγέλιον is used 77 times.

In one instance only does John allow himself the use of the verb κηρύσσειν, twice the use of εὐαγγελίζεσθαι, once of the noun εὐαγγέλιον, and all these are found in the Apocalypse, which the best modern critics assign to a period twenty-five years before the composition of the fourth gospel, when the evangelist was still, we may assume, to some extent under the influence of the original evangelical terminology. On the other hand, the verb μαρτυρεῖν occurs 47 times in St. John's writings and only twice elsewhere, while the noun μαρτυρία is used 31 times by him and 7 times by other New Testament writers. With the words κήρυγμα, κηρύσσειν, καταγγέλλειν, εὐαγγελίζεσθαι, εὐαγγέλιον, John must have been very familiar. From their constant use by the Synoptists and the apostle Paul it is clear that they formed an essential and marked characteristic of the original or oral gospel, and that they or their Aramaic equivalents were the words deliberately chosen and employed by Christ and his great Forerunner to express the leading significance and feature of their mission. And in this they are in perfect harmony with the Messianic forecasts of the Old Testament and apocryphal literature and with the usage of the Septuagint. This studied and complete avoidance on the part of the author of the fourth gospel of the commonly accepted terminology of the great and ever-expanding evangelical circle is very striking; but it is impossible at this distance of time to divine any adequate reason for it. His object may have been to bring the proclamation (κήρυγμα) of the good news (εὐαγγέλιον) into closer relation to the personal experience and convictions of the proclaimer (κῆρυξ), and to emphasize the important fact that, while preaching is necessarily an announcement of great historical facts, it is still more the utterance of such truths transmuted into vital elements of experience and personally attested by the preacher's own spiritual life. This purpose evidently influenced both the author's selection of materials from the common evangelical tradition and his mode of treating them. In the Synoptists Christ is a *preacher* of good news to the people; in John's gospel he is uniformly in conflict with the Jewish authorities—a *witness* against their moral and intellectual obtuseness and organized hypocrisy. In the former he is the Herald of the kingdom; in the latter he is both in intention and effect a martyr to the cause of truth.

But whatever may have been the motive of this marked departure from the fixed terminological vogue and usage of the early Church, or its passing effect on contemporary Christian thought, it evidently produced no permanent impression, nor has it perceptibly tinctured the subsequent current of Christian literature. Christianity is characteristically and essentially an *evangel*, boldly and aggressively *proclaimed* to the world, and not merely a conviction courageously and faithfully *attested* by the believer when called upon or compelled to appear before the bar of the world. It is more an ever-living and spontaneous *message* to the ignorant and indifferent multitude than an occasional and involuntary *testimony* against a few powerful gainsayers who are willing to use their influence and authority as representatives of the civil power for its suppression.

CHAPTER V
The Theme of Preaching

Πᾶσάν τε ἡμέραν ἐν τῷ ἱερῷ καὶ κατ' οἶκον οὐκ ἐπαύοντο διδάσκοντες καὶ εὐαγγελιζόμενοι τὸν Χριστὸν Ἰησοῦν.—*Luke* (Acts v, 42).
Ἡμεῖς δὲ κηρύσσομεν Χριστὸν ἐσταυρωμένον.—*Paul*.
Σπάρταν ἔλαχες, ταύταν κόσμει.—*Laconian Proverb*.

1. The Only Saving Name.

CHRISTIANITY does not challenge the attention of the world simply as a competitor with other religions for popular acceptance and belief; nor is it content to take its place as one among other ethical forces that have been, and are to-day, working for the moral uplift and amelioration of mankind. Its position is lofty and exclusive. It professes not only to contain in itself the few fragments of essential truth found in mutilated shape and in alliance with various errors in pre-Christian and extra-Christian cults, and present them in purer and nobler forms, but to supplement them with disclosures indispensable to the complete moral and intellectual development and spiritual well-being of mankind. Its contention is that there can be no adequate conception of God or of man; no sufficient rule of life, or standard of character, or mastery of moral evil or perfect human happiness, here or hereafter, apart from the manifestation of the Son of God. It claims to be the one eternal and absolute religion ultimately destined to universal and undisputed sway. Consistently with this claim it ascribes to its Founder an unapproachable moral grandeur and an unrivaled authority—insisting that his person, mission, and work shall be the sole center of religious interest, and constitute the abiding substance of Christian doctrine and discourse.

"Sparta is your lot and choice," ran the motto of Laconian loyalty. "Show off Sparta to the best advantage." And a devotion equally single-hearted and sincere is required of him who aspires to be a publisher of "the glad tidings of good things." "Christ is your inheritance and hope," cries the Church to her chosen spokesmen and representatives. "Let him be the burden of your thought and witnessing; do your best for him. For 'him hath God exalted with his right hand to be a prince and a Saviour, for to give repentance to Israel and the forgiveness of sins.' 'Neither is there any other name under heaven given among men whereby we must be saved.'"

2. The Person of Christ.

It is needless to say that the man who approximates, however remotely, to the ideal of the Christian preacher, contemplated in the New Testament, must take high ground as to the person of Christ. His conviction and attitude as to this will ever be the great determinant of his spirit, character, message, and success. Christ is much to the world or little according as the doctrine of his person is construed; according as *reason*, working within its own circumscribed limits and hampered with the immense difficulties that beset it, persists in retaining him on the plane of ordinary humanity, or *faith*, reverently bowing to the authority of the revealed word, concedes to him "a name which is above every name," and sees him exalted to a place "far above all heavens that he might fill all things." Great as have been the learning and eloquence, the philanthropic activity and public-spiritedness, the dialectical dexterity and skill, and, what is of still greater consequence, the high moral character and purpose of many of those to whom belief in Christ's absolute and proper divinity was like grasping the mist or building on the sand; powerfully as some of these men influenced scientific and intellectual advancement in their times, not one of them has left any deep mark as a preacher of the Christian salvation. And there was a reason for their failure. A religion which insists on explaining or dissipating all mysteries does not necessarily justify itself to human reason, while it leaves the nobler elements of man's nature—his heart and imagination—untouched. The power of Christianity has always lain in the incomprehensible sublimity and grandeur of its fundamental truths, and in the charm they have exerted over man's imaginative and emotional, not less than over his intellectual, susceptibilities. The Roman augurs, in performing the solemn functions of their office, are said to have laughed each other in the face because it seemed to them that in examining the smoking entrails of the slaughtered animals they saw all that was to be seen and knew all that was to be known; and that hope or fear or forecast based on the condition of the omens was nothing but the sheerest superstition. The proclaimer of the stupendous marvel of human redemption has no temptation to be frivolous. The Christian Church is a generator and nurse of the faith and adoration both of angels and men,* because she is the depository and propagandist not of a group of vague and senseless superstitions, but of the hidden secret of the ages†—the mystery (τὸ μυστήριον) which, though it open to the approach of faith, yet broadens with the expansion of human thought and deepens with the growth of man's nobler life and experience, and ever moves in advance of his intellectual march like the pillar of cloud by day and the pillar of fire by night which guided Israel's wanderings in the desert. It was no inadequately trained exponent, but the master mind of the first great cycle of Christian thought—a thinker whose influence on the course of Christian civilization has been incalculable—commanding the respect of men of light and leading for nigh two thousand years—who

---

* Eph. iii, 9, 10; 1 Pet. i, 12. † Eph. iii, 9.

wrote in a letter to his young friend, "Confessedly great is the mystery of godliness; he who was manifested in the flesh, justified in the spirit, seen of angels, preached among the nations, believed on in the world, received up in glory."*

Nor can it be complained that Christianity, in exclusively confining its ministry to the proclaiming among the nations of the transcendent mystery of Christ's manifestation and the salvation thereby accomplished and provided, tends to contract the legitimate range of human interest and narrow the realm of man's intellectual freedom and research. It is said of the celebrated European singer, Caffarelli, that, after having been kept practicing, in spite of frequent protests and complaints, some elementary yet difficult vocal exercises, for seven years, his master one day put his hand on his head and said fondly and complacently, "Go forth, my son, to wealth and fame; you are the finest singer in Europe." Similarly the simple discipline of the cross of Christ patiently submitted to is the secret of all greatness, moral and intellectual, giving men and nations complete mastery over their powers and leading them to the happy fulfillment of their mission and destiny.

The system of thought that contemplates the nature, offices, and work of the Son of God, as set forth in the Christian documents, can never be superficial and narrow, but must be deep, discursive and elevated, making more or less intimate acquaintance with many departments of knowledge, and necessarily with the noblest and mightiest truths of all. A single word with its profound and comprehensive significance selected from among others, relating to different aspects of Christ's many-sided nature, will show how strikingly this is so. The epithet Firstborn ($\pi\rho\omega\tau\acute{o}\tau o\kappa o\varsigma$), applied to him as the "Image of the Invisible God" in Col. i, 15, occurs five times in the New Testament, and in these five instances the place and function assigned to Christ may be

---
* 1 Tim. iii, 16.

The Theme of Preaching

said to offer a true, complete, and satisfactory solution of every serious problem of life, thought, and destiny. (1) He is placed in relation to the cosmos—its genesis, order, life, and government, as its originator and upholder, the reason of its being, the determiner of its goal. He is, in fact, the firstborn of the physical creation (πρωτότοκος πάσης κτίσεως) on whom the system of universal nature depends and in whom it hangs together.* He thus supplies the answer to the deepest questions at once of ancient philosophy and of modern science. (2) He stands in relation to redeemed humanity as its creator, head, exemplar, and standard of perfection. He is the firstborn among many brethren (πρωτότοκος ἐν πολλοῖς ἀδελφοῖς)—the eternal moral archetype to which every true-born child of God is predestined to be conformed.† He thus holds the key to every problem of the heart and the conscience, and throws a flood of light on the dark and often appalling enigmas of divine Providence. (3) He is the first begotten from the dead (πρωτότοκος ἐκ τῶν νεκρῶν)—the Moses of our triumphant exodus *from* the Egypt of the grave;‡ and the firstborn *of* the dead (ὁ πρωτότοκος τῶν νεκρῶν)§—pledge and prophet of our immortality. (4) He is the preeminent one, *the* firstborn (ὁ πρωτότοκος); absolute and supreme Head of all created being, concerning whom, at the inauguration of the new and everlasting economy of the future, it is to be said, "And let all the angels of God worship him."‖ Such is one of the many broad glimpses afforded us in the New Testament of the divine and adorable personality whose exalted name, saving power, and inexhaustible wealth of resource have been the unwearying theme of those who, for sixty generations, have joyfully heralded everywhere the

---

* Col. l, 15. † Rom. viii, 29. ‡ Col. l, 18.
§ Rev. i, 5. The best ancient authorities as represented by Lachmann, Tregelles, and Tischendorf omit the preposition ἐκ of the *Textus Receptus;* so that the phrase seems to convey the idea of Christ's supremacy over the dead as the pledge of the survival of his saints and the final judge of the wicked. ‖ Heb. i, 6.

tidings of God's love and mercy to mankind, amply justifying the words of a recent writer when he says, "Christ is Revelation, its soul, its substance, its center and circumference, its all in all."*

3. Our Great Exemplar.

But if the person of Christ is to be proclaimed as offering to the mind of man, in its manifold and wide-reaching significance, a world of thought and contemplation at once progressive, luminous, comprehensive, and sufficient, not less is he to be presented as the one infallible standard of morals and arbiter of human conduct. To only one born of woman has it been given to make to hostile scrutiny the daring challenge, "Which of you convinceth me of sin?" Of one only could it ever be said without obvious exaggeration that he was "holy, harmless, undefiled, and separate from sinners." To one alone could the discriminating bystander point the finger and say, "Behold the Lamb of God, which taketh away the sin of the world." This gives Jesus of Nazareth a place unique in the history of morals. He stands in an ethical order of his own, the first in it and the last. The light of his example shines through all the avenues of human life in its almost bewildering multiformity of phase and variety of experience, penetrating even every corner of the unseen realm of motive. "Over against all false and meager ideals of man's capacity and destiny he represents the great reality; he is the Son of man." By the subtle self-adjustment and far-reaching application of the principles which his spirit and acts involve he offers infallible ethical guidance to all. "Born a man and a Jew, in a carpenter's family, he can be equally claimed by both sexes, by all classes, by men of all nations. . . . . Each race has its special aptitudes, its 'glory and honor,' and as the glory and honor of each na-

* Clifford's *The Inspiration and Authority of the Bible*, p. 98.

tion has been brought within the light of 'the holy city'—the versatility and intellect of the Greeks, the majestic discipline of the Romans, the strong individuality of the Teutons—each in turn has been able to find its true ideal in Jesus of Nazareth, not as a dream of the imagination, but as a fact of observation, and has marveled how those that were in Christ before them could be blind to the presence in him of what they so especially value. Looking around us we search in vain for a perfect manhood, nor can we find any promise or potency of such an ideal within ourselves, but as soon as we contemplate the manhood of Jesus we find at once both the condemnation of what we are and the assurance of what we may be. As Son of man he claims and exercises over us a legitimate authority, the authority of acknowledged perfection; as Son of man he shows us what human nature is to be individually and socially, and supplies us with the motives and the means for making the idea real." *

This is the immense significance and value for the ministry of all time, of the human life and example of Christ. The first great demand and triumph of the Gospel was a complete reversal of the current of popular thought, a widespread and radical change ($\mu\varepsilon\tau\acute{a}\nu o\iota a$) of individual minds, but this only as preliminary to its main object, namely, the reformation of conduct, the renewal and reconstruction of the individual soul and of society, the practical and cordial conformity of men to the eternal law of righteousness as revealed and exemplified in Christ. The early Christians were more remarkable for the singular purity of their morals and the sublime unselfishness of their disposition and deportment than for the novelty of their beliefs and teaching, which were never very peculiar except as regards the person of Christ. Men were certainly more impressed with what they *did* and the manner

---

* Dr. Gore's, *The Incarnation of the Son of God*, pp. 183, 185.

and motive of their doing it than with what they *believed*. From this peculiarity sprang one of the most appropriate and suggestive of the many designations by which the first followers of Christ were popularly known, namely, men of "the way" (ἡ ὁδός), or method.* They were *Methodists* after no narrow, conventional, or modern fashion, but in the deepest and broadest sense, inasmuch as the line of conduct which distinguished them aimed at nothing short of the establishment of an absolute rule and standard of morals and a complete revolutionizing of the prevailing disposition and manners of society as embodied in that comprehensive triad of vices—"the lust of the eye, the lust of the flesh and the pride of life." In the entire expression of their inward life; in their faith and mutual love and benevolent care for the indigent and helpless; in their habit of daily prayer and praise as "breaking bread from house to house they did eat their meat with gladness and singleness of heart," they proclaimed Christ as their living model (ἡ ὁδός), whose spirit and purpose it was their delight to share and exemplify. In the warmth, freedom, and purity of their fellowship they presented to the eye of the observer the *microcosm* of a redeemed and regenerated social order. They trod a path which tended ever upward and heavenward, and showed no footsteps of retreat. And whatever may have been the changes that have passed over ethical law and science and the constitution of human society since that time, they have not proceeded so far as to render obsolete or inapplicable the example of Him who "went about doing good," and who says to-day as he said of old, "He that heareth these sayings of mine, and *doeth* them, shall be likened unto a wise man, which built his house upon the rock:

---

*Comp. John xiv, 4, 6; Acts xvi, 17; xviii, 26; xix, 9, 23. It is "a way" distinguished by various epithets, all of them having a marked ethical significance; "the way of salvation," "the way of God," "the way which they call heresy," in allusion to its practical divergence from the inferior code of conduct commonly adopted, "a more excellent way," "the way into the holiest," "a new and living way which he hath consecrated," "the way of truth," "the right way," "the way of righteousness."

and the rain descended, and the floods came, and the winds blew, and beat upon that house; and it fell not: for it was founded upon a rock."

4. Teacher of His People.

Equally deep and undying is the interest of the race in Christ as the prince of teachers. In this aspect, too, he is to be presented as one claiming universal and exclusive authority, between whom and the most eminent and exalted of his followers there yawns an impassable chasm. "One is your Master"—leader, teacher (καθηγητής)—"even Christ," he said, "and all ye are brethren." This assumption of didactic supremacy has a perennial significance and the broadest application. While, on the one hand, it denies the right of any *Augustus* or *Pontifex*, baptized or pagan, or any *imperium*, no matter what its antiquity or pretensions, to "lord it over God's heritage," on the other, it reduces the great Protestant question as to the seat of authority in religion, so much discussed in our time, to little better than an impertinence. "The Church to teach and the Bible to prove;" therefore "Hear the Church," is the cry of the Anglican, as he clamors for the attention he imagines to be due to the voice of the historical hierarchy and the great general councils of Christendom.* "Let Reason speak and let her critical findings be adhered to and her dictates be obeyed," is the plea of the liberal school of Channing, Theodore Parker, Freeman Clarke, and James Martineau, emphasizing the sufficiency of the inward light and the exclusiveness of the individual's responsibility to God—totally oblivious of the obvious lesson of all history that "human reason can never generate religious certitude. "The Bible, and the Bible alone, is the religion of Protestants," is the vague and illusive contention of the old-fashioned evangelical, as he clings to the threadbare motto

---

* Dr. Gore's *Bampton Lectures*, p. 203.

which he owes to one who was emphatically "a reed shaken by the wind," and of whom it may almost be said that he

Was everything by turns and nothing long.*

"There is a triple coordinate source of faith and dogma, namely, Revelation, Reason, and the Church," is the averment of a school of recent birth represented by the distinguished American Hebraist, Dr. C. S. Briggs; while the Catholic is content with the Jesuitical formula that the hilt of the sword of authority rests at Rome in a hand that makes its sharp point penetrate everywhere and its keen and ruthless blade sever every knot that won't untie. Amid this ecclesiastical Babel of conflicting voices a divinely illumined and living ministry could hardly propose to itself a nobler or worthier task than that of bringing relief alike to the thoughtful few and to the busy and half-educated thousands by simply and earnestly insisting on the sole and sufficient authority of Christ in all matters pertaining to religion and the soul. "I am the way, the truth and the life;" "I am the bread of life; he that cometh to me shall never hunger, and he that believeth on me shall never thirst;" "I am the door of the sheep; I am the good shepherd, and know my sheep, and am known of mine. My sheep hear my voice, and I know them, and they follow me: and I give unto them eternal life;" "This is the work of God, that ye believe on him whom he hath sent;" "Let these words sink down into your ears;" thus spake he who taught "as one having authority, and not as the scribes;" he concerning whom the voice from heaven bore witness, "This is my beloved Son; hear him."

Obvious and admitted, however, as is the claim of Jesus to supreme and exclusive authority over the souls of men, the superior excellence of his teaching is not to be sought where one would naturally expect it. He does not profess

*See " Essay on Chillingworth " in Dr. A. Barry's *Masters in English Theology.*

to make every lesson he teaches so plain that it cannot be missed. Great moral principles, with their limitless breadth of scope and infinite variety of application, cannot be imparted in any such form. Few errors have been more insidious and hurtful than that embalmed by common consent in the innocent-looking phrase "the simple Gospel." The Gospel is not a superficial and easily mastered scheme of salvation, or a system of life and thought in any sense implied in these words, but a profoundly heart-searching spiritual discipline from first to last. Jesus purposely placed many precious truths where they could not be got at without self-denying exertion, hiding them deep, like the "treasure hid in a field," which had to be sought for and obtained at a self-bankrupting cost. The moral and spiritual advantages he offers to his followers are great and abiding, but the ground taken in the conditions is exacting and high. "This is a hard saying, who can hear it?" has been murmured more than once by the timid and doubtful on the threshold of his kingdom, as in the instance of the admiring scribe who, yielding to a passing spasm of conviction, offered to embark with the company of the apostles only to have his enthusiasm cooled by quiet reminder of the cost, or in that of the amiable young Crœsus who, drawn perhaps by sympathy with some single and conspicuous feature of Christ's character, came to him "*running*" to "*walk* away sorrowful."

It is true Jesus invites men to himself that he may lighten their burdens and commit to them the golden secret of a deep and enduring spiritual repose. But the moral and intellectual discipline he imposes is really not lighter, but severer, more difficult, more continuous, than that required by other professed masters of the human mind. "Strait is the gate," he said, "and narrow is the way that leadeth unto life, and few there be that find it."* "The Mosaic

---

* Matt. vii, 14.

law," says a judicious writer, "says exactly what it means; you have only to take it and obey it; but the Sermon on the Mount sets a man thinking; it perplexes, it often baffles; it is only by patient effort to appreciate its spirit that it can be reduced to practice. The same is true of the parables which our Lord used to teach the people. They stimulate thought, they suggest principles, they arrest the attention, but they do not give men spiritual information in the easiest and most direct form. Our Lord, then, taught, and especially taught his disciples, so as to train their character and stimulate their intelligences; he worked to make them intelligent sons and friends, not obedient slaves. He would have them set ends above means and principles above ordinances, as when he said, "The Sabbath was made for man, not man for the Sabbath." Speaking elsewhere of the practical genius of Christianity, the same writer says: "It is not satisfied that one or two of the Christian community should do the positive work of religion for the rest. It desires to see the whole community an organized body in active cooperation, a royal priesthood in consecrated service. It is because it thus desires to enlist all men and the whole man in positive service that the best kind of authority refuses to do too much for men, refuses to be too explicit, too complete, too clear, lest it should dwarf instead of stimulating their higher faculties." *

5. Pacifex Maximus.

But now, if Christ be regarded as preeminently the Teacher of his Church, his own presentation of himself as our sacrifice for sin and Saviour from its guilt, penalty, and power must necessarily occupy a place in the ministry he has instituted corresponding to the prominence it held in his own mind as the consummation of his earthly mission and the realization of God's redeeming purpose. As the

---

* Dr. Gore's *Incarnation of the Son of God*, lecture vii.

revealer of God to men he bears witness to the truth.*
And the truth is the fan in his hand wherewith he purgeth
his threshing floor. It sifts men's motives, tests the depth,
strength, sincerity, of their attachments, sometimes disclos-
ing a lamentable failure of faith and courage, sometimes a
positive alienation of the heart from all goodness. The
chaff yields to the breeze, and the solid grain attests its own
weight and worth by keeping its place on the threshing-
floor. An ill-considered profession of discipleship like that
of the scribe who said, "Master, I will follow thee whither-
soever thou goest," is met by, "The foxes have holes, and
birds of the air have winter shelters, but the Son of man
hath not where to lay his head." After the searching discourse on the "Bread of Heaven," and his strong insist-
tence on the superior claims of the spiritual life, "many
of his disciples went back and walked no more with him."
Even the inner circle of the twelve began to show signs of
wavering, and he asked, with a blending of rebuke and
tenderness in his tone, "Will ye also go away?" To which
Peter answered, "To whom shall we go? Thou hast the
words of eternal life." It required the impersonation of the
truth in Christ to make it acceptable and welcome even to
the noblest and most candid minds. Standing alone, as
an abstraction, truth is hard and exacting and tends to
repel. It is Sinai covered with blackness and darkness and
tempest, and reverberating with the voice of words. Embodied in a gracious personality by whose spirit and action
it is made lovely, by whose tone of sympathy and love its
harshest notes are made sweet and musical, by whose self-
sacrificing death its lofty claims become invested with the
highest of all sanctions, it impresses and attracts. Where
Christ's utterance of the naked truth tended to repel men
his personality of perfect love held them in thrall. In him
sovereignty and fatherhood, truth and love, necessity and

---

* John xviii, 37.

freedom, moral self-surrender and spiritual triumph, found their point of coincidence and reconciliation when "he suffered to the lowest bent of weakness in the flesh and triumphed to the highest pitch of glory in the spirit." The truth as the transcript of God's holy nature demanded recognition of its unabated claims; but human nature without the awakening of some deeper motive than it had heretofore known was unequal to that demand. The Teacher of truth must bear the cross, must sacrifice himself for those who have hopelessly lost the precious secret; and his sacrifice, unlike the willing martyrdoms of his followers, which illumine with a supernal splendor some of the darkest periods of history, must be equal to and worthy of the truth it is offered to attest. He who would uphold and honor the law and yet show mercy to lawbreakers must needs die for those whose acquittal and salvation he would secure. As Longfellow beautifully says:

The depths of love are atonement's depths.*

"Thus it behooved Christ to suffer and to rise from the dead the third day," was his own explanation, to his bewildered disciples, of what had happened, when the tragedy was completed, "and that repentance and remission of sins should be proclaimed in his name among all nations, beginning at Jerusalem." The cross of Christ, as the central fact in the history of the race, has had an incalculable influence on the destiny of individuals and nations, and has, to-day more than ever, an inexhaustible interest and significance for human thought. It is the *Pacifex Maximus*, "the grand resolvent of all difficulties;" and the preacher who discerns not the paramount value and importance of it and of the truths which grow out of it, or stand intimately related to it, and employs the time and attention of his people to discuss questions of the hour—transitory problems which change

---
* "Children of the Last Supper."

complexion almost while he is in the act of speaking of them—is surely "blind and cannot see afar off." Says a thoughtful American preacher, after naming questions sufficient, if attention were given them, to occupy nearly all the fifty-two Sundays in the calendar—" the money question, the tariff question, the tenement question, the labor question, the immigrant question, the agricultural question, the tramp question, the war question, the Afro-American question, the Roman Catholic question, the education question, the municipal question, the woman question, the geological question, the descent-of-man question, the inspiration-of-Scripture question, the immortality question, and a host of others that need not be named "—" I confess I have been at times much depressed with my inability to solve them satisfactorily; . . . yet in all my perplexity and regret one thing has stood forth in my consciousness, the incarnation of the Son of God, the crucifixion of the Son of man. The cross of Christ seems to come nearer and nearer to my eyes and to sink deeper and deeper into my soul, and there grows up in me a conviction . . . that the cross is the one thing in all the world that it is necessary for me to know and understand; that on the knowledge and the understanding of the meaning of Jesus Christ crucified the answers to all the world's hard questions can be given, not fully, perhaps, but sufficiently for the daily needs of the life of mankind. I am convinced as well for myself as for you and others that we do not give the proper attention to the central fact of God's revelation of himself to man in the person of his Son. We let our minds be diverted from the crucifixion—that great tragedy of evil and yet victory of love, that event in which all the interests of the world met, by which all the questions of mankind were answered—and we fix them on the things that lie in the shadows of Calvary, the things that long were put to flight by the outcome of its power."*

---
* Prall's *Civic Christianity*, p. 181.

"But even were it practicable, would it be wise," it might be asked "in these days, when to a degree unknown in any previous age the life of man is touched on so many sides and his mind and character influenced by a hundred different topics, for any public teacher to confine himself to the one theme of Christ and his salvation? Even if it be admitted, as Horace Bushnell said, that 'the soul of all improvement is the improvement of the soul,' is not said improvement of the soul a very complex affair? Does it not involve the promotion of science, the progress of art, the growth of literature, the study of social and economic questions and attention to politics and government—municipal and national—as well as to questions of international policy, law, and jurisprudence? And can any man have a comprehensive idea of human well-being or contribute what he ought to promote it who rigidly confines his sympathy and interest to religion and religious truths?"

To this the answer is that, while confining himself, in the pulpit, as the ambassador of Christ, to those truths and considerations which go to the very taproot of all the evils which afflict society and hurt the individual—truths which touch the springs of thought and motive more deeply than anything else can, inspiring men with those ideals, energies, and hopes which are ever the great factors, alike of civil and religious progress—the Christian minister ought to seize every opportunity as a citizen and a friend of humanity to lighten the burden of labor, to multiply the consolations of poverty, to promote purity, sobriety, industry, thrift, and general enlightenment, and advance and support the principles of good government. While so preaching the doctrine of the cross as to make it clear that "its significance is broader, deeper, higher than all the thought of man, because its height, and depth, and width are conterminous with the love of Jesus Christ, which is the love of the infinite and eternal God," his personal example, active sympathies and general attitude toward great public questions ought to be the best practical illustration of the reality and power of the truth he proclaims.

6. Pledge of our Completed Manhood.

And just as the problems of history and of individual life find their best and fullest solution in the death of Christ, so the completion and coronation of our manhood are guaranteed by his resurrection. Through him comes the hope that "this corruptible shall put on incorruption, and this mortal immortality"—the confidence that when "the earthly house of our tabernacle is dissolved we have a building from God, a house not made with hands, eternal in the heavens."* By his cross sin is atoned, for and its power broken ; by his resurrection faith is confirmed, and death and the grave, which are the natural and instinctive aversion of all healthy minds, become the royal road to the promised glory. To the most enlightened and most cheerful of ancient peoples Death was the most inexorable of adversaries, in whose presence the aid of both gods and men was unavailing, and from whose unrelenting grasp there was no escape. He is the only one among the gods who regards no gifts and has no altars, and to whom no pæans are sung.† "It is not right for me to behold the dead,"‡ Eurpides makes the goddess Artemis say to the dying Hippolytus as she prepares to leave him to shift for himself in the final struggles of mortality. She may not stain her pure, godlike vision, she explains, with the sight of deathlike expirations. Homer in the *Odyssey* makes Ulysses congratulate Achilles on his supremacy and power in the under world or "land of

---

* 1 Cor. v, 1.
† Lessing, in the *Laocoon*, quotes from Æschylus the line
  Οὐδ' ἔστι βωμὸς οὐδὲ παιωνίζεται.
‡ —— ἐμοὶ γὰρ οὐ θέμις φθιτοὺς ὁρᾶν
  οὐδ' ὄμμα χραίνειν θανασίμοισιν ἐκ πνοαῖς
  ὁρῶ δὲ σ' ἤδη τοῦδε πλησίον κακοῦ.—*Hippol.*, v. 1437.

the Cimmerian men," but the noble Greek finds life in the world of shades so empty, poor, and pitiless that he scornfully rejects the well-meant consolations of his living friend and expresses his very decided preference for the meanest and most miserable pauper's lot in the world of the living to the princeliest place and power in the realm of the dead.* Such were men's views of death and of the state of being beyond its dark veil before the "Day-star" arose in their hearts and the thick mists were lifted from everlasting scenes by Him who

> Captive led captivity,
> And robbed the grave of victory
> And took the sting from death.

And apart from faith in the Risen One the eternal outlook is as gloomy and forbidding as ever. "What went before me and what will follow me," says one of the most refined and most scholarly of modern skeptics, "I regard as two black, impenetrable curtains hanging down at the two extremities of human life and which no living man has yet drawn aside. Many hundreds of generations have stood between these curtains with their torches, guessing anxiously what lies behind. On the curtain of futurity many see the shadows of themselves, the forms of their own passions enlarged and put in motion, and they shrink back in terror at this image of themselves. Poets, philosophers, and founders of States have painted this curtain with their dreams, more smiling or more dark as the sky above them was cheerful or gloomy, and their pictures deceive the eye when viewed from a distance. Many jugglers, too, make profit out of this our universal curiosity; by their strange mummeries they have set the outstretched fancy in amazement. A deep silence reigns behind this curtain. No one once within will answer those he has left without. All you can hear is the hollow echo of your question as if you

---
* *Odyssey*, book xi, 474.

shouted in a cavern."* Thus sad is the plight and predicament and comfortless and cold the confession of modern skeptical philosophy. With this depressing note of despair it is the noble privilege of the proclaimer of "Jesus and the Resurrection" to contrast the bright and exhilarating hope of "the Gospel of the grace of God." By him who brought life and incorruptibility to light the "black, impenetrable curtain" of materialism is rent in twain from the top to the bottom. "I commend you to the care of divine Providence," wrote Ralph Waldo Emerson, in bidding affectionate farewell to his parish in the city of Boston, in 1832. "May he multiply to your families and your persons early genuine blessings and whatever discipline may be appointed to you in this life, may the blessed hope of the resurrection which he has planted in the human soul and confirmed and manifested in Jesus Christ be made good to you beyond the grave."

7. "Our Most Worthy Judge Eternal."

Once more: As the risen Redeemer of men and Perfecter of their souls, whose sphere of mediatorial activity is the invisible realm of thought, will, conscience, and affection, Christ is also the only sure discerner of spirits and the only competent arbiter of human destiny. His assumption of our nature made him perfectly familiar with all the most trying situations of our life and with all the deeper problems of the soul. All the essential elements of our probation found their burning focal point in his personal consciousness. His experience was full, comprehensive, and varied enough to be typical and to provide the clew for an accurate and just judgment of every man's character and desert. It gave him in his own personality a standard in which spotless purity and perfect pity, truth and tenderness, justice and mercy, meet and blend. "He was tempted

---

*G. J. Holyoake's, *Logic of Death*.

in all points like as we are, yet without sin." He learned obedience by the things which he suffered. "For it became him, for whom are all things, and through whom are all things, in bringing many sons unto glory, to make the author of their salvation perfect through suffering." Hence to him are given "the keys of Hades and of death, and he is ordained to be the judge of quick and dead. In his glorified manhood men will see themselves approved or condemned according as they have assimilated to or degenerated from the divine ideal embodied in the 'Son of man.'"

Within the cycle of truths thus briefly outlined, dominated by the love of God as revealed in Christ and appropriately designated the good news (τὸ εὐαγγέλιον), minds the most refined and most cultivated, and minds narrow and undisciplined, find ample room to roam, and hearts laden with sin, sorrow, and anxiety find exhaustless springs of consolation. Beyond this there is no need to travel. "A Christian preacher ought to preach Christ alone and all things in him and of him. If he find a dearth in this; if it seem to him a circumscription, he does not know Christ as the πλήρωμα—the fullness. It is not possible that there should be aught true or seemly or beautiful in thought, word, or deed, speculative or practical, which may not and which ought not to be evolved out of Christ and the faith in Christ; no folly, no error, no evil to be exposed or warned against which may not and should not be convicted and denounced for its contrariance and enmity to Christ. To the Christian preacher Christ should be in all things and all things in Christ; he should abjure every argument which is not a link in the chain of which Christ is the staple and the staple ring."*

Beyond the group of vital and saving verities of which Christ is the source, center, and subject, the Spirit of God re-

---

* R. W. Church, in *Masters in English Theology*, edited by Dr. A. Barry.

fuses to bear witness; for he is only concerned to teach, demonstrate, attest, and administer the truths which relate to him "who through the eternal Spirit offered himself without spot to God, that he might purge your conscience from dead works to serve the living God;" he witnesses only to the things of Christ, and he who is ever eager to escape from the inspiring and exhaustless theme of Christ and his salvation is doomed to a ministry of sterility and failure. Once away from this center of light and solace the preacher is like the camels which bore the dead body of the distinguished Jewish scholar, philosopher, physician, and rabbi, Maimonides, across the Egyptian desert from Cairo to Tiberias. It is said that the noble animals on leaving the tomb traveled round and round, in a wide circle, till, hungry and exhausted with their wanderings, they dropped down and died. The man who abandons that deep and inexhaustible fountain of salvation—Christ and him crucified—to discourse on topics of limited range and ephemeral interest hews out for himself and for his people "broken cisterns that will hold no water." He spends "money for that which is not bread, and labors for that which satisfieth not." He wanders in waste places, fertile only in disappointment and despair.

CHAPTER VI

The Bugbear of the Present-day Evangelical Pulpit

The prevalence of doubt about all truths and to some extent, also, the general eagerness of preachers to find out and meet the people's desires and demands, these two causes together have created the impression that the ministry had no certain purposes or definite message; that the preacher was a promiscuous caterer for men's whims, wishing them well, inspired by a general benevolence, but in no sense a prophet uttering positive truth to them which they did not know before, uttering it whether they liked it or hated it. Is not that the impression many young men have of the ministry?—*Bishop Phillips Brooks.*

I have said preach plainly and preach earnestly; I now say preach with moral courage. Fear no man, high or low, rich or poor, taught or untaught. Honor all men; love all men; but fear none. Speak what you account great truths frankly, strongly, boldly. . . . Put faith in truth as mightier than error, prejudice, or passion, and be ready to take a place among its martyrs.— *William E. Channing's Advice to a Preacher.*

1. An Important Question.

"Is the doctrine of future retribution neglected by the evangelical pulpit of our day? If so, why?" was the question the present writer was asked to introduce at the fortnightly meeting of a large association of evangelical ministers of all denominations in an old and beautiful New England city a few years ago. Interest in the subject was evinced by a much larger attendance than usual, and the opening essay was followed by a warm and general discussion. In the absence of the laity and of reporters (by a rule of the association) a full and free expression of opinion was elicited, and a much wider diversity of view was disclosed than anyone anticipated. Even men who had labored side by side for years, and esteemed each other to be veritable Abdiels in loyalty to evangelical truth, and each other's pulpits to be *faces et foci*—the fires and the hearthstones—of orthodox zeal, seemed surprised at the wide departure from the recognized and traditional faith of their respective denominations as to "last things" (τὰ ἔσχατα) which the discussion brought to light. One thing was clear: a large landslide from the old lines of teaching on the subject of eschatology had taken place, almost without anyone being aware of it, beyond a vague feeling that the doubt and uncertainty of one's own mind were only a part of the general consciousness. One spoke of the inevitable recoil from the harsher features of Calvinism, and read copious extracts from Jonathan Edwards's sermon on "Sinners in the Hands of an Angry God;" which he had raked from the "dustheap of oblivion," or picked from some "wormhole of long-vanished time." Another pastor of venerable aspect eloquently emphasized the instinctive shrinking, from every form of pain, that is so marked a characteristic of the age. A third pointed out what he considered a growing conviction of the essential weakness of all appeals to an inferior order of motives, such as fear, self-love, other-worldly prudence. Several *nodded* a vigorous assent to the old position who did not *speak*, while Swedenborgians present and Adventists of various shades of opinion seized the occasion to exhibit the superiority of their respective theories of "the world to come." The argument of the paper, which was commended in terms which the writer felt to be hardly warranted, was not discussed at all, on its merits, except by one or two. Feeling after the lapse of several years an increasing conviction of the gravity and importance of the question for the pulpit of to-day, the author ventures to insert the essay here substantially as it was read before the association, but supplemented with some references to present-day developments of opinion. An exhaustive and complete discussion of the problem it did not then, and does not now, pretend to be.

2. Significance and Bearings of the Inquiry.

The question which forms the subject of this paper is one very difficult for a minister in harness to answer with any degree of confidence. Working up to the collar all the time, as most of us are doing; wholly preoccupied with the manifold and various duties that daily claim attention and thought, with no inclination to meddle with other men's affairs, and with very few opportunities of hearing each other preach, how shall anyone say what doctrines are regularly taught from evangelical pulpits? in what relative proportion taught? and according to what rule of theological perspective? And what are neglected—consigned to that limbo, large and broad, in which things transitory and vain only should be received? The very fact, however, that this question is suggested by an association of evangelical pastors must be allowed to have its own significance. Men do not pause and deliberately and anxiously propound such inquiries without sufficient reason. The question is a soliloquy in which the soliloquist challenges his own faith and courage aloud, and such challenge, unprovoked by charge or insinuation from any hostile source, always creates suspicion of a condition of unsettledness and unrest in the mind of the questioner. By the first interrogatory the allegation of neglect is tacitly admitted, and in the second a hint is given not of rebuttal, but only of condonement or justification. The mere mooting of such an inquiry then, taken in conjunction with the general trend of modern religious thought, and especially the prevailing tone and character of present-day eschatological literature, is our warrant for concluding, without attempt at formal proof, that the doctrine of last things has been allowed to drop out of its proper place in a true perspective of Christian teaching. We do not openly disavow our faith in a "wrath to come" ($\mu\acute{\epsilon}\lambda\lambda o\nu\sigma a$ $\grave{o}\rho\gamma\acute{\eta}$). We offer no argument for its disproof. We are simply afraid of it as an item of Christian doctrine, and are willing to contribute toward its painless extinction by taking part in a conspiracy of silence against it. There are doubtless exceptions to the truth of this statement, but it is believed they are notably few.

As to the causes which have led to this uncertainty and hesitation of the religious mind in regard to an important article of Christian faith, it is much easier to say what they are not than what they are. We shall endeavor, however, to state them both negatively and positively.

3. Doctrine of Future Retribution, no Figment of the Mediaeval Fancy.

The evangelical pulpit of to-day is not silent as to the eternal fate of the finally lost, because, as has often been erroneously alleged, the doctrine of future punishment is discovered to be a figment of the mediæval imagination. The early creeds of the Church up to the Council of Nicæa are simplicity itself, being for the most part recitals of historical facts, but it is indisputable that the hopeful and inspiriting representation of the eternal state of the just has always been attended by this foil—this shadow of gloom and despair overhanging the ultimate destiny of the unsaved. If Christian thought on this problem during the last few centuries has been morbidly apprehensive and fearful, the distemper which afflicts it is a very inveterate one, for it has been inherited from the very earliest ages of Catholic Christianity, as the writings of the earliest Christian fathers clearly show.*

Nay, it has a deeper seat still. It is inherent in our intellectual constitution, springing from a far-reaching psychological root which makes our whole mental experience a

---

*Καὶ κρίσιν δικαίαν ἐν τοῖς πᾶσι ποιήσηται, τὰ μὲν πνευματικὰ τῆς πονηρίας καὶ ἀγγέλους τοὺς παραβεβηκότας καὶ ἐν ἀποστασίᾳ γεγόντας καὶ τοὺς ἀσεβεῖς καὶ ἀδίκους καὶ ἀνόμους καὶ βλασφήμους τῶν ἀνθρώπων εἰς τὸ αἰώνιον πῦρ πέμψῃ.—*Irenæus Contr. Hær.*, lib. i, c. 10, §1.

Et judex eorum, qui judicantur, et mittens in ignem æternum transfiguratores veritates et contemtores Patris sui et adventus ejus.—*Contr. Hær.*, lib. iii, c. 4, § 2.

series of contrasts. All our abstract ideas exist in pairs and stand over against each other in sharp antitheses. We could have no notion of high without low, of great without small, of power without weakness, of pleasure without pain, of sweet without bitter, of light without darkness, of rest without labor, of holiness without sin, of order without confusion, of good without evil, of heaven without hell. No doubt many errors, half truths, and abnormities in philosophy, ethics, and religion sprang up during the intellectually active times of Erigena, Scotus, Bernard, Abelard, Anselm, and Aquinas, but this idea of a world of eternally lost souls was not one of them. The clause about the "descent into hell," indicating Christ's dominion over the souls in prison, though not found in the Apostles' Creed earlier than the age of Rufinus, exists in one or other of its forms—*descendit ad inferos, vel ad infera, vel ad inferna, vel ad infernum*—in many early symbols, and was certainly a part not only of premediæval, but of apostolic, teaching.*

4. No Lack of Definite Statement in the New Testament.

Nor is the doctrine of a "wrath of God revealed from heaven"† neglected because it is not definitely and frequently taught in Holy Scripture. The magnitude and gravity of the problem, the solemn and far-reaching issues that depend on its settlement, call for care and exactness in its treatment, and demand a devout sense of dependence on the eternal Spirit, whose promised light and guidance alone can secure the most scholarly, critical, and cautious investigation against erroneous interpretation of the inspired word; but the limits of this paper do not admit of a full and exhaustive discussion of the question here. We will only say that recent attempts, as in Row's *Eternal Retribution*, for example, and very recently in Dr. Beet's *Last Things*, to elim-

---

* See Hahn's *Bibliothek der Symbole und Glaubensregeln der Alten Kirche*, and Dr. Schaff's *Creeds of Christendom*. † Rom. i, 18.

inate the idea of endless duration from such phrases as εἰς τοὺς αἰῶνας τῶν αἰώνων, to the ages of ages; χρόνοις αἰωνίοις, through times eternal; αἰώνιος θεός, the eternal God; ζωὴ αἰώνιος, eternal life; ὄλεθρον αἰώνιον, eternal destruction; τὸ πῦρ τὸ αἰώνιον, the fire which is eternal, taken in conjunction with εἰς τὴν γέενναν τοῦ πυρός, into the Gehenna of fire; αἰώνιον ἁμάρτημα, eternal sin; αἰώνιος κρίσις, eternal judgment; κόλασίς αἰώνιος, eternal punishment; τὸ πῦρ τὸ ἄσβεστον, the fire unquenchable—the elimination from these and similar phrases of the idea of a proper eternity can only be regarded as an exhibition of pitiable exegetical perversity. For though it cannot be denied that αἰών often signifies an age or dispensation of indefinite limit, and that the adjective αἰώνιος, formed from it, often has a similar signification, it is equally indisputable that αἰώνιος, as applied to God and as descriptive of the future condition of saved men and the retribution awaiting the finally lost, was intended to convey the notion of unending duration—eternity proper—as in the *Timæus* of Plato.*

Something must be grievously wrong when the stern exigencies of dogmatic theory require the rendering of such a phrase as αἰώνιος θεός, "the age-long God." What does such a phrase mean? That the duration of God's being, though indefinitely extended, is yet bounded by limit? Strange idea! Yet this is the logical and inevitable conclusion if the rendering of Dr. Beet and those who think with him is legitimate. How can θεός, the name of a Being who is essentially self-existent, eternal, and independent, be qualified by an epithet which strips him of one of his essential and necessary attributes? The phrase "age-long God" contains within itself an obvious contradiction. And yet if this ingenious but palpably absurd interpretation breaks down, the second probation and annihilation theories break down along with it. For if αἰώνιος θεός is the eternal God

* *Timæus*, 38, c. 38. So *Lycurgus*, 162, 24. εἰς ἅπαντα τὸν αἰῶνα.

who lives (χρόνοις αἰωνίοις) through times eternal, and rewards his servants with eternal life (ζωὴ αἰώνιος) and, punishes those who are found guilty of eternal sin (αἰώνιον ἁμάρτημα) with eternal destruction (ὄληθρον αἰώνιον) in eternal fire (εἰς τὸ πῦρ τὸ αἰώνιον), which is not annihilation either swift or slow, but an eternal chastisement (κόλασις αἰώνιος) under an eternal judgment or condemnation (αἰώνιος κρίσις), then there is no place found for the doctrine of universal restoration or of conditional immortality, or the theory of the eternal hope, which, after all, is only another name for everlasting despair; and, curiously enough, even Dr. Beet, while denying the natural immortality of the human soul, admits that the duration of the penalty reserved for the wicked "extends to the utmost limit of man's mental horizon," and that there is "no ground to hope that the agony of the lost will ever cease."*

If the original Scriptures, construed according to strict grammatical law and in harmony with the *usus loquendi* of the writers, are to decide this much-debated question, there is no escape from the conclusion that men's destiny in another world is eternally determined by their character and conduct here, and that as no peril after death overshadows the well-being of the saved, so there is no hope of deliverance—*post-mortem*—for the finally lost. Both good and bad reap in eternity what they have sown in time. As to what that future harvest is there is no dispute. In the case of the "holy" it is life everlasting actually possessed now; in the case of the wicked and lawless it is not some arbitrarily inflicted punishment, but the natural result of a known law working now. Men live by law—"the law of the spirit of life in Christ Jesus."† And men morally degenerate and die by law—"the law of sin and death."‡ Scripture simply corroborates and confirms the inference drawn

---
* See the further discussion of this point in Appendix to this chapter.
† Rom. viii, 2.   ‡ Rom. viii, 2.

from the facts of life, "that sinful character means retributive character, and that permanent and sinful states mean permanent penal states."

The fixed and eternal doom of the unrenewed soul is death ($\theta\acute{a}\nu a\tau o\varsigma$) and moral corruption ($\phi\theta o\rho\acute{a}$)—the inevitable concomitant and consequence of death. It is an incurable *depravation* arising from a hopeless *deprivation*. In the God-abandoned consciousness of the hopelessly corrupted and lost soul the worm that does not die gnaws and the fire which is not quenched burns. In enunciating this solemn fact the manifest object of Jesus is not to gratify our curiosity or to terrorize our minds with the possibility of some indefinite and dread calamity, but to stimulate us to a right use of life and impress us with a due sense of its responsibility.

5. The Doctrine Essential to a Complete and Well-articulated System of Christian Truth—Fourfold Apocalypse.

But if it is not for want of definite inspired authority that the pulpit of the day plays the part of a muffled drum on this most solemn question, neither is it because of its nonessentiality to a complete and thoroughly articulated system of Christian truth. Christianity is essentially a revelation of the eternally existent, a disclosure ($\dot{a}\pi o\kappa\acute{a}\lambda\upsilon\psi\iota\varsigma$) of certitudes. And as regards the future, this apocalypse or unveiling is distinctly fourfold: 1. There is to be an unveiling of the glorified Christ, whose kingly majesty here was hidden, being enshrined in our lowly human form and obscured by his humiliation and sorrow (1 Pet. iv, 13). 2. There is to be an unveiling of the sons of God ($\dot{a}\pi o\kappa\acute{a}\lambda\upsilon\psi\iota\varsigma\ \tau\tilde{\omega}\nu\ \upsilon\dot{\iota}\tilde{\omega}\nu\ \Theta\epsilon o\tilde{\upsilon}$), whose present subjection to various trials and temptations and prejudgments and manifold mortal ills conceals from view their destined royalty and blessedness (Rom. viii, 19; 1 John iii, 2). 3. There is to be an unveiling of the New Economy ($o\dot{\iota}\kappa o\upsilon\mu\acute{\epsilon}\nu\eta$), "the new heavens and new earth"—the divinely adjusted environment or new conditions of existence which are to conserve and enhance the joy of those who have demonstrated their desert and capacity for blessedness in a world of temptation, sin, and sorrow. Accordingly the Christian prophet who sees the "Holy City, New Jerusalem," descending out of heaven from God, prepared as a bride adorned for her husband, is the author of an apocalypse (Rev. xxi, 1-4). 4. Lastly, there is to be an apocalypse "in the day of wrath" (ἐν ἡμέρα ὀργῆς) of the righteous judgment of God, who will render to every man according to his work (Rom. ii, 5, 6).

Now, these apocalypses are integral and necessary parts of one great providential scheme of the future, of which the whole past history of the world, with its drama and melodrama, tragedy and comedy, trials and triumphs, declension and advancement, is nothing more than a sort of prologue or preparatory rehearsal; and such is the vital connection and close interdependence of these several disclosures that to omit or suppress one of them is like breaking a link in a chain. It dismembers and disturbs the entire system of revealed truth and interrupts the gracious purpose of God. While theological system may be artificial and arbitrary in its arrangement, its several parts being developed, displaced, or even dispensed with at will, as has always been the case more or less, no such method can be applied without serious mischief to the scheme of redemption, which grows according to laws of its own like a "tree of life" out of the nature of God. Each apocalypse is the unveiling of previously existing facts; of truths, laws, relations that, having their root and reason in Eternal Being, cannot be altered, but become successively and seasonably ripe for disclosure like the leaves, blossoms, and fruit of a tree.

Now, the systematic neglect of any of these essential phases of the divine scheme of the future produces a maimed and mutilated type of Christianity, and presents in place of the God-given evangel, where the harshest note is essential to the fullness and completeness of the music, a parody and a caricature which requires all the training, ability, eloquence, courage, tact, and adroitness a man can muster to save it from becoming jejune, tedious, and tiresome to the common mind beyond all mortal endurance. The biographer of Paganini tells us how, when playing before a large and critical audience in Cremona, the home of the great makers and masters of the violin, his first string broke. The musician, with the dogged pertinacity and love of charlatanry that characterized him in spite of his consummate artistic skill, seemed not to notice the mishap, but proceeded to play out the piece on three strings. But it was admitted that, while the performance did credit to the matchless courage and incomparable art of the violinist, it scarcely did equal justice to the music, to the sweet-toned and precious Stradivarius he pressed against his jaw, or to the audience which had come expecting not so much to see and applaud the expertness of Paganini, for whom personally the people of Cremona had no special liking, as to hear the thrilling strains of his peerless and almost perfect music. If Paganini had paused and secured his broken string, the delay might not have enhanced his fame, but what the performance would have lost in brilliance and bizarreness the music would have gained in fullness and harmony. And surely no one called to the high and honorable ambassadorship of the Gospel ministry can afford to withhold from his people from any motives of fear or prudence, or personal ease or prospect of temporary advantage of any kind, what he has reason to believe is a vital item in the divinely inspired counsels of salvation.

6. No Theodicy in Silence.

Nor is there to our mind an excuse for silence in the alleged difficulty of reconciling the execution of eternal penalty on the ultimately lost with the infinite compassion and goodness of God. Those who really feel this difficulty ought to find it at an earlier stage, namely, in the introduction and continued existence of sin in the world. The objection squints in the wrong direction, inasmuch as it looks forward instead of backward. It ought to be dated from the point where the great epic poet begins his beautifully sad and tuneful strain, namely, with

> Man's first disobedience and the fruit
> Of that forbidden tree, whose mortal taste
> Brought death into the world and all our woe
> With loss of Eden.

The greatest evil conceivable is not the suffering which naturally follows sin, but the sin which ever leads to suffering. And this is true whether the suffering be of long or of short, of endless or limited, duration. Suffering does not corrupt the soul and atrophy its moral powers, but sin does. Nor is it conceivable that to a moral being, whose essential happiness must ever largely consist in the sanity and free play of moral faculty and function, any element of pain or disaster extraneous to the soul itself can materially add to that essential anguish which must always be consequent on its own self-chosen or self-caused deterioration. Singularly enough, the future fate of lost souls is described as a harvest of corruption—of blasted and putrescent grain—reaped under the domain and action of natural law.* We look around us and we see natures as noble and strenuous as our own, capable of as large and lasting a happiness as we are hoping ourselves to attain, defiled, degraded, ruined, by the giant vices of idleness, intemperance, lust, the love of mammon, etc., and every thoughtful man accustomed to look beneath the surface of things feels that endless pain, as such, is nothing compared with this apparently hopeless and eternal corruption of a moral and responsible being. That is

---

* Gal. vi, 8.

Bugbear of Present-day Evangelical Pulpit 137

merely the shadow; this is the dark substance that casts it. That is an accident only; this is the essential fact. Yet this ruin wrought by sin is something that confronts us every day, and if we believe in the existence and reign of a wise, holy, and gracious God at all, we are compelled to believe this mystery of mysteries—sin—to be consistent with his spotless character, universal supremacy, absolute and beneficent rule. As Dr. Salmond observes: " The greatest thinkers have felt that if the problem of the *existence* of sin and sinners could be made clear to us, we should the more easily understand the problem of their *continuance*." Meanwhile, if we admit the *root* of evil to be consistent with God's wisdom and love, why find any difficulty in admitting the *fruit* of it to be so too? The objection should be taken earlier, otherwise we "strain out the gnat and swallow the camel."

7. Causes Operating Positively toward Alleged Neglect.

Looking now at the question on its positive side, there are doubtless several considerations operating powerfully to bring about the doubt and hesitation which tend to seal the preacher's lips as to the future of the lost. We can only advert briefly to the chief of these.

1. There is—perhaps it is only a passing mood—the absence even in the religious, but much more in the unrenewed, mind of any vivid sense of the exceeding sinfulness and ill-desert of sin. Its eternally offensive nature, its corrupting and polluting power, its far-extending and eternal consequences are not clearly apprehended nor deeply felt in our day. Even in its worst forms it is condoned as misfortune, as the result of human frailty or false environment, or both; often as the error of noble but misdirected impulses, meriting more the pity both of God and man than the severe blame of either. It is a missing of the mark ($ἀμαρτία$) through the ignorance, infirmity, want of moral precision of

the marksman; or it is a false step, a blunder (παράπτωμα), rather than a deliberate stepping over the forbidden line (παράβασις)—a conscious and intentional disregard of divine authority, or a habitual contempt and defiance of law (ἀνομία), or a wrong with a double aspect (ἀδικία)—a course of conduct unjust alike to God and to men. And this failure to discern the real inwardness of moral evil—this tendency to emphasize sin in its character of error and weakness, and to minimize or ignore its preponderating scriptural aspect of moral offense, perversity, guilt, and condemnation—makes the holy and unceasing antagonism of God's nature to it seem "much ado about nothing," and the preacher's faithful denunciations of its inevitable doom a vain beating of the air.

2. There is, too, more than ever a tendency of reason to usurp the place of faith. Not reason disciplined and sobered by the difficulties of life, of science, and philosophy—reverently cognizant of mystery alike in nature, providence, and religion, and instructed by divine revelation. To this God makes his appeal. But it is reason arguing over-confidently from her own dubious and fallible premises, and acting as the self-constituted judge of those universal, eternal, and incomprehensible principles which are the essence of God's moral character and the immovable basis of his moral government.*

---

* Dr. Oliver Wendell Holmes quotes, in his delightful volume, *Over the Teacups* (pp. 253, 254), the words of Mr. John Morley, concerning "the horrors of what is perhaps the most frightful idea that has corroded human character, the idea of eternal punishment," and remarks, "All the reasoning in the world, all the proof-texts in old manuscripts, cannot reconcile this supposition of a world of sleepless and endless torment with the declaration that 'God is love!' Where did this frightful idea come from? We are surprised as we grow older to find that the legendary hell of the Church is nothing more nor less than the Tartarus of the old heathen world. It has the mark of coming from the cruel heart of a barbarous despot."

To this it may be answered:

1. The "reconciliation" of eternal punishment with God's essential love is not more "hopeless" than the reconciliation of many other coexistent and indisputable facts, such, for example, as the tender mercy and absolute power of God with the indescribable "horrors of the middle passage," as it was called, or the miseries of the modern slums, where the present well-being of thousands of helpless children is sacrificed to adult intemperance, improvidence, and debauchery. But God is no more responsible for the hells of the future than for those of the present, both being obviously the result

3. Then the natural result of this tendency to enthrone reason in its narrower sense where faith should reign is a state of general theological unsettledness affecting the whole of Protestant Christendom. Everywhere traditional beliefs are being overhauled and theological conviction is in a state of flux. The most conservative of Churches are tearing their old confessions and standards of faith to pieces. Already the age has seen some of the most familiar and venerable of dogmas

> Fold their tents like the Arabs,
> And silently steal away.

Many have felt the old homestead of faith coming down over their heads and have left it before the roof fell in, and not having found either time or inclination to build themselves another shelter, are out in the cold. And like Æneas, who stands afar off and sees Troy sink in flames,* they are doomed apparently to encounter many storms, to be tossed on waves of doubt, and to wander in desolate places abounding only in anxieties and sorrows.

In periods of great intellectual activity in the history of the Church each of the cardinal doctrines of Christianity has come in succession into the hot crucible of controversy,

---

of the perverseness of the human will in resisting the necessary and benignant laws of the divine government.

2. There is absolutely no evidence that either the *Hades* or the *Gehenna* of the New Testament was adopted from heathen mythology. Even were it so, Christianity never claimed a monopoly of fact and truth. The word Tartarus is met with only once in the New Testament writings, namely, in the Second Epistle of Peter (ii, 4), which was received late into the Christian canon, but the idea of hell long antedated Peter's adoption of the term *Tartarus*.

3. So far from having "every mark of coming from the cruel heart of a barbarous despot," the author and chief exponent of the doctrine is Jesus Christ, in whose authentic teaching it is firmly imbedded. Is it a sign of cruelty of disposition when a mother reminds her beloved child that fire burns and sharp instruments inflict hurtful wounds when carelessly handled, and when she warns him not to play with them? Does the teaching of Jesus and of his apostles go beyond the simple unveiling (ἀποκάλυψις, Rom. i, 18) and definite statement of the eternal law which governs the relation of the sowing of to-day to the reaping of the hereafter—the link which inseparably connects present character and eternal destiny? Christianity does not *create* the facts and laws it *unfolds*. Neither is he a despot who, himself knowing, mercifully makes known the morally inevitable to men blinded by vice and passion, and not only provides a reasonable method of escape, but urges them to use it by accepting the conditions.

* " Tum vero omne mihi visum considere in ignes
Ilium et ex imo verti Neptunia Troja."
—*Vergil*, Lib. ii, 624.

but somehow, without taking the precaution to mark the heated vessel with a *crux*, in the manner of the old chemists, to prevent the devil from marring the refining process, Christian thinkers have ever got the precious deposit of revealed truth out of the testing jar in an improved rather than in a deteriorated condition. At one time the subject of investigation and dispute has been the divinity of Christ, leading slowly but surely to the development of the doctrine of the Trinity and the formation of the Nicene Creed. At another it has been the nature and extent of the atonement, resulting in the construction respectively of the Calvinistic and Arminian systems of Soteriology. At another it is, as at present, the literary composition, age, authorship, value, and validity of the documents of the Christian faith, mainly of the Old Testament, or, again, it is the doctrine of the life to come. To-day it may be said that there is scarcely any Protestant Church or denomination within the limits of Christendom that is not more or less agitated by the question as to the final state of unrenewed souls; and of course the natural consequence of this uncertainty is silence all round—profound, oppressive, ominous, almost unbroken silence.

Is this silence excusable? It may be true, as Dr. Salmond, Professor of Theology in the Free Church College, Aberdeen, contends in his able and scholarly discussion of "The Christian Doctrine of Immortality," that "a true theology will confess its own limitations, and will not presume to give an answer to every difficulty; will recognize that the Christian revelation is given not to utter all the secrets of another world, but to make God known to us and to bring him near; will seek to be positive up to Christ's word; will not be ambitious to be wise beyond it; will be satisfied to be silent where Christ's voice has not spoken, and will leave much that is dark in man's life, here and hereafter, to the eternal wisdom that keeps so much in reserve;

in a word, it will be content to see that all is in the hand of a God of grace, and its assurance will be that the farthest future can discover nothing that will not be consistent with the perfect love and righteousness which are revealed in Christ." But, on the other hand, as Dr. Salmond is careful to observe, we are warranted in concluding that "Christ's own teaching gives the significance of finality to the moral decisions of the present life. If there are possibilities of change, forgiveness, relaxation of penalty, or cessation of punishment in the future life, his words, at least, do not reveal them. He never softens the awful responsibilities of this life even by the dim adumbration of such possibilities. His recorded sayings nowhere suggest the provision of ministries of grace, whether new or continued, in the after-existence. They nowhere speak of a place of repentance unto life in the other world. They nowhere open the prospect of remedial discipline in the disembodied state, or of terminable award in the condition which follows the great day. They bring the two events, death and judgment, into relation, and give no disclosure of an intermediate state with untold potentialities of divine love and human surrender. They never traverse the principle that this life is the scene of opportunity, and this world the theater of human fates."*

APPENDIX TO CHAPTER VI.

It is possibly a fact of some consequence in this controversy, as Dr. Beet, the author of *Last Things*, seems to insist that Plato, indorsing the opinion of his master, Socrates, teaches in the *Phædo* (105^e–107^e) "the natural immortality and indestructibility of the soul" ($\psi v \chi \dot{\eta}$ $\dot{a}\theta \dot{a}\nu a$-$\tau o\nu$ $\kappa a \dot{\iota}$ $\dot{a}\nu \dot{\omega}\lambda \epsilon \theta \rho o\nu$)—*Last Things*, p. 194. But it is surely a fact of still vaster significance that this doctrine has been

* "The Christian Doctrine of Immortality," by Stewart D. F. Salmond, M.A., D.D.

held and supported by the almost unbroken consensus of Christian thinkers for nearly nineteen centuries; and as this doctrine professes to be derived by them not from the master of the Academy, but from a careful study of the explicit and implicit teachings of the Christian Scriptures, it will scarcely be contended that the earlier and smaller fact, standing alone, is any adequate explanation of the later and larger phenomenon, as Dr. Beet evidently wishes us to believe. That would be like an attempt to poise the pyramid of argument on its apex. Dr. Beet admits that the Pharisees in the lifetime of Christ and the New Testament writers held this opinion of the soul's natural immortality as distinctly as Plato or Cicero. If it be necessary to seek the origin of this view anywhere outside the New Testament, why derive it from a remote source in Plato and ignore its proximate explanation in the well-known teachings of the Pharisees? Is not this a case of carrying coals to Newcastle?

The author of *Last Things* labors through three hundred scholarly pages with the poor result, as it seems to us, of reducing the New Testament teachings to vagueness, paradox, and confusion. In his Appendix he pierces every positive conclusion of contemporary writers on the subject with the sharp spear-thrust of his logic, but tantalizes the reader by never arriving at any definite conclusion of his own. As an example of his hesitancy and confusion of mind in this sort we quote the following contradictory *dicta* from his pages: "The ultimate fate of the lost is not precisely defined in the Bible" (p. 282). "We know so little about the ultimate punishment of sin and the dissolution of the universe that analogy affords no sure basis for argument or even conjecture" (p. 272). The dogma of the eternal conscious suffering of the lost is "a doctrine which lies open to serious moral objection" (p. 275), and "is contradicted by *the clear and abundant teaching of the New Testament*" (p. 293). "The theories of annihilation and universal restoration are destitute of sufficient evidence, the latter being *contradicted by the plain teaching of Christ and of Paul*" (p. 271).

Now, if "the ultimate fate of the lost is not precisely defined in the Bible," it would be interesting to know just what definite doctrine as to the fate of lost men "the clear and abundant teaching of the New Testament," which so conclusively disproves Universalism, on the one hand, and "contradicts" the doctrine of conscious, endless suffering of the lost, on the other, refers to. How can there be "clear and abundant teaching" on a subject which is "not precisely defined" and about which "we know so little?"

In his careful and exhaustive discussion of the meaning of the adjective αἰώνιος Dr. Beet forgets that in the increasing light of the New Dispensation Old Testament words (and especially the more vaguely defined and more elastic terms) naturally acquire a deeper meaning, as they have to express a larger and fuller revelation of God's mind and of the future. The meaning of a word in the Old Testament must, of course, be a more or less safe clew to its true import in the New, but the *limit* of its meaning in the former cannot be the *measure* of its significance in the latter. Now, if in determining the precise sense of any word in the New Testament its clear and indisputable meaning in the vast majority of instances where it is employed be allowed to have any weight, there can hardly be any question as to the primary and pivotal sense of the adjective αἰώνιος. For of the seventy places in which it is used forty-three occur in the phrase "eternal life," as Dr. Beet himself points out, and the meaning in all these cases is admitted by all to be beyond dispute. In twenty of the remaining cases it ascribes to the object it qualifies a proper eternity. In hardly any of the small residue of instances can its import be said to be doubtful. With such a preponderance of evidence showing its true meaning to be *endlessness* one cannot but regret that polemical necessity obliges a scholar and theologian like Dr. Beet to limit its significance to *age lasting*. The phrase πρὸ χρόνων αἰωνίων (Tit. i, 2) he makes to mean "before long periods of time past," transferring the limited sense of the word in the Old Testament to the pages of the New. It will probably, however, be admitted that such "long periods of time past" antedated the creation of man, and as the Lamb of God is said to have been slain from the foundation of the world, so in view of and in conjunction with that sacrifice, eternally projected and purposed in the divine mind, God promised or purposed in himself, before times eternal—πρὸ χρόνων αἰωνίων—to bestow eternal life on those who should believe, these having been "chosen in Christ (Eph. i, 4) before the foundation of the world" (πρὸ καταβολῆς κόσμου), "that they should be holy and without blame before him in love." All the fundamental verities and institutions of revealed religion emerging in time under the aegis and action of divine Providence are based on eternal archetypal ideas, and as these ideas have their root and reason in the nature of God, they are eternal in the same sense that he is eternal. Dr. Beet's exegetical device, therefore, though ingenious, only excites distrust, and is certainly not without some risk of bringing the great "science of theology" into the "contempt" which he so earnestly and justly deprecates.

The present writer disavows any personal or polemical interest in the decision of this question of the final fate of the lost one way or the other. For many years he was undecided, now leaning to this solution and then to that, as the weight of evidence and argument swayed him in the course of a patient and protracted study of the whole problem. Latterly, in spite of the enormous difficulties which he still feels to beset the question, he has reached the conclusion that the plain and obvious drift of the teaching of Jesus and his apostles is toward the doctrine held and taught almost unanimously by the Christian Church, early, mediæval, and modern, east and west, Protestant and Catholic, for more than eighteen hundred years.

Though compelled, however, to disagree with many of the positions assumed by the author of *Last Things*, the present author cannot but regret that Dr. Beet, having had the courage to publish his views, has not had the firmness to sustain them and resist the pressure put upon him by a committee of the Wesleyan Conference to withdraw his book from sale and circulation in England. The motto of theological as of all other truth is, " He who wrestles with me strengthens me."

CHAPTER VII
Homiletical Craftsmanship

It seems to me that I built into my house every one of those superb autumn days which I spent in the woods getting stone. I did not quarry the limestone ledge into *blocks* any more than I quarried the delicious weather into *memories* to adorn my walls. Every load that I sent home carried my heart and happiness with it. The jewels I had uncovered in the débris or torn from the ledge in the morning I saw in the jambs or mounted high on the corners at night. Every day was filled with great events. The woods held unknown treasures. . . . When you bait your hook with your heart the fish always bite.—*John Burroughs.*

Character and experience form the quarry from which the only material of any value can be drawn; they supply the only force which carries it home; and they are its only effectual and adequate illustration. . . . There are a great many excellent sermons that are spoilt in the minds of the hearers because side by side with the sermon as it proceeds so beautifully there is the personality of the preacher.—*James Chapman.*

1. Personality of the Craftsman.

IN preaching, as in many other noble callings, much less depends on method than upon the man. In every position of responsibility personality is largely the secret of power, but nowhere quite so emphatically as in the ministerial profession. In science, philosophy, statesmanship, law, literature, art, handicraft, or common industry, where, if anywhere, proficiency and eminence would seem to be independent of character, the *work* to a shrewd and practiced observer bears unmistakably the sign-manual of the *man*. No marvel, surely, that in view of this fact the moral tone and status of the occupant of the modern pulpit should be more and more regarded as the one supreme and vital consideration. The preacher of to-day is required not alone to proclaim and expound, but to personally embody and exemplify that trinity of moral and spiritual excellence which is the goal of all salvation worthy of the name—"the true, the good, the beautiful" (τὸ ἀληθές, τὸ ἀγαθόν, τὸ καλόν). To him it is given to preach "the unsearchable wealth of Christ;" to be "a steward of the manifold grace of God." And of this exhaustless and varied good his own well-instructed and thoroughly disciplined soul must be a depository. The prince of Roman poets, at the opening of his song, announces a double theme. He sings of "arms" and of the "man" who bore them. But quite naturally his strain is mainly concerned with the personality and prowess of the hero, since it is these alone which make the arms worth singing about. So here, in speaking of homiletical method, the main emphasis must be placed on the character and capability of the craftsman. On him presses with peculiar gravity in these days the obligation which finds expression in the familiar lines:

> Thou must be true thyself,
>   If thou the truth wouldst teach.
> Thy soul must overflow, if thou
>   Another soul would reach.
> It needs the overflowing heart
>   To give the lips full speech.
>
> Think truly, and thy thought
>   Shall the world's famine feed.
> Speak truly, and thy word
>   Shall be a fruitful seed.
> Live truly, and thy life shall be
>   A great and noble creed.

The great artist who constructed the immense shield of Minerva for the Acropolis of Athens, in the golden age of Greece, felt so sure he had "cast bread upon the waters which would be seen after many days" that he did not hesitate to commit his fame as exemplified in the product of his art to the custody of posterity. So skillfully did he manage to insert the letters of his name amid the matchless carvings of that monument of genius that it was impossible to erase them without injuring the shield itself. And if Phidias was proud enough of the offspring of his well-disciplined talent to be willing to risk his reputation on its artistic merits for untold generations, how much more ought the master of a far nobler craft to feel himself called upon to cultivate a moral and intellectual personality which he will not be ashamed to find stamped ineffaceably on the work of his life? The art of the preacher as far transcends the art of the painter, the sculptor, or the architect as the value and durability of moral impressions are greater than those of sensuous and æsthetic emotion, and the living character of a Washington, a Gladstone, or a Lincoln is of more worth to the world than the stereotyped beauty of a thousand Apollo Belvederes. What Fra Angelico did for the cells of San Marco, and Michael Angelo did for the ceiling of the Sistine Chapel, a true proclaimer of "the Gospel of the grace of God" like Savonarola, Luther, Wesley, or Spurgeon does for the souls that are privileged to hear him. He paints images of moral loveliness—visions of truth and personal rectitude—on walls that cannot crumble or decay. "Let your light so shine among men," said Christ to the Galilean fishermen, who were in subsequent years to catch men by "baiting the hook with their hearts," "that they may see your good works ($\tau\grave{a}$ $\kappa a \lambda\grave{a}$ $\check{\epsilon}\rho\gamma a$—noble and honorable deeds), and glorify your Father which is in heaven" (Matt. v, 16). The phrase is one which the Greeks were accustomed to employ in expressing their admiration of the highest order of plastic, pictorial, or oratorical art, as well as of the loftiest types of moral conduct. Did ever master-artist present to his pupils a loftier standard of excellence or address to them a nobler incentive to godlike endeavor than this?

2. Power of the Ideal in Sermon-making.

It is the more necessary to insist on this inward preparedness in the man who aspires to be a workman beyond reproach or shame, "rightfully dividing the worth of truth," inasmuch as such highly developed spiritual condition alone renders possible the ideal which makes a difficult and often discouraging task attractive and pleasant, illumining and transfiguring human nature and human life, and enabling the preacher to see the possibilities of sainthood in every Magdalene, a rock of fidelity and firmness potentially in every impulsive and vacillating Peter, a guileless Israelite in the man who incredulously asks, "Can any good thing come out of Nazareth?" an apostle of love in the youth who seeks authority and encouragement to invoke the consuming fire of heaven upon the heads of his opposers. Of the awards bestowed at the Greek athletic contests Walter Besant says: "The actual prize was of little or no worth—a cloak in the Athenian games, but at the greater games a mere handful of parsley, a few sprigs of pine or wild olive. The prize had only an intellectual or moral value, yet Pindar's verse (in which the prizemen's achievements are celebrated and idealized) are all of gold and wine and flowers." What John Burroughs says of the observer of nature is true, in even a deeper degree, of the man whose business it is to study human life with sympathy and insight, and interpret and apply the revealed mind of God to man's various needs. "One secret of success in observing nature," says this high priest in the Temple of the Cosmos, "is capacity to take a hint; a hair may show where a lion is hid. One must put this and that together and value bits and shreds. Much alloy exists with the truth. The gold of nature does not look like gold at the first glance. It must be smelted and refined in the mind of the observer. And one must crush mountains of quartz and wash hills of sand to get it. To know the indications is the main matter. People who do not know the secret are eager to take a walk with the observer to find where the mine is that contains such nuggets, little knowing that his ore-bed is but a gravel heap to them. How insignificant appear most of the facts which one sees in his walks, in the life of the birds, the flowers, the animals, or in the phases of landscape or the look of the sky!—insignificant until they are put through some mental or emotional process and their true value appears. The diamond looks like a pebble until it is cut. One goes to nature only for hints and half truths. Her facts are crude until you have absorbed them or translated them. *Then the ideal steals in and lends a charm in spite of one. It is not so much what we see as what the thing seen suggests."* *

It is this suggestiveness of nature, of history, of human life, of God's revealed word, which the preacher needs to perceive and appreciate. And it is this capacity to supply the ideal which differentiates the true interpreter of divine and human things from the false; the fruitful from the barren; the man of power in the pulpit from the prosy mumbler who once a week makes the "house of God" a cemetery or sleeping place for those who are not yet quite dead. It is this which gives each fragment of inspired truth power to kindle thought, making the text chosen like a diamond of many facets, flashing light from many sides. It is this which gives the preacher's rhetoric its sparkle, vividness, and charm; his argument its vigor, scope, compactness, and power to convince; his illustrations luminosity and aptness; his appeal its impressiveness and force. It gives warmth and color, life and movement, to his thought, energy to his style, precision and fluency to his expression, melody and richness to his voice, and propriety and fitness to his manner and action. It is the direct result of the indwelling Holy Spirit's power on the soul of the preacher, and its presence or absence makes or mars the sermon, no matter who the man who preaches it, or what the thoughtful care and conscientious toil employed in its construction.

---

* *Signs and Seasons*, p. 33.

Homiletical Craftsmanship 151

3. Unity of Theme and Thought.

Then this ideal as inspired and sustained by the Holy Spirit offers service to the craftsman of the pulpit in another way. It makes the text selected a living revelation to the preacher's soul, and his sermon an authoritative message to his hearers. It enables him to contemplate his subject clearly and steadily, and to grasp it whole; to see the desired destination from the start. "An artist," says Frith, the English Royal Academician, "must see his picture finished in his mind's eye, or he will never be an artist at all." And a preacher who is not mind-full, heart-full, and conscience-full of his theme will never preach impressively and with profit to his hearers. When one grand thought inspires the mind, and an absolute singleness of purpose illumines its sight, directs its effort, and absorbs its energy, discursiveness and vagueness of treatment become next to impossible. The ruling idea keeps the mind on its guard against the most tempting allurements to turn aside, and sustains its resolution to pursue the straightest and shortest course, with a view to the earliest possible arrival at the desired goal. It secures concentration of all the powers of the soul on the one work of the moment. The entire man preaches, and when the complete manhood of the pulpit preaches the undivided manhood of the pews listens and is blest.

"It is impossible to do a thing badly that fills the whole soul," especially if it has been filling the whole soul for some time and gradually developing into ideal form, as "a thing of beauty" and κτῆμα εἰς ἀεί—a thing forever precious. The sermon-making faculty ought at least to be as studiously and severely cultivated as the noblest of the fine arts. Every homily ought to be as truly an expression of the preacher's consecrated life and powers as the picture or the oratorio is an expression of the painter's or the musician's undivided soul. Until this is done evangelical preaching, which is showing indubitable signs of decay, will never become that joy to the preacher and that blessing to all the people which it was manifestly meant to be.

Modestly disclaiming any special aptitude as a pulpit orator, a man whose labors as a lay preacher have been signally owned of God says: "The success which, in the mercy of God, has attended my own weak efforts in the pulpit and some of the remarkable incidents of visible conversion to God I have been permitted to witness, is a great secret to me, and one I cannot explain." He actually, however, though unwittingly, lets drop the very secret which, humanly speaking, "explains" everything, when he says: "A man to be successful in his work must be at it, hard at it, and always at it—his home life, his business life, his social life, his church life, all made subservient to this one great work of preaching the Gospel." "This one thing I do" is, to use the phrase of Carlyle, "significant of much" in every department of intellectual activity, and nowhere of more than in this noblest department of all.

Mrs. Macfadyen, "the sermon-taster" of Drumtochty in *Beside the Bonnie Brier Bush*, listening critically to the Highland preacher, McTavish, thought herself master of the situation when "the great trumpet which shall be blown" (Isa. xxvii, 13) was duly announced as "a leeteral trumpet, a heestorical trumpet, a metaphorical trumpet, and a speeritual trumpet." But when the preacher, in defiance of all the homiletical unities, blew first one trumpet, then another, crossing and recrossing his own division lines without a moment's warning, she grew perplexed. And yet the worst was to come; for when at nine o'clock at night, after preaching three full hours, he said, "We will now consider Satan in all his characteristics," she grew pale with vexation, lost all patience, began to shuffle her feet, and thus hopelessly stained her faultless record for reverent behavior in church. In its very extravagance the situation is typical. The present writer listened to a sermon preached in a college town to a score of college professors, a hundred and fifty students, and about a hundred other educated and thoughtful auditors. The text announced was the beautiful and inspiring promise, "And I, if I be lifted up from the earth," etc. But the central thought of the text, the moral grandeur and attractiveness of the divine self-sacrifice and victim—the thought which fascinated even the skeptical soul of Shelley when, in *Prometheus Unbound*, he sang:

> I alit
> Upon a great ship lightning split,
> And speeded thither on the sigh
> Of one who gave his enemy
> His plank, then plunged aside to die,

was never even remotely approached during the whole service until the sweet-voiced choir led in the hymn, "In the cross of Christ I glory." As the author stood singing with tears filling heart and eyes and voice he thanked God for the gracious compensation offered in that noble strain against a dismal disappointment, and said to himself, "What a mercy it is we sing hymns in church!" Brimful as the best of them are of the finest evangelical sentiment, they are often a disappointed and hungry people's one unfailing crumb of comfort after the poverty and failure of the sermon.

4. Selection of Materials.

Now, aimless and purposeless vagrancy of this kind is as gratuitous and unnecessary in the pulpit as it is harmful and blameworthy. For when once the mind of the sermon-builder fully surrenders itself to the all-inspiring and dominant idea of the text, materials for the sermon-structure rapidly accumulate and are easily selected, or rather assimilated—the true sermon being much less an intellectual creation than the evolution of a moral and spiritual force, expressing itself in terms of the intellect. If the central thought has, as it always ought to have, a sublimity, grandeur, fullness, and suggestiveness of its own, it will have no need to be flattened out thin, like gold leaf, in order to cover the ground required; no need to descend from its high plane or deflect from its straightforward course in search of means of development, expansion, and illustration. Sovereign ideas, like royal personages, do not impoverish themselves by traveling. As in the progress of a reigning prince through a loyal country there is not only a large retinue of willing servitors, courtiers, and attendants, but homage, aid, hospitality, contributions for ornament and decoration, *vectigal* of various kinds and the freedom of cities are freely brought and offered at the halting stages, without the necessity of turning aside a moment from the predetermined line of march; so the broad fields of nature, the realms of science, the world of art, the page of history, the groves and porticoes of philosophy, the treasures of literature, and the gleanings of travel offer themselves freely for the elucidation of the essential and eternal verities of revelation. Should the germ-thought decided upon prove poor in kindred and powerless to attract a sufficient amount of homogeneous and illustrative matter, to set it off to advantage and make it forcible and impressive to an audience, that is the best reason for a timely abandonment of the desolate and unpromising topic and the selection of another of nobler pedigree, of more suggestive character, and of greater wealth of kin. It is fabled that when Minerva found, by looking into a fountain near Mount Ida, that playing upon her favorite flute distorted her looks and made her a laughing-stock to her sister goddesses—Venus and Juno—she threw the beloved instrument into the water, pronouncing a melancholy death on anyone who ventured to take it out again. The preacher should avoid every bare and barren theme, no matter what its attraction, whose treatment is

Homiletical Craftsmanship 155

likely to cost him more labor, anxiety, and painstaking than he can give of edification and help to his hearers.

And the appositeness and relevancy of the subsidiary matter should always be obvious and easy to perceive. It is hardly to be expected that the more subtle and less apparent relations of thought to thought will be as quickly discerned and as fully appreciated in the pews as they are in the study and the pulpit. A preacher may easily commit the fatal mistake of underestimating the intelligence, culture, and capacity of his audience, but there is at least an equal danger of overrating not their *ability* but their *willingness* to think. On the whole, it is safer to be ultra-plain and simple than excessively profound. "Recollect that you are addressing people who need to be taught like children," is the warning to the young men of his college of that very distinguished and successful preacher, Mr. Spurgeon; "for though they are grown up, the major part of our hearers, as to the things of God, are still in a state of childhood, and if they are to receive the truth, it must be made very plain and packed up so as to be carried away and laid up in the memory."*

Metaphysical speculations, loose, disjointed thinking, far-fetched and irrelevant allusions, promiscuous snatches of poetry and prose, with the violent transitions they often involve, are unedifying, offensive even to uncultured minds; while nothing is more satisfactory than lucid and logical statement, well-compacted argument, and a clear-cut issue. No audience cares to be jogged too much at homiletical switches.

The principle of selection, too, ought to be determined not so much by the intrinsic value and interest of the material itself which happens to be on hand, as by the immediate object of preaching and the needs of the souls whose present and eternal welfare is earnestly desired and sought. Every man truly designated of heaven to the

---
* Inaugural address to the students of the Pastor's College.

evangelical ambassadorship will have no difficulty in nodding a cordial assent to the words of the great Baptist preacher. "God," says he, "deserves the best oratory, the best logic, the best metaphysics, the best of everything, but if ever rhetoric stands in the way of the instruction of the people, a curse on rhetoric; if any educational attainment or natural gift which we possess should make it less easy for the people to understand us, let it perish. May God rend away from our thought and style everything which darkens the light, even though it should be like a costly veil of rarest lace." Elsewhere descanting on the tendency to sacrifice the great end of preaching to literary form, elegance of style, accuracy of dogmatic statement, etc., he says: "A man must have a stout digestion to feed on some men's theology—no sap, no sweetness, no life, but all stern accuracy and fleshless definition, proclaimed without tenderness and argued without affection; the Gospel from such men rather resembles a missile from a catapult than bread from a Father's table. Teeth are needlessly broken over the grit of systematic theology, while souls are famishing. To turn stones into bread was a temptation of our Master, but how many of his servants yield readily to the worse temptation to turn bread into stones! Go thy way, metaphysical divine, to the stoneyard, and break granite for Macadam, but stand not in the way of loving spirits who would feed the family of God with living bread. The inspired word is to us spirit and life, and we cannot afford to have it hardened into a huge monolith or a spiritual Stonehenge, sublime, but cold; majestic, but lifeless."

5. Simplicity of Structure.

Not less important to the craftsman than the spiritual nutritiveness and digestibility of the material is the simplicity of the structure of the sermon. A preacher's loftiness of aim and earnestness of purpose reveal themselves in this as much as in anything. What the naturalist of the Hudson says of architecture contains a principle which is largely applicable to sermon-building. "The great monumental structures of the Old World show no pride or vanity, but, on the contrary, great humility and singleness of purpose. The Gothic cathedral does not try to look beautiful; it *is* beautiful from the start, and entirely serious. London Bridge is a heroic resolution in stone, and apparently has but one purpose, and that is to carry the paved street with all its surging masses safely over the river." The very lines of strength and evidences of weight and stability which the practiced eye craves in architecture the ear also desires in a sermon. "It prefers the broad, conspicuous lines of structure to the small, fine lines of finish and ornament." The hearer likes to have the motive of the discourse and the principle of its construction open and apparent. He likes to see how the whole thing stands up and is held together; that it is not a structure of pasteboard and paint and gilding; that every paragraph, every sentence, every word, is a necessary part of the whole, a stone alive with purpose, which cannot be displaced from its position in the wall without weakening the building and marring the effect. It is a relief and a pleasure to him to see that the structure does not need to be anchored against the wind or buttressed against the settling of the foundation. The words of Burroughs are as true of the pulpit as of the street, as applicable to a certain kind of sermon as to a certain style of domestic architecture. "Go to the city," he says, "walk up and down the principal thoroughfares and see what an effort many of the buildings make to stand up. What columns and arches they put forth, where no columns or arches are needed! There is endless variety of form and outline, great activity of iron and stone, when the eye demands simplicity and repose."*

---

* Signs and Seasons, p. 288.

6. Homeliness of Illustration.

Nor ought this principle of simplicity to be confined to the organic structure of the sermon. It is equally applicable to its illustrative matter. In nothing is Christ, as supreme Teacher of his Church, more obviously a model for the preacher of all time than in the aptness, homeliness, and transparency of his analogues and illustrations. In many things he is inimitable and must ever stand alone—the peerless prophet of the New Dispensation to whom "all bare witness and wondered at the gracious words that proceeded out of his mouth," as "he taught them as one having authority, and not as the scribes." Here, however, his footprint is plain; his example invites and encourages emulation. To him nature, in all her variety of mood and aspect, and human life, in all its wide range of type, occupation, and experience, half suggested and half concealed great spiritual verities. The suggestion of Milton:

> What if earth be but the shadow of heaven;
> And things therein each to each other like
> More than on earth is thought!

He decisively confirmed as in simile and parable he unveiled and illumined the mysteries of the "kingdom of God." The raven of the sky; the lily of the plain; the housewife leavening her meal, or mending old clothes with patches of new cloth, or anxiously sweeping the floor of the dark room for a missing coin; the sower scattering grain on the terrraced slopes of the Judean and Galilean hills; the shepherd seeking his lost sheep in the wilds, adjacent to the fold, and returning exultant with success; the children playing in the market, now at funeral and now at wedding, now shedding the tear of mimic sympathy, now piping to induce a dance, in the vain attempt to oblige and please their disaffected playmates; the lone traveler pausing by the wayside to compassionate and help the half-murdered victim of human cupidity and violence; the inexperienced and way-

Homiletical Craftsmanship 159

ward youth who leaves his home for freedom and adventure, and whose sanity and sense of manhood return to him amid scenes of infamy, degradation, and shame—such are examples of the homely parabolic method by which present and visible things were made to speak to the innermost soul of man of another and a nobler world beside and beyond the present material and visible one. Says Keble:

> Two worlds are ours; 'tis only sin
> Forbids us to descry
> The mystic heaven and earth within
> Plain as the sea and sky.

To reveal this "mystic heaven and earth within," and make it plain and familiar as the sea and sky to the popular thought and conviction, is the supreme aim and sublimest achievement of the Christian preacher.

To do this effectually only requires an open and appreciative eye and ear and a soul intensely in sympathy with divine and human things. The sermon-maker's best "Encyclopedia of Illustrations" is the world around him and the life of man as lived in history and in the passing hour. Here he may pick the flower as he wants it fresh from the stem. Here, almost any day, he may set his trap to catch the sunbeam, though, when he has caught the luminous hint, he should leave it hovering angel-like in its ethereality and freedom on the outskirts of the imagination. He should not try to pinion or imprison it in literary form, emulating the mythical truant schoolboy in his attempt to tie the rainbow to a tree. Elaboration in such cases is the martyrdom of beauty. "The freshness of first thought is lost in the finish of reflection." If

> To be possessed with double pomp,
> To guard a title that was rich before,
> To gild refined gold, to paint the lily,
> To throw a perfume on the violet,
> To smooth the ice, or add another hue
> Unto the rainbow, or with taper-light
> To seek the beauteous eye of heaven to garnish

were "wasteful and ridiculous excess," it is surely no less foolish to hide nature's spontaneous hints and obvious analogues in a haze of brilliant rhetoric. What would have become of "the sower who went forth to sow," or "the good Samaritan," or "the prodigal son," or "the wise and foolish virgins" in such a process of refinement and elaboration? As Tennyson wisely observes:

> Truth in closest words shall fail,
> *When truth embodied in a tale*
> *Shall enter in at lowly doors.*
> And so the word had breath, and wrought
>   With human hands the creed of creeds,
>   In loveliness of perfect deeds
> More strong than all poetic thought,
>   Which he may read that binds the sheaf,
> Or builds the house, or digs the grave,
> And those wild eyes that watch the wave
>   In roaring round the coral reef.

And yet a distinguished living preacher and churchman of the time, regardless of the example of Christ, and oblivious of the requirements of the common mind and the conditions of successful Gospel preaching, commends, in Jeremy Taylor's famous sermons of the *Golden Grove*, a homiletical vogue, which, were it as prevalent to-day as it once was, would do more than almost anything else to enslave the homilist, discredit preaching, and weaken the hold of the pulpit on the popular conscience and affection. "We," he says, "who are but the pickers-up of learning's crumbs; we who in the Church of the present day can hardly count five profoundly learned men, stand incapably amazed before the sermons of the seventeenth century in their inexhaustible, their prodigious fertility. . . . An ordinary sermon of the present day, compared in point of splendor, variety, and erudition with a sermon of Jeremy Taylor's, is like a squalid brick Bethesda in some poverty-stricken Dissenting village in comparison with the high embowered roofs and storied windows of a Gothic cathedral. What a range of reading —Hebraic, Hellenic, theological, literary—we encounter in these discourses of *Golden Grove!* The historians, the philosophers, the orators of Greece; the poets, the satirists, the epigrammatists of Rome; the Greek fathers, the Latin fathers, the schoolmen, the casuists, the scholars, the Italian poets, the classicists of the Renaissance; French romances, Arabic legends; this μυριόνος ἀνήρ seems to be familiar with them all. And what wealth of illustration! Persian kings, glittering among the satraps of Asia, Roman banquets, Chian wines in purest crystal, Lamiæ that turn to serpents, Lybian lions, Pannonian bears, stags whose knees are frozen in icy streams; statues decapitated to make room for other heads; 'poor Atilius Aviola (as though everyone knew all about him);' the 'condited bellies of the Scarus," drinking of healths by the numeral letters of Philenium's name; the golden and alabaster houses of Egyptian Thebes; the quaint, the pedantic, the imaginative, the marvelous, the grotesque—these alternate with exquisitely natural images derived from the green fields and the violet and the thrush's song."* But if the prime object of preaching is not pedantic ostentation, not the manipulation of a literary kaleidoscope for the entertainment and amusement of the people, but to impress, convince, persuade, admonish, edify, and comfort human souls, this homiletical panorama, this "prodigious fertility" of learned allusion is a mistake. It is arming the "ambassador for Christ" with a bludgeon in place of "the sword of the Spirit." It is equipping the heels of the evangelical *Mercurius* with wings of lead rather than with feathers of flame. It is to divert men's minds from "the simplicity which is in Christ," and blind them to the vital and immediate issue—their personal relation and duty to God under the Gospel. And, as Archbishop Leighton observes: "He who would teach men the precepts of spiritual wisdom before their minds are drawn off from foreign objects, and

---

*Archdeacon Farrar's "Jeremy Taylor," in *Masters in English Theology*, edited by Barry.

turned inward upon themselves, might as well write his instructions, as the sybil wrote her prophecies, on the loose leaves of trees, and commit them to the mercy of the inconstant winds."

7. Adaptedness to the Spiritual Needs of the People.

The one consideration, which however, perhaps more than any other, tends to simplify the labors of the sermon-builder, and needs to be constantly kept in sight, is the spiritual condition and requirements of the people. He who has adapted the rays of light to the tender structure and extreme sensitiveness of the eye, and the vibrations of sound to the delicate organism of the ear, and "tempered the wind to the shorn lamb," has with still greater skill and care adjusted the provisions of redemption to the needs of man's nature. The Gospel of the grace of God existed in archetype and idea before the soul, and is greater than the soul. It is the expression of an infinite and unfathomable love—a depth in which the plummet of human and angelic thought is lost.* But whether regarded as a gracious purpose, quiescent during countless ages, in the eternal mind, or fighting its way, as a saving power, through the darkness, error, and hindrance of history, toward embodiment and realization in individual life and destiny; whether administered by men or by angels; by patriarch, priest, prophet, apostle, or evangelist; by the Incarnate Christ, or by the Comforter, in the Old Dispensation or in the New, it has steadily kept in view the needs, dangers, difficulties, of the soul, and has modified its message and its ministry to meet them.† And the study of men in their variety of condition, temperament, character, culture, social and domestic environment, is as vital to success as the study of current thought and opinion, of the inspired word of God, or of the art itself of presenting the truth as it is in Jesus.

There ever has been and perhaps ever will be a wide

---
* Rom. xi, 33; 1 Pet. i, 12.　　　　　† Matt. xix, 8; Acts xvii, 30.

difference in the moral capacity and aptitude of men to receive the divine message. Even in the ministry of the Son of God the light and shadow of acceptance and rejection curiously alternate. "The common people heard him gladly."* On the other hand, "It cannot be that a prophet perish out of Jerusalem."†

"Among the chief rulers also many believed on him," remarks the apostle John.‡ "Because I tell you the truth ye believe me not," is his own solemn charge on another occasion.§ "Now we believe not because of thy saying, for we have heard him ourselves, and know that this is indeed the Christ, the Saviour of the world," ‖ say the Samaritans. "He looked round upon them with anger, being grieved for the hardness of their hearts,"¶ notes the evangelist Mark. Of the great prophet who came to announce his coming and to prepare his way Jesus said, "John came unto you in the way of righteousness, and *ye* believed him not, but *the publicans and harlots believed him*."** Of Jesus John said, "There standeth one among you whom ye know not."††

The same inexplicable moral phenomena meet us in the record of apostolic labor; now a strain of triumph, and now a note of defeat and deprecation. "And many of them that heard the word believed."‡‡ "Ye do always resist the Holy Ghost; as your fathers did, so do ye."§§ The Bereans "were more noble than those in Thessalonica."‖‖ And as, in reporting the last appearance of the risen Lord to his disciples in Galilee, Matthew observes: "And when they saw him, they worshiped him: *but some doubted*,"¶¶ so, in closing his record of the apostolic cycle, Luke significantly says of the Jews in Rome who visited Paul in his own hired house, "And some believed the things which were spoken, and *some believed not*."***

---

* Mark xii, 37.   † Luke xiii, 13.   ‡ John xii, 42.   § John viii, 45.
‖ John iv, 42.   ¶ Mark iii, 5.   ** Matt. xxi, 32.   †† John i, 26.
‡‡ Acts iv, 4.   §§ Acts vii, 51.   ‖‖ Acts xvii, 11.   ¶¶ Matt. xxviii, 17.
*** Acts xxviii, 24.

These are types which still survive. These are items of apostolic experience which are encountered by the earnest and faithful pastor and preacher of to-day. The craftsman of the modern pulpit cannot afford to ignore this diversity or to be indifferent to the vital problem it suggests. He will never be able satisfactorily to solve it; he cannot afford to leave it unconsidered. That he "may not run in vain, neither labor in vain," he needs to make a careful personal diagnosis of the moral and spiritual condition of his people as far as time and opportunity permit. He needs to "know their state," not only that he may be "all things to all men, that he may by all means save some," but that he may be to the fullest possible extent a comforter, counselor, sympathizer, edifier, admonisher, friend, and guide to the souls over whom he is appointed to "watch as one that must give account."

CHAPTER VIII
The Christian Ministry and the Masses

I dare say some of you in this hall are accustomed to speak of this great metropolis with pride, of its size, of its wealth, of the teeming millions that inhabit it. I give you my assurance that no thought of pride has any connection in my mind with the idea of London. I am always haunted by the awfulness of London; by the great appalling effect of these millions, cast down, as it would appear, by hazard on the banks of this noble stream, working each in their own groove and their own cell without regard or knowledge of each other, without heeding each other, without having the slightest idea how the other lives, the heedless casualty of unnumbered thousands of men.—*Lord Rosebery.*

Living in the midst of the Church of God is like sailing down the Nile in a boat. One is charmed with the luxuriance of either bank and with much that is beautiful around; but, alas! at a little distance on either side lies a vast uncultivated, we had almost said hopeless, desert. Some are at rest, because they never look beyond the borders of the Church, but those whose sympathies reach to all humanity will have to carry a lifelong burden.—*C. H. Spurgeon.*

1. Condition of the Masses.

IN the large modern city, with its poverty, immorality, overcrowding, and imperfect sanitation, the statesman and the philanthropist find themselves confronted with the thorniest of present-day problems. In many respects the city of to-day, seen from the outside, seems all-sufficient for itself. Its great and ever-growing wealth; its keen, argus-eyed intelligence; its world-wide commercial relations; its industrial activities and professional skill; its political, social, educational, and religious institutions; its art, its science, its literature, its public pageants and amusements, make life amid its surging crowds seem very desirable to the uninitiated rustic. But an interior and deeper view is not so prepossessing. With a glimpse of its vice, crime, pauperism, poverty, suffering, and sorrow, there comes a strong revulsion of feeling. The broad suburban avenue, with its big shade trees, close-shaven lawns, and stately homes, and the crowded and gay thoroughfares of traffic, suggest the swiftest thought of wealth's comfort and contentment; the lepers' quarter, with its congested tenement dwellings, low saloons, brothels, thieves, and gamblers' dens, narrow and dirty streets full of garbage and refuse, and alive with half-clad children breathing the odors of an atmosphere not at all suggestive of attar of roses, disillusionizes one and spoils the glory of one's dream. One discovers at a glance that what may be the *paradise* of the rich is likely, also, to be the *purgatory* or even *pandemonium* of the poor, and that the big city is a community with its head high up in the clouds and its feet deep-sunk in the intolerable mud.

With the phenomenally rapid growth of many civic communities there are being gathered to points of concentration all the worst as well as the best elements and energies of human nature. One of the most striking paragraphs in a remarkable book, published some years ago—Jenkin's *Devil's Chain*—is that in which the author describes the steady stream of human beings, pouring itself night and day from all parts of the earth—from the cities, towns, and villages of the United Kingdom, from the countries of the Continent of Europe, and from quarters more remote—into that great receptacle of the financially, socially, morally, and spiritually bankrupt, the city of London. Some seek the great centers of industrial and business activity, impelled by mistaken hopes and ambitions; others are drawn there by flattering professional openings, or by the prospect of employment, or the bait of some bogus advertisement. Many betake themselves there as political refugees from other lands, or to forget and hide some stain of reputation, or in the hope of finding an asylum from the hot pursuit of justice. The vicious and criminal are at home at once in the jostling crowd. The virtuous and honest, coming from quieter scenes, are liable to find the pulse of life in the city too quick and hurried and its competition too keen for them. They are unable readily to adjust themselves to the new conditions, and get stranded. Failing to secure or retain employment, they become homesick, discouraged, and slowly sink down to the social stratum below them. And finding after repeated efforts of self-extrication that escape is impossible, the last gleam of light in the soul—the "hope" which is said to "spring eternal in the human breast," but does not—expires. This is the natural history of more than half the vice, crime, poverty, and misery of London, Paris, New York, Chicago, and other overgrown communities in Europe and America. The steady depletion of rural populations, together with the unbroken influx of foreign immigrants, to feed the insatiable maw of the larger cities, has become a constantly increasing peril, demanding the immediate and practical attention of the thoughtful statesman, the social reformer, and, above all, the leaders of the Christian Church.

Miss Jane Addam, of the Hull House University Settlement, Chicago, thus describes the cosmopolitical character of the densely populated region of the city where she and her colaborers are at work: "Between Halstead Street and the river live about ten thousand Italians, Neapolitans, Sicilians, and Calabrians, with an occasional Lombard or Venetian. To the south, on Twelfth Street, are many Germans, and side streets are given over almost entirely to Polish and Russian Jews. Still farther south these Jewish colonies merge into a huge Bohemian colony so vast that Chicago ranks as the third Bohemian city in the world. To the northwest are many Canadian French, clannish in spite of their long residence in America, and to the north are many Irish and first-generation Americans."*

---

* *Philanthropy and Social Progress*, p. 28.

A precisely similar condition of things exists in London,* in New York city, and in smaller degree in many other large communities in Europe and the United States.

As to the moral, social, industrial, and sanitary condition of the people thus crowded together, some idea may be obtained from the fourth annual report of the United States Commissioner of Labor. The report is professedly "based on statistics gathered from twenty-five cities, North, South, East, and West, and may be taken as truly representative of the country at large." As it does not profess to deal with the status of the very lowest class of workers, the tale it tells, sad as it is, is still not an adequate account of the trials, privations, and miseries endured by thousands of the toiling masses. Describing the conditions under which many of the people earn their bread in New York city, the commissioner says: "As respects ventilation, a properly regulated workshop is the exception. The average room is either stuffy and close, or hot and close, and even where the windows abound they are seldom opened. Toilet facilities are generally scant and inadequate, a hundred workers being dependent sometimes on a single closet or sink, and that too often out of order." In Philadelphia "the worsted yarn mills employ very young girls, sometimes violating the law against child labor." "The older mills" [of Providence, R. I.] "are defective in light, ventilation, and space, are often without dressing rooms, and frequently the ordinary sanitary arrangements are disregarded." Speaking of the toilers' homes, the report says that in Brooklyn "whole *streets* and *districts* of tenement houses are given over to poverty, filth, and vice, the sanitary and moral unwholesomeness of which is manifest." In Cincinnati "the streets" where the laboring classes live

---

* In London there are Irish, 250,000; Scotch, 120,000; Asiatics, Africans, Americans, 45,000; Germans, 60,000; French, 30,000; Poles, 7,000; Jews, 40,000. In New York city it is computed that from seventy to eighty per cent are foreign-born or the children of foreign-born people.

"are dirty and closely built up with ill-constructed houses, holding from two to six families. Many poorer parts of Cincinnati are as wretched as the worst European cities, and the population looks as degraded." As to New York city, the crowded condition of the poor and struggling is beyond belief unless actually witnessed. This brings with it disease, death, immorality, etc. Tall rear tenements block up the small air-spaces that are insufficient even for the front, and often a third house stands behind the second. Sewerage is lacking or defective, and stenches of all kinds prevail in the poorer quarters."*

Dismal as this picture is of the kind of life lived by thousands of the wage-earners of American cities, it may be duplicated almost anywhere, with even deeper shadows, in a district containing a population of from eight to nine hundred thousand in the east of London. "Narrow alleys—so narrow that two can hardly pass each other, and the adjacent houses seem almost to meet overhead—hotbeds of smallpox and fevers, so impure and pestilential that any stranger visiting these haunts could scarcely breathe the fetid air, and would sometimes have been literally driven backward on opening suddenly some attic door or diving into the darkness of some cellar, those cellars, damp, dark, and cold, reeking with rotten vegetable matter and the accumulated filth of years, so that it seemed almost impossible for the starved cats of the neighborhood to shelter there. But, incredible as it may seem, human beings crowded nightly to these wretched cellars, which, in some instances, were rented out at a dollar a week and used as homes by large families. Tenements with rotten, creaking stairs, and roofs through which the rain and snow could find an easy access to the garrets, were common. All the rooms were much of the same character as the cellars and garrets, so far as cleanliness is concerned—filth, stench, discomfort, every-

---

* *Congressional Report*, 1893.

where."* As an indication of the hopeless poverty and improvidence of large numbers of the people, it is significant that of the three hundred thousand huddled together in the large London parish of St. George's-in-the-East *forty-seven per cent* are buried by the parish. "Dante was said to have copied the horrors of his *Inferno* from the Hades of Greek and Roman mythology, but Dante said he found all his hells in Florence. We need not go to any far antiquity to find with exactness every human torture reflected in its fables. In London you shall find many an Ixion bound fast upon his never-pausing wheel. The bent back of Toil goes round with the revolving year, knowing only the hard routine of a life without knowledge, bitter days going down to nights of stupor, all in the unsunned Hades of Drudgery. Sisyphus still rolls away the ever-returning stone, his weary labor passing on from father to son, from mother to daughter, with no hope of ending. The rock-bound Titan is visible in every victim of lust or drink, preying vulturelike on his vitals. The pauper Tantalus moves hungry amid the tables of luxury."†

'Tis a somber and melancholy story. And yet, though the poverty, degradation, and misery of the people in the congested quarters of the city are sufficiently appalling, this is not the only dark and ominous feature with which present-day civilization confronts the Christian Church and her leaders. Social submergence in the city often finds its counterpart in the privations and pauperism, the sins and sorrows, of village life. "It is when I go down from our house to the village," says Mrs. Humphrey Ward's Marcella Boyce—the fair young socialist of Mellor Park—"when I see the places the people live in, when one is comfortable in the carriage and one passes some woman in the rain, ragged and dirty and tired, trudging back from her work, when one realizes

---

* Mrs. Ballington Booth's *Beneath Two Flags*, pp. 91, 92.
† Moncure Conway's lecture on "London."

that they have no *rights* when they become old, nothing to look to but charity, for which *we*—who have everything—expect them to be grateful, and when I know that every one of them has done more useful work in a year of their life than I shall ever do in the whole of mine, then I feel that the whole state of things is *somehow* wrong and topsy-turvy and *wicked.*" * " Amazing ! " is the pitying exclamation ; "starvation wages, hardships of sickness and pain, horrors of birth and horrors of death, the meanest surroundings, the most sordid cares of this mingled cup of village fate every person in the room had drunk, and drunk deep. . . . Dependent from birth to death on squire, parson, parish, crushed often and ill treated according to their own ideas, but bearing so little ill will, amusing themselves with their own tragedies even, if they could but sit by a fire and drink a neighbor's cup of tea."†

2. The Problem Stated.

How comes it to pass that under a system of religion and morals professedly containing "the power of God unto salvation," ‡ and after nearly two millennia of effort and experiment in preaching, teaching, creed-making, and theological controversy, spurts of reforming zeal, styles of ritual, modes and forms of worship, and methods of ecclesiastical administration, we are still confronted, in Christian lands, and at the close of the most enlightened and progressive century the world has known, with a state of festering, *positive* heathenism, in many respects worse than the most dismal *negative* heathenism anywhere yet discovered ? §

Let us look at the problem as it stands. We find ourselves as churches in the midst of the masses of the people who are, now as of old, as sheep scattered abroad by the

---

* Mrs. Humphrey Ward's *Marcella*, p. 104.   † *Ibid.*, p. 84.   ‡ Rom. i, 16.
§ The heathenism that is such *in spite* of the light of divine revelation and the active ministries of the Christian Church may properly be called *positive* as compared with that which is such simply for *want* of the Gospel message.

wolves that prey upon them without a shepherd. In every aspect of their being, in all their most vital interests, they are pursued, bitten, torn; or are waylaid, ensnared, deceived, destroyed, by the predatory classes that hold them in thrall, pander to their worst propensities, and fatten upon their ruin. "Talk about Dante's hell," says William Booth, "and all the horrors and cruelties of the torture chamber of the lost! The man who walks with open eyes and with bleeding heart through the shambles of our civilization needs no such fantastic images of the poet to teach him horror. Often and often when I have seen the young and the poor and the helpless go down before my eyes into the morass, trampled under foot by beasts of prey in human shape that haunt these regions, it seemed as if God were no longer in his world, but that in his stead reigned a fiend, merciless as hell, ruthless as the grave." *

In their labor the people are the victims of the keen and relentless competition of capitalists and sweaters, who, Shylocklike, insist on having their "pound of flesh," "according to the bond," even when it cannot be had without "the blood," to which they have not the audacity to pretend any claim. In their miserable dwellings in which they find shelter, but no kind of a home, they are at the mercy, on the one hand, of the uncurbed and insatiable cupidity of real estate proprietors and their frequently unprincipled agents, and, on the other, of the remissness, neglect, corruption, of venal municipal authorities, who expose them to the perils of insanitation at their own doors, by which their health is permanently injured, and they become hopelessly handicapped in the severe and ceaseless struggle for a livelihood.† In

---

* *In Darkest England*, p. 13.
† In a letter to Fleischer, editor of the *Deutsche Revue*, who requested his opinion on the action of the Emperor of Germany in summoning a conference of nations in 1890 on the labor question, the late Cardinal Manning said: " The condition of wage-earning people of every European country is a grave danger to every European state. The hours of labor, the employment of women and children, the scantiness of wages, the uncertainties of employment, the fierce competition fostered by modern political economy, and the destruction of domestic life resulting from all these and other kindred causes have rendered it impossible for men to live a human life.

some countries, like Germany and Russia, for example, the belated barbarism of despotic governments cripples and discourages the people's industry, demanding the best years of the able-bodied male population for military service in order to maintain enormous standing armies and throw the shadow of a perpetual menace over the peace of Europe; the result being that thousands of young men seeking refuge from the military conscription of their own lands enter the unequal contest for places and prizes in the broad but overcrowded arena of American industry. As to their morals and domestic happiness, thousands of wage-earners are the helpless prey of the saloon, the brothel, the gambler's dive, the money lender, the easy-terms-of-payment furniture dealer, the low music hall, the dime museum, and some of the foulest literature issued from the modern press; while as to their religious nature, with its instincts, hopes, and aspirations, it is crushed to death between the hard millstones of their own stolid indifference, on the one hand, and the criminal indolence of the Christian Church, on the other.

Now, if it is clear that the salvation of the people—temporal and eternal—depends, humanly speaking, on two great factors, namely, their own exertions and the active ministries of Christianity, it is equally obvious that the former of these can only be expected as a response—slow, partial, reluctant, often discouragingly cold—to the warm and persistent appeals of the latter, and that the fatal apathy of the people will never be broken up except by a thoroughly wide-awake and continuously aggressive Church. Can it be said that the Church and the ministry of to-day are giving adequate and substantial attention to the all-important and urgent problem? "The exceeding bitter cry of the disinherited,"

"How can a man who works fifteen or sixteen hours a day live the life of a father to his children? How can a woman who is absent from home all day long do the duties of a mother? Domestic life is impossible; but on the domestic life of the people the whole political order of human society reposes. If the foundation be ruined, what will become of the superstructure?"

says the most sympathetic and practical student of the people and their miseries the present century has produced, "has become to be as familiar in the ears of men as the dull roar of the streets or as the moaning of the wind through the trees. And so it rises unceasing, year in and year out, and we are too busy or too idle, too indifferent or too selfish, to spare it a thought. Only now and then, on rare occasions, when some clear voice is heard giving more articulate utterance to the miseries of the miserable men, do we pause in the regular routine of our daily duties, and shudder as we realize, for one brief moment, what life means to the inmates of the slums. But one of the grimmest social problems of our time should be sternly faced, not with a view to the generation of profitless emotion, but with a view to its solution. . . . Why all this apparatus of temples and meeting houses to save men from perdition in a world which is to come, while never a helping hand is stretched out to save them from the inferno of their present life? Is it not time that, forgetting for a moment their wranglings about the infinitely little or infinitely obscure, they should concentrate all their energies on a united effort to break this terrible perpetuity of perdition and to rescue some, at least, of those for whom they profess to believe their Founder came to die?"*

3. Failure of the Church to Solve the Problem.

Such, at any rate, would seem to be the obvious dictate of Christian duty. But what is being done? It is true that many churches of straitened resources, as to workers and money, are doing their utmost to stem the swelling tide of popular ignorance, apathy, improvidence, irreligion, immorality, and pauperism around them; but it is also true that the majority of large and wealthy churches in the cities are heedless of and indifferent to the rampant heathenism often

---

* *In Darkest England*, p. 15.

lying closely contiguous to the regions where they dwell and worship. By their united exertions they might contribute effectively toward the moral and social transformation of the godless masses near them if only they could be convinced that they have any reserve of time, money, and spiritual energy to cope with a task and a duty which, while they offer nothing to denominational vanity, pride, or ambition, present the boldest challenge to Christian self-denial, patience, faith, and courage. But the plea, even where wealth abounds, is that they are too poor and feeble to undertake new responsibilities, and the little that is done by the rest makes no deeper mark on the growing areas of poverty, vice, and misery than would be produced by a baby's fingers scratching a granite bowlder.* Putting aside, for the moment, the notorious fact that, in consequence of the hopelessly divided condition of Protestant Christendom, "energies and resources," even where churches are comparatively poor, "are poured out freely," not that souls may be won for Christ, but that proselytes may be gained for sects and sets; that there are hundreds of village communities where four or five men are stationed to do the work that one of them could do, and probably do better than the five; that, in consequence, considerable sums of money are raised to gratify denominational prejudice or vanity which might be expended with the happiest result in evangelizing the neglected quarters of the cities setting all this aside, let us take the wealthiest church in English-speaking Christendom and study its behavior face to face with the heathenism of the city of London. From an article on "The Wasted Wealth

---

*A comparison of the census of church attendance, taken Sunday, October 18, 1891, in the large city of Liverpool, with one taken in 1881, showed a falling off of 2,000 in spite of the fact that during the ten years 52 new places of worship had been erected with accommodation for 18,513 additional worshipers; that additional pastors had been appointed and additional auxiliaries and organizations had come into existence. From these findings the editor of the *Daily Post* drew the following inferences: " 1. There is an evident decay of interest against which the most earnest clergymen struggle in vain. 2. In many districts it is only too evident that the Church has completely lost its hold upon the population by which it is surrounded. 3. It is impossible to resist the conclusion that a large portion of the clergy have mistaken their vocation in life."

of City Churches," which appeared a few years ago in *London*, a journal of civic and social progress, published in the great city whose name it bears, we learn that there are sixty churches in the oldest and most central portion of the British metropolis with a total income of over $310,000, although the constantly dwindling population has fallen to 37,705.* The incumbent of All Hallows, Barking, receives a stipend of $10,000 a year and a further $3,000 a year for the maintenance of the church, while the total population of his parish is 447. At St. Andrew, Undershaft, with a population of 218, the clergyman has a house, $10,000 a year, and an additional $1,750 for the church. On a recent occasion when the congregation was counted it amounted to 45. At St. Edmund-the-King the incumbent has a house, $6,500 a year, and $1,500 annually for the church account, with 172 parishioners; the Sunday congregation recently amounted to 31 out of the 172. At St. Ethelburga, Bishopsgate, the stipend is $5,250, with a church account of $1,500, the population being 158. At St. Margaret, Pattens, the stipend is $5,300, with a house; there is a further income for the church of $1,500 a year; the total population is 116, and the congregation on a recent Sunday was 36. At St. Catharine, Coleman, the stipend is $4,150; church account, $1,450; population, 237. In this case the incumbent actually receives a grant from the ecclesiastical commissioners for the stipend of a curate. At St. Mary, Woolnoth, the stipend is $6,000 a year; church account, an additional $1,000; population, 208; congregation, as recently counted, 19. At St. Stephen, Walbrook, the stipend is $4,750; population, 124; congregation, 13. At St. Olave, Hart Street, the parson has $10,400, a house and $1,250 for church expenses, with a population of 364. At St. Peter-upon-Cornhill the stipend is $10,750, a house, with $1,750 for church expenses,

---

* The city of London proper extends only about a mile in every direction from St. Paul's Cathedral as a center.

and a population of 162. When most of the churches between the Tower of London and the Bank of England were recently visited it was found that three of them were actually closed. St. Magnus, London Bridge, with a stipend of $2,900 and a church account of $2,500, was closed. St. Mary-at-Hill, with a stipend of $2,000, a church account of $2,500, and a population of 173, was closed. St. George, Botolph Lane, was closed, and on the door, barred by an iron rod, was the following notice: "By order of the Bishop of London, with the consent of the rector and church warden of the parish, this church will be closed in consequence of the unsafe condition of the fabric and the lack of funds with which to repair it." In this case the rector, Rev. M. Mac-Coll, M.A., a well-known writer in various first-class magazines, receives $2,455 a year, a house, which presumably was not so much out of repair as to be unfit to live in, and $1,250 for the maintenance of the church. Inquiry as to what Mr. MacColl was doing to repair the fabric and reopen the doors of his church failed to elicit any satisfactory information.

While these and other incredible scandals exist in one form or another in most of the Churches is it any marvel that Christianity fails to reach and reform the wage-earning classes? that a sullen alienation and apathy, if not latent antagonism, hold them far aloof from all elevating or consolatory moral and spiritual influences? that intemperance, improvidence, and want, with all the ghastly catalogue of miseries that follow in their train, abound? and that infidelity and atheism exult and triumph? Is it not clear that lukewarm and worldly churches and church members are often, without knowing it, by far the most dangerous and deadly enemies of the religion they profess?

4. Remedies Suggested.

The age in which we live, however, while markedly one of doubt, criticism, and studied reserve of judgment, is also one of courage, hope, and enlightened altruistic sentiment. Thousands of thoughtful men and women have grown restless under social and industrial arrangements which are practically nothing better than organized abnormities, dooming the toiler to a condition of hopeless poverty, privation, and dependence, and forcing the weak to the wall; making it increasingly difficult for even the virtuously disposed to do right, and increasingly easier for the viciously inclined to do wrong. There probably never was a time when so much earnest, practical attention was given to the question of the people's salvation in the broadest and most comprehensive sense of the word. The last few decades have witnessed a genuine renaissance of philanthropy—a philanthropy inspired by nobler feelings and pledged to wiser methods than the old charity organizations which may be said to have had their day. To this new and deeper sense of humanity and brotherhood that has come we are indebted for the parliamentary exertion of such men as the late Lord Shaftesbury with a view to the protection of factory workers and children under age, the efforts of George Müller, C. H. Spurgeon, J. T. Barnardo, George Peabody, Loring Brace, and others, and the ambitious social betterment scheme of General Booth. It has created a distinctive school of social and political economy. It has produced a literature of its own in fiction, philosophy, and economics, varying in style and method of treatment from Jenkins's *Ginx's Baby* and Riis's *How the Other Half Lives* to the more philosophical *Social Evolution* of Mr. Benjamin Ridd. It has influenced legislation, has stirred the pulpit, and tinctured more or less deeply the current of common thought and feeling.

To be sure, the remedies suggested are often crude, Utopian, impracticable, but few of them are without some intrinsic value as steps toward the ultimate solution. By three classes chiefly, each of which ought to be a powerful factor in their moral and social elevation, the people have been "severely let alone "—(1) by the wealthy, (2) by the intellectual, (3) by the conventionally devout. And in each of these cases the law of reaction is vigorously asserting itself to-day. The protest against the exclusiveness of aristocratic and plutocratic principles has come in the form of socialism. The reaction against contemplative, not to say barren and contemptuous, intellectualism is found in the University Settlement movement in such cities as London, Boston, Chicago, with its object of "relieving the over-accumulation at one end of society and the destitution at the other, as these are most sorely felt in social and educational advantage." The recoil from a self-absorbed and churchly piety declares itself in the resolute and noisy evangelism—in the drum, tambourine, and stained and tattered banner of the Salvation Army barracks and street procession. Curiously suggestive was the reception the "Army" met with at first from some of the most prominent leaders of the religious world. After visiting the barracks of the "Army" for the first time, during his stay in London, Bishop Phillips Brooks wrote to his brother thus: "I went on Thursday to a tremendous dinner party at the Baroness Burdett-Coutts's, with swells as thick as huckleberries. Then for variety I went on Thursday night with K—— to an all-night meeting of the Salvation Army, what they, in their disagreeable lingo call 'all-night with Jesus.' They close the doors at eleven and do not let anybody go out till half past four A. M. The meeting was noisy and unpleasant, but there was nothing very bad about it, and I am not quite sure that it might not do good to somebody."* The transition from "swells as thick as huckleberries," not one of whom probably had ever felt himself called upon to forego a single meal or deny himself the expense of a choice buttonhole flower for the benefit of others, to "an all-night with Jesus," whose object was to bring divine strength and con-

* *Letters of Travel*, p. 292.

solation to those who by sin and vice had forfeited their inheritance of hope for time and eternity, was evidently too sudden for the good bishop. But curiously enough, though no communion in Christendom cultivates more assiduously stately ecclesiastical forms and imposing ceremonies than that of which Bishop Brooks was so distinguished an ornament, unless, indeed, it be that of the

> Milk-white hind, unspotted and unchanged,

that Church is the only one that has cared to attempt any direct imitation of the organization and methods of the "Army;" and from it the "Army" has obtained some of the ablest and most successful of its recent leaders. Speaking of her first acquaintance with the movement, Mrs. Maud B. Booth says: "I heard them sometimes when the singing sounded muffled through the stained-glass windows of our church, and it could hardly have been said to break the sacred stillness, yet I could catch the oft-repeated words, 'O you must be a lover of the Lord,' and sometimes they would come to my ears mixed in a strange way with the familiar sentence, 'Lord, have mercy on us miserable sinners.' Ah, little did I know then that these people were sinners forgiven seeking sinners lost.

"But I pass at once to days when I learned to look anxiously and lovingly through the rectory windows for the approach of their blue-bordered flag, until I pause at *the* day when I myself, in an 'Army' hall, saw Jesus my Saviour as I never had seen him before, and gave up my life entirely to God—*my* God, the 'Army's' God, and the drunkard's God. Then I received into my heart the love and fire that have sent me forth to do God's will and to follow the steps of Christ of Calvary.*" The whole secret of the "Army's" success, as General Booth assured the present writer during some pleasant hours spent together, some years ago, on the

---

* *Beneath Two Flags*, pp. 6, 7.

eastern coast of England, is its absolute freedom from conventional forms of reverence and solemnity.

1. Now, as to all schemes of salvation which look toward a reconstruction of society on a socialistic basis, it may be objected that, though of the most comprehensive and most radical character, and consequently difficult of realization, they yet propose to risk everything on a doubtful experiment; and, further, that they propound legislative, economic, and industrial remedies for what, after all, is, at root, a moral disease. "So far," says Mrs. Ward, "as socialism means a political system—the trampling out of private enterprise and competition, and all the rest of it—I find myself slipping away from it more and more. . . . As I go about among the wage-earners the emphasis—do what I will—comes to lie less and less on possession, more and more on character. I go to two tenements in the same building. One is hell—the other heaven. Why? Both belong to well-paid artisans with equal opportunities. Both, as far as I can see, might have a decent life of it. But one is a man, the other, with all his belongings, will soon be a vagabond."

2. Precisely the same objection of inadequacy may be urged against the University Settlement scheme. It is doubtless quite true that "the best speculative philosophy," to use the words of Miss Addam, "sets forth the solidarity of the human race; that the highest moralists have taught that without the advance and improvement of the whole no man can hope for any lasting improvement in his own moral and material individual condition;" that "nothing so deadens the sympathies and shrivels the power of enjoyment as the persistent keeping away from the great opportunities of helpfulness and a continual ignoring of the starvation struggle which makes up the life of at least half the race."* Still it is important that we recognize the real nature and full extent of the work we propose to do, and resolutely prepare ourselves,

---

* *Philanthropy and Social Progress*, p. 11.

at whatever cost, to comply with the only conditions which promise genuine and enduring success. Nothing is more certain of ultimate failure than a scheme of amelioration which makes no direct appeal to man's spiritual nature and ignores his need of moral transformation by the grace of God.

3. With the immense advantage conferred by this conviction the Salvation Army has brought new life and hope to thousands who must have perished without its aid. During the three decades of its existence it has extended its operations to every continent and to almost every civilized country of the globe. And yet, though by no means lacking in courage, resolution, and fertility of expedient, its poverty of material sources, the fewness of its steadfast and reliable adherents in any given locality, and the backward state of education among its local leaders will always be in marked contrast with the magnitude of its plans and of the problem that confronts it. While scarcely anything could be better adapted to save men from the slum and the gutter, hardly any form of Christianity could be more ill suited to develop the many-sided nature of man when once restored to himself. It is, in fact, as it professes to be, an empire under despotic military rule; not a Christian Church after the New Testament type, seeking under constitutional spiritual government and the sacramental forms and ministries instituted by Christ* to develop individual character and leaven the world with eternal principles of morality and religion. As an autocracy it is opposed to the whole genius and spirit of Christianity, and is a glaring anachronism in an intensely democratic age. Nor are there lacking evidences within its own ranks of its want of harmony with the requirements of the time.†

---

* Eph. iv, 11–14.

† Since this chapter was written the rebellion of Mr. Ballington Booth, leader of the "Army" in America, against the autocratic rule of his father, the general, has taken place, leading to the organization of a separate movement, much to the disappointment and regret of the general's family, as the present writer recently learned from his sister, Mrs. Booth-Tucker, of New York.

Even among those who were born in the household in which it also had its birth, whose natural and spiritual life was cradled to the strains of its rude but rousing music, who have labored, planned, and prayed for its expansion, who have born its "banner with a strange device" through many a storm and carried its message of life and salvation into many a dark and dismal alley of the city, there appear symptoms of dissatisfaction with its rigid and inelastic polity—its unyielding and merciless despotism.

5. The True Solution.

The more thoroughly the problem of the salvation of the unreached majority is considered the more plainly will it appear that responsibility for its true solution rests with the ministry and membership of the organized Christian Church. It is not the manner of God to impose obligation where there is not sufficient power and opportunity to meet it. The rule of heaven, in this as in other things, is a law of truth and equity. "To whom much is given of him will much be required." The Churches have the talent, the education, the moral stamina, the spiritual experience, the social prestige, the historical antecedents, the pecuniary resources, the unbroken record of mercy and philanthropy, and the divine authorization required to inaugurate and sustain a general movement for the moral, social, and spiritual redemption of the people. All that is needed is a full and frank recognition of their responsibility and the intelligent and hearty adoption of some course of action in harmony therewith.

The first result of such recognition will be an effort to get near the people and devise some practical method of reconciling the obvious social tendencies of Christianity, on the one hand, with its avowed spiritual mission and sympathies, on the other. These tendencies and sympathies are now in hopeless conflict. Religion tends legitimately and inevitably toward the creation of wealth and the promotion of education, intelligence, refined taste, exalted character. The most natural result of its active principles is to quicken thought, encourage noble aspiration and endeavor, and confer reputation, capacity, status, manhood. On the other hand, it is part of its very essence to insist on self-denial and self-sacrifice; on tenderness, pity, and considerateness toward others; on genuine sympathy with the lowly, the needy, the fallen, and the lost. It calls for the cultivation of a warm and vivid sense of brotherhood and positively forbids the creation of a social chasm between the Church and those outside her pale.

Jesus affected no carefully guarded seclusion like Buddha or Mohammed; no superiority of caste like the modern Brahman. He loved the people, encouraged their approach, lived, taught, dispensed his healing ministrations in the midst of them. The companions of his choice were taken from the masses and remained in loving touch with them. "The common people heard him gladly." As of the impersonal Wisdom of the Old Testament it is said, "His delights were with the sons of men," so at the close of the New Testament canon it is solemnly reiterated, "Behold, the tabernacle of God is with men, and he will dwell with them, and they shall be his people, and God himself shall be with them—their God." *

Among the people Christianity, as a vital and active force, had its start, and with the people it is destined forever to abide or perish. "To help the world," says Miss French, "we must take it as we find it, and we find men and women with trivial perplexities and interests ready and longing for the life which is of God. . . .

"To reach the people who are, in some senses, below you, you must touch them first on their own plane, show that you are interested in the things—trivial though they

---
* Rev. xxi, 3.

The Christian Ministry and the Masses 185

often are—that interest them, and then you can by degrees raise them to your own plane. This mounting a stage, stretching a hand down to some one on the ground, and expecting that person to keep pace with you as you run along, is not practical; it is too much of a strain on the other person's muscle."

To get back to the people, then; to take Christ to them in our living personality—in our whole life as having to do with society, politics, and trade; with science, art, and literature; with legislation, government, industrial improvement, and church enterprise—that is the first necessary step toward reaching and reclaiming the, as yet, unevangelized millions of the people.

Along with this sympathy with the unchurched multitudes will come the power and facility to recognize their ideals and to interpret their best thoughts and aspirations without insisting on translating them into the, often to them, unintelligible lingo of religion. Whoever will study carefully the political watchwords and party cries of wage-earners will find that they are not such total strangers to noble conceptions of life as they are sometimes supposed to be. Often they will be found to be blindly craving the very boon religion offers as its highest good. For example, on every public structure of any pretensions in the city of Paris the visitor sees inscribed the gospel of the Revolution—*Liberty, Equality, Fraternity.* Could anything be grander than the ideal of social relation embodied in those potent words? As one of the most scholarly and influential of English bishops has recently pointed out, that revolutionary triad which captured the imagination of millions of workingmen in Europe are nothing more than the social application of the Pauline triad, "Righteousness, peace, and joy in the Holy Ghost." And when the religion which yields righteousness, peace, and joy in the Holy Ghost in the individual soul dominates public as well as private life, then will have come safely and beneficently the reign of Liberty, Equality, Fraternity, in a deeper and broader sense than has been hitherto dreamed of.

The people are not slow to appreciate any genuine effort to understand and benefit them. "The child of the people," says Paul Sabatier of St. Francis d'Assisi; "he knew all their material and moral woes and their mysterious echoes sounded in his heart."* Was not this the secret of Paul's power over men wherever he went—the key to such scenes as that which transpired at his parting with the Ephesian elders on the Milesian shore? Was it not the secret of Wyclif's success in sowing broadcast, by means of his poor friars, the word of God in the England of his day? The secret, too, of Luther's, of Wesley's, of Whitefield's, of Bunyan's, of Spurgeon's, of Moody's, of General Booth's work? From first to last the religion of Jesus has in view the sorrows, temptations, trials, and spiritual necessities of the people; and, instead of crying to them from afar, it hastens to the spot where they suffer to offer its help and leave its quenchless ray of light and joy. As Professor Drummond points out, "Its purpose is by means of the Christian society to give the world liberty, comfort, beauty, joy. This program deals with a real world. Think of it as you read, not of the surface world, but of the world as it is, as it sins and weeps and curses and suffers and sends up its long cry to God. Limit it, if you like, to the world around your door, but think of it—of the city and the hospital and the dungeon and the graveyard; of the sweating-shop and the pawnshop and the drinkshop; think of the cold, the cruelty, the fever, the famine, the ugliness, the loneliness, the pain. And then try to keep down the lump in your throat as you take up his program and read, 'To bind up the brokenhearted; to proclaim liberty to the captives; to comfort all that mourn; to give unto them beauty for ashes,

---

* *Life of Francis d'Assisi*, p. 15.

the oil of joy for mourning, the garment of praise for the spirit of heaviness.'"

Finally, when the Christian Church and ministry are resolved to stand fearlessly full front to the obvious duty of the hour, they will put themselves unequivocally on record against all forms of evil that antagonize and imperil the present and eternal well-being of the people, degrading and cheapening their toil, debasing their social pleasures and amusements, corrupting their morals, draining their resources, cursing and embittering their lives. There will be no more disposition to indulge in the easy duty of colorless deprecation of sin in general, but there will be plain, straight, definite preaching of evangelical repentance, showing sin as it is, in its dark nature, enslaving power, and ruinous effects; exhibiting it as it lives in trade, in politics, in social usages and phenomena; individual sin, collective and corporate sin, class selfishness, class prejudices and antagonisms; the whole bad heritage of centuries as it has been allowed to crystallize in the antichristian principles, laws, and customs of to-day.

Specifically against war, intemperance, licentiousness, greed, gambling, narcotism, and vile literature will the warning word of an awakened ministry be definite, decisive, outspoken, continuous. These surely are the "seven last plagues" reserved in the retributive providence of God for a wayward and rebellious race. In these, whatever may be hidden from our sight in the shadowy background of the future, "the wrath of God is revealed from heaven upon all ungodliness and unrighteousness of men who hold down the truth in unrighteousness."*

The civilized world of to-day is little cognizant of the insidious manner in which all that is most precious and most ennobling in human life, character, and destiny is constantly threatened by evils which even the victims them-

---

* Rom. i, 18.

selves often regard with in appalling levity. Take the item of war, for example. Leaving out of sight the bloodshed and slaughter, the hardship and suffering, the waste of treasure and destruction of property, of actual conflict, the mere preparation for it imposes a burden beneath which humanity groans with an increasing sense of oppression and restlessness. In introducing a measure a few years ago in the British House of Commons for the reduction of the "bloated armaments" of Europe, in the interests of "justice, humanity, and religion," Sir John Lubbock contended that, whatever might be the case in dealing with barbarous tribes, the resort of civilized nations to exhibitions of brute force was "repugnant not only to our moral but also to our common sense." In the course of his argument that distinguished scientist and statesman disclosed the astounding fact that at the time of his speaking the peace establishments of Europe comprised 3,500,000 men, the war establishments over 10,000,000; that when the proposed arrangements for enlarging the armies, then being made by infatuated rulers of Europe, had been carried out 20,000,000 men would be ready to slaughter one another. Even the nominal cost of these insane and wicked arrangements was over $1,000,000,000 a year. But, as the continental armies were to a great extent under the degrading yoke of the conscription, the actual cost was far larger. If all this did not end in war, it led to ruin and bankruptcy. During the last twenty years the debt of Italy had risen from $2,415,000,000 to $2,580,000,000; that of Austria from $1,700,000,000 to $2,900,000,000; that of Russia from $1,700,000,000 to $3,750,000,000; that of France from $2,500,000,000 to $6,500,000,000. In 1890 Herr Richter stated in the German Parliament (Reichstag) that since 1870 Germany had expended $2,400,000,000 on its army. In 1870 the government debts of civilized nations aggregated $20,000,000,000. In 1890 they had reached the startling sum of $30,000,000,000, and were still increasing.* In fact, as Sir John Lubbock remarks, there never is any peace under such a condition of affairs. Nations live "practically in a permanent state of war, happily without battles or bloodshed, but not without terrible suffering." One third of the whole national income of Great Britain is spent in paying for the wars of ancestors ; one third in preparing for future wars ; one third only is used to promote the well-being and happiness of the citizens. And the military craze is hardly less felt on this side the Atlantic. Already the demand for forts and fleets and convenient naval coaling stations is involving the nation in the expenditure of millions of dollars. All this in spite of the indisputable fact that the prosperity, happiness, and independence of nations everywhere bear a strict proportion not to their military and naval strength, but to their moral and intellectual training. "Switzerland spends as much money on education as on soldiers and their costly equipment; Denmark half as much, and Belgium about a third, and these are all prosperous and contented little States. But the great empires which clutch territory and ignore men spend prodigally upon their armies and parsi-

---

* In an article in the *Nineteenth Century* for May, 1898, an English writer, having access to reliable sources of information, points out that "Europe is piling up its expenditure on armaments in an alarming manner to the sacrifice of sound finance." He shows that the military expenditure of England between 1868 and 1896 rose from $130,000,000 to $201,000,000 ; that of France from $100,500,000 to $180,000,000 ; that of Russia from $82,000,000 to $157,500,000 ; that of Italy from $42,000,000 to $75,000,000 ; that of Austria from $40,000,000 to $75,000,000 ; that of Germany from $53,500,000 to $156,500,000—an increase of 78.6 per cent, while the populations in these six States had only advanced 44 per cent. To this must be added the enormous and steadily increasing items of naval expenditure for these countries, some idea of which may be obtained from the fact, as stated by an authority in the British navy (Sir W. H. White, Director of Naval Construction), that from April 1, 1887, to March 31, 1898, there has been spent on ships, machinery, gun mounting, etc.—*exclusive* of guns and ammunition, which of themselves cost $66,000,000—very nearly $247,500,000. In the *seventy-four years* preceding 1887 the increase in naval expenditure had aggregated $135,-000,000 ; for the past *ten years* the increase has been $285,000,000. Well might Sir W. H. White say, "These are striking figures." Nor have our distance from Europe and hitherto avowed attachment to the Monroe doctrine preserved us from the contagion of this warlike passion. A chaplain of the United States navy informs us that during the past fifteen years we have appropriated $387,987,840 for ships and guns—almost half that sum within the last five years. And yet the outbreak of the late war between Spain and this country found us none too well prepared. Not too soon has a leading actor in this gigantic conspiracy against the peace and well-being of the world proposed a pause. Meanwhile the civilized world will await with anxiety the result of the contemplated International Congress on the Czar of Russia's proposals.

moniously on their people. In Prussia education obtains scarcely a fifth of the amount lavished on preparations for war; in England only one sixth the amount; in Italy less than a tenth; and in Russia five hundred dollars are squandered on turning peasants into soldiers for every five spent on making peasants fitter to perform their duties in the world."* As one has justly observed, "What drinking is in the individual, militarism is in the race, a sort of national drunkenness; a lust of pride of power of blood. In the mad temper of war everything else is submerged."

The havoc and misery wrought by drink are apparent everywhere, and the mere transfer to other industries of the money now embarked in the liquor trade would immediately secure for every human being ample work and wages. The liquor trade is the one of all others which gives the minimum of the product of industry to labor and the maximum to capital. For every twenty-five dollars spent on shoes from eight to ten go to the workman. For every twenty-five spent on earthenware from ten to eleven go to the wage-earner. For every twenty-five spent on drink not more than a dollar goes to compensate labor. In the north of England a large and well-known iron company with a capital of $7,500,000 employs 3,000 men. In Scotland a large distillery of the same capital employs 150. Brewers and distillers quickly become millionaires, and the gains of the trade offer a powerful inducement to men to leave useful and honorable industries and callings and seek the more profitable employment of saloon-keepers;† while in prohibition States like Maine, for example, it is impossible

---

* Address delivered before the Irish Literary Society by Sir Charles Gavan Duffy.
† A Cincinnati Methodist minister, writing to the London *Methodist Times*, says of that city's population of 300,000, 54,000 are Germans. The Germans run the city, and the brewers run the Germans. There are as many breweries as Methodist churches, and more than twice as many people employed in the liquor business as are members of Methodist churches. Poverty is so rife that the secretary of the Associated Charities says there are 70,000 poor who never deposit a dollar in a bank or saving society. Pauperism, vice, and crime keep the asylums and prisons crowded, and the workhouse is in the midst of a dull season when it contains less than 600 inmates.

to enforce the prohibitory law because a profit of eighty per cent constitutes a temptation to run the risk of raiding, arrest, and fine or imprisonment too great to be resisted. Of intemperance and the liquor trade licentiousness in its worst forms is the twin sister, while gambling, narcotism, the foul print, and the obscene drama, as birds of similar feather, haunt the same resorts. Who can contemplate the colossal magnitude and sleepless activity of these foes of human purity and peace without feeling that the time has well arrived for a dead-lift effort on the part of all who love the souls of men to raise and attune the public heart and mind to the high measure of that grand hymn of paradise wherewith the happy parents of our race, according to Milton, began their morning toils?

> Hail, universal Lord! be bounteous still
> To give us only good, and if the night
> Has gathered aught of evil or concealed,
> Disperse it, as now light dispels the dark,

that thus by the united prayer, faith, and self-denying exertions of the thousands of Christian ministers and the millions of Christian people, a quicker approximation may be made to the ideal Christian state and civilization; where the laws shall be administered equally to all in the name of justice and humanity; where the poor, sick, and lonesome shall be wisely and tenderly cared for; where children and youth shall be trained in noble thoughts and courteous manners and lofty ideals; where art and literature and science shall flourish; where the welfare of all shall be the delight and solicitude of each; that fair city of God, in a word, which the last of the apostles saw descending in spotless and transparent beauty out of heaven from God; where tears are no more; where the voice of complaining is not heard in the streets; where disease and pauperism and crime and drunkenness and gambling and debauchery are forgotten insanities of a dismal and buried past.

CHAPTER IX
Missions and Missionaries of the Twentieth Century

Καὶ εἶδον ἄλλον ἄγγελον πετόμενον ἐν μεσουρανήματι ἔχοντα εὐαγγέλιον αἰώνιον εὐαγγελίσαι ἐπὶ τοὺς καθημένους ἐπὶ τῆς γῆς καὶ ἐπὶ πᾶν ἔθνος καὶ φυλὴν καὶ γλῶσσαν καὶ λαόν.—*Apocalypse of John.*

§. Christianity an Apocalypse.

THE genius of Christianity is essentially apocalyptic and prophetic. It makes no pretense of having invented the great moral remedy it offers for the sins and sorrows of mankind, nor claims to have originated the sovereign truths it proclaims, but only to make a plain announcement of verities as old as God and as immutable and enduring as the eternal nature. This characteristic was distinctly perceived and duly emphasized at the outset, and its divine author is accordingly designated "a light for the unveiling (ἀποκάλυψις) of the nations." The aim of the new evangel is not only to remove from men's souls the veil of darkness beneath which the world of spiritual and eternal realities, with its exhaustless wealth of truth, beauty, power, and blessedness has so long and so completely lain concealed, but to disclose to the heathen mind the unsuspected value of the fragmentary and distorted truths it may still retain —the hidden and residual meaning of its myths, legends, and traditions, and to point out the goal toward which its religious thought and aspiration have toiled through many weary centuries in vain. Where culture and philosophy have been obliged to halt, and in confession of their limitations, have erected, on the confines of their narrow domain, the pathetic memorial of a hopeless search—an altar "to an Unknown God"—the Christian evangel extends the frontier of religious knowledge ; widens the empire of light and certainty; says even of the Unsearchable himself, "He is not far from each one of us; for in him we live, and move, and have our being." The entire address of the apostle Paul to the men of Athens is a striking example of the way in which Christianity, intelligently and skillfully interpreted and applied, is capable of exhuming and revitalizing the buried treasures of the ethnic mind. Instead of being jealous of truths discovered outside its own authentic records—instead of being like Isaac Walton's "River of Epirus," whose waters put out every lighted torch and lighted every one which had been extinguished, it welcomes every ray that relieves the darkness of the soul, and refuses to "break the bruised reed or quench the smoking flax."

"Deep-seated in our mystic frame" are hidden truths whose profounder meaning has never yet been unfolded to human thought. Whatever may be the state of intellectual atrophy or moral degradation in which man is anywhere found, he is always innately nobler than he seems. The traces of God's image in him are often too obscure and faint to be easily detected, yet when he is better understood there are found, shining

> Through all his earthly dress
> Bright shoots of everlastingness.

In the depths of the soul the glory of God is written in plainer and more enduring script than on the midnight sky, and to the infinite of thought and the greatness of the soul philosophy and religion owe a deeper debt than to the infinite of space and the magnitude of material nature. Nowhere and at no time has the eternal Wisdom disowned mankind. From of old he has "rejoiced in the habitable part of the earth, and his delights are with the sons of men."

> In joy and inward peace, or sense
> Of sorrow over sin,
> He is his own best evidence;
> His witness is within.

>   No fable old, no mythic lore,
>   Nor dream of bards and seers;
>   No dead fact stranded on the shore
>   Of the oblivious years.
>   But warm, sweet, tender even yet
>   A present help is He.

"God has never left himself without witness. But in every nation he that feareth him, and worketh righteousness, is accepted of him."

2. A Hundred Years of Missions.

To facts like these a century of missionary labor and experiment, of partial success and partial failure, has given a nobler import and a larger value than they ever had before. It was hardly to be expected that in complete ignorance of the history and character of the various types of the ethnic mind, of its religions, philosophies, sacred literatures, beliefs, ideals, and idioms of thought, the best methods of dealing with it should be at first adopted or the best results obtained. Indeed, it is astounding that with small and unpromising beginnings, with an utterly inadequate equipment and a precarious support, and in the face of thousands of difficulties, the early missions of the present century should have made so profound and enduring an impression on the heathen world and have reaped so large a measure of success. The successful evangelization of nearly three millions of heathen people and the planting and maintenance of several thousands of churches and schools, together with the translation of the Scriptures, in whole or in part, into three hundred different tongues and dialects, and the wide diffusion of some of the best religious literature of modern times, is an achievement whose full significance it is difficult to estimate.

But that is not all. Down to a period "within the memory of living men the classic lands of history, of the Bible, and of romance were surrounded with high walls and gates barred against Christian missionaries. The Turkish empire, the Mogul empire, the Chinese empire, the empire of Japan, and that of Morocco were all in this manner fenced around. The remote parts of Africa were guarded by darkness and death themselves. And in southern Europe rare were the spots where it was not an offense, punishable by the police, to circulate the Bible, or to preach or to worship except under forms prescribed. But over the walls has passed the scepter which eye seeth not, and they who before could only blow slender blasts outside the ramparts now march up straight before them, and in the name of Jesus of Nazareth enter in."

But the most striking result of missionary toil and devotion during the period was probably the last to be anticipated, as it certainly is the most doubtful and most disquieting in its character and tendency. The object sought and hoped for was the multiplication of docile and devoted Christian disciples, but a large portion of the harvest is found to be a number of dispassionate investigators and keenly questioning critics. The latent skepticism of the human mind, which is the natural substratum of superstition in all lands, Christian and heathen alike, acquires, from its growing acquaintance with Christian philosophy, literature, and life, an aggressive energy and a power of expression which are often startling. And the missionary to the peoples of the older civilizations faces problems to-day which his predecessors never encountered; he consequently requires a wider knowledge of heathen philosophy, beliefs, and literature, and a nobler faith and courage to meet his difficulties, than have heretofore been considered essential.

Realizing the necessity of familiarizing the heathen mind in its earlier more impressionable and more plastic stages with Christian doctrines, ideals, and habits of thought, most Protestant missions early instituted schools and emphasized the important work of education. The result, notably in old civilizations like India, China, Japan, has been the development of a faculty of independent and discriminating criticism not always favorable to the claims of the Christian religion. Thousands of high-caste Hindu youths, for example, have been weaned from their ancestral faith—discredited alike by the light and science of the West and the teachings of the Christian Church—but they have not transferred their attachment to Christianity. Deplorable and discouraging as this is, the wiser course is not to indulge in lamentations over it, but to find out how it comes to pass and consider carefully what its precise significance is.

It must be borne in mind that neither in India nor elsewhere does the cultivated intellect wake up from its slumbers as a child which one may lead by the hand just where one pleases, but as a factor to be fairly reckoned with in the ever-widening world of thought. Like a colt which has long been tied up and has broken loose, it is in no hurry to commit itself to any new suitor for its faith and loyalty. It prefers to look around with care and discrimination and see just what the new situation is. It ought not to astonish us if at times it asks awkward and even startling questions, such as his Zulu collaborator asked Bishop Colenso about the dimensions of the ark, giving birth to a controversy whose deathless and ever-widening echoes are heard even in our own day—questions we would never ask ourselves, perhaps, without suggestion from the doubter, but which yet it were well for us to be prepared to answer.

It is not surprising that the educated devotee of Brahmanism, or Buddhism, or Confucianism, or Taoism should be as anxious to obtain a critical knowledge of the philosophy, religion, and moral condition of Christendom as the missionary and the student of comparative religion is to know the character and contents of the *Rig-veda* or the *Laws of Manu* of the Brahmans, or the three *Pitakas* of the Buddhist, or the *Shi King* of Kong-fu-tse; and the sins and errors of the peoples who respectively accept these scriptures as their rule of life. Christianity is destined to be known in the life and manners as well as in the beliefs and teachings of its adherents, by the intelligent heathen as fully and accurately as the missionary and the friends of missions are anxious to know him in his creed and in his moral and religious condition; and unless for this searching scrutiny which is coming we are much better prepared than we are now, it is obvious that as soon as the actual condition of modern Christian civilization is known the missionary, as its representative among educated heathen, will be more and more exposed to the stinging retort of which even the perfect One admitted the general force, but did not feel the specific application, " Physician heal thyself." " If Christ can save men from the power of sin, your religion must be divine," said some Brahman officials of the government in the Punjab to a Wesleyan missionary* who had lectured to them weekly on the gospel of St. John at their own request, "but where are the people saved from sin by this Christ? There may be one or two saved, but what about the thousands around here [English residents—soldiers and civilians] that are evil and vicious?" "You complain that you do not make converts among us," said Dharmapala, the eloquent and scholarly Buddhist priest at the Parliament of Religions in Chicago. "You preach a God of love, but in your actions you are selfish. You make of an ignorant or an unsophisticated man a perfect hypocrite. You have used the story of a life-crushing bloody Juggernaut to secure the means to save alleged heathens. Juggernaut has been popularized by Christian missionaries, and yet a commission composed of eminent Englishmen has declared that the Christian idea of Juggernaut was a myth, that death and

---

* Rev. J. H. Bateson's speech at Wesleyan Missionary Anniversary, London, May, 1896.

blood were repulsive to our people. This Christian story has been exploded. It has gone into oblivion."*

In some such strain of dignified resentment, on the one hand, or of close judicial cross-questioning, on the other, is intellectually awakened India destined to test the hitherto unquestioned claims of the Christian religion. Nor ought any missionary of the Anglo-Saxon race to complain of this. For in this very mood of reserve and cautious thoughtfulness his ancestors received the message of the Roman missionaries in the far-back dawn of English civilization. Having received the apostle of the Church and his companions, observes the historian Green, " sitting in the open air on the chalk-down above Minster, where the eye nowadays catches miles away over the marshes the dim tower of Canterbury," King Æthelbert, in 597, listened patiently to the long sermon of Augustine as the interpreters the abbot had brought with him from Gaul rendered it in the English tongue. "Your words are fair," he said, "but they are new and of a doubtful meaning."† And time was asked to consider them. Does anyone, looking back over the history of Anglo-Saxon Christianity for more than a thousand years, regret such slow deliberation and counting of the cost?

3. Present Outlook.

It is perfectly clear that the Christian Church as she looks across the threshhold of the twentieth century will be required in her missionary policy and operations to grapple with a situation almost entirely new and growing more and more difficult every day.

1. In the first place, from the new point of elevation on which his training under Christian auspices, and his more or less intimate acquaintance with the life and literature of

---

* Address in Chicago, 1893.
† J. Richard Green's *History of England*, vol. i, p. 41.

Christendom have placed him, the enlightened devotee of paganism perceives his advantage, and uses it without scruple. Not only is he unprepared to sever himself from the past, disavow the traditions of his family, tribe, and caste, and proclaim himself a foreigner among his own people, by embracing a foreign faith, but he boldly assumes the rôle of reformer and apologist at once. He insists on reading a new and nobler meaning into the philosophy and religious literature, customs, and institutions of his people, and aggressively compares the religion of his ancestors—the growth of his native soil—in the new guise he thus gives it, with its less venerable rival, coming from afar, greatly to the disappointment and disadvantage of the latter. In this work of rehabilitation and defense he finds himself cordially commended and assisted by many representative scholars of Europe and America, who have not only studied with sympathy and insight the sacred literatures of the great religions of the East, translated them into good idiomatic English, and in this way placed them in the hands of Western readers, but commented, in transports of enthusiasm and delight, on sentences of rare "moral beauty" found scattered over their voluminous pages like green oases here and there, relieving the dreary yellow acres of the desert.

In his recently published lectures on the Vedânta philosophy the distinguished Sanskrit scholar Max Müller invites an attentive hearing for the profounder thoughts of Indian thinkers about the soul and God, and reminds us that, if it seem strange that sages whose names were long ago consigned to the limbo of forgetfulness should have known more about the soul than the philosophers of Greece, of the Middle Ages, or even of modern times, we must remember that "the observatories of the soul have remained much the same," and that the repose and quiet which are requisite for accurate observation of the movements of the human spirit "were more easily found in the silent forests of India than in the noisy streets of your so-called centers of civilization."

2. Side by side with these efforts to recast the native cult in the terms of modern thought and philosophy a policy of imitation is sometimes adopted, and where rivalry by reform is out of the question, and academic and argumentative opposition would be powerless, and persecution would be impracticable or of no avail, the sarcasm of counterfeiture has proved a marked success. In a curious manner the truth is being afresh brought home to the conviction of the thoughtful missionary, that if he trusts to the mere accidents and externalism of his religion—its rites, ceremonies, institutions, dignities, titles, terminology, and usages, or even to its superior rational and ethical elements—to recommend it and secure its triumph, he is building hope upon the sand. For in none of these respects is Christianity beyond more or less successful copying. The revival of Buddhism in Ceylon, for example, where twice over, during the last three and a half centuries, Christianity seemed to have nearly extinguished the native cult,* is solely owing to the discovery of the fact that all the distinguishing external features of the Christian Church may be appropriated and paraded with immense popular advantage without the trouble on the part of the imitating cult of an inward transformation. Within the last few years the Buddhists of Ceylon have begun to keep the anniversary of Buddha's birth, just as Christians have celebrated annually for nearly nineteen cen-

---

* Three and a half centuries ago the Portuguese found Ceylon a Buddhist land. They compelled the people to become Christian, pandering to their oriental vanity by giving them high-sounding baptismal names, and by interfering slightly, if at all, with idolatrous ceremonies. A century after the Dutch pursued a similar policy, and multitudes who had been Roman Catholic Buddhist Christians became Protestant Buddhist Christians. A profession of faith, with baptism, was demanded from any person seeking government employment even in the humblest capacity. As a consequence Christianity became duplex, degenerate, without saving salt. Less than a century ago, when Britain took the country, eighty per cent of the people were Christians, but in ten years the temples had increased sixfold, and half of the Christians had gone back to Buddhism.—*Speech of Rev. T. Moscrop, in Exeter Hall, London*, 1894. See also Copleston's *Buddhism*.

turies the advent of Christ. Carols are sung in the early morning hours, including a version of the well-known Christmas hymn, "Christians [Buddhists], awake, salute the happy morn." Lanterns and other transparent devices are borne through the streets of Kandy and Colombo displaying the audacious parody, "Glory to Buddha in the highest, on earth peace and good will toward men." Christians are scornfully alluded to as "the heathen of the land," and the theosophic Buddhist priests are styled Rev. Dharmapala, Rev. Buddhagosha, etc. They have established week-day and Sunday schools, published catechisms full of ideas and forms of expression stolen barefacedly from Christian catechetical manuals, and in some instances have copied that peculiarly Methodist institution, the class meeting. If this policy of mimicry is at times grotesque or even malicious, it is, nevertheless, tactful, adroit, alert, aggressive. And now Christianity in heathen lands finds satire and ridicule harder to face than were the lions of the Roman arena, the tortures of the rack, or the fires of martyrdom to the Christians of yore; for as Gibbon, himself a past master in the sardonical art, triumphantly asks, "Who can answer a sneer?"

3. Only rarely and as a last resort does the pagan *protégé* of evangelical philanthropy resent the unsolicited interest taken in his welfare and become a persecutor. Of late years the Chinese and the Turks are the only people who have continued to employ brutality and violence in opposing Christian missions, and the incentive to this policy of outrage and murder, which is directed by the governing classes of both nations, alike against missionaries of all denominations, is said to be not patriotism nor excess of zeal for their native cults, but dread of the civilizing forces which the life and labors of the missionaries everywhere set in play. "The influence of Western civilization," says Mr. Valentine Chirol, who was at Peking as correspondent of the London *Times* during the recent war between China and

Japan, "in whatever shape it manifests itself, is an abomination in the eyes of the rulers of China, whose days would be counted were it ever to persecute the masses. The hatred directed against the missionaries is only a peculiarly virulent form of hatred directed against Europeans generally, and it is easy to understand why it should be a peculiarly virulent one. Missionary work is practically the only agency through which the influence of Western civilization can at present reach the masses. . . . The missionary alone goes out into the byways as well as the highways, and, whether he resides in a treaty port or in some remote province, strives to live with and among and for the people. The life which he lives, whether it be the ascetic life of the Roman Catholic missionary or the family life of a Protestant missionary, with wife and children, is in itself a standing reproach to the life of gross self-indulgence led by the average mandarin. But in the eyes of the latter it becomes a public scandal when, in glaring contrast to every vice of native rule, the foreign missionary in his daily dealings with the people of his district conveys a continuous object lesson of justice and kindness, of unselfishness and integrity." *

The same explanation holds, in a large degree, of the genesis and motive of the Turkish barbarities in Armenia, whose harrowing reports have operated like successive fits of nightmare on the paralyzed and impotent sympathy of Christendom. It is not so much zeal for Islam that makes the ruthless sword of the "unspeakable Turk" leap from its scabbard on the slightest pretext or provocation as it is the dread that the standard of fair dealing, justice, and humanity quietly set up and steadily maintained by the lives and teachings of the missionaries will be a standing reproach to official corruption, rapacity, and lawlessness, and generate

---

* *The Far Eastern Question*, chap., "The Genesis of Missionary Outrage in China," p. 78.

a sense of wrong and resentment in the breasts of the oppressed.

4. Policy of Success.

Now, taking a broad survey of the heathen field to-day, a policy adequate to the situation requires:

1. A careful study of ethnic systems and the relation of Christianity to them as they live in the thought, worship, and literature of modern heathendom. To these systems Christianity, with its high claim to universal dominion, owes something more than an attitude of uncompromising antagonism and a duty of wholesale denunciation. It is impossible now to take for granted that heathen morals are unmitigatedly corrupt, and heathen religions systems of unmingled fraud and falsehood, to be condemned and rejected in the lump. Men who have stood face to face with them for years, and have studied them in their genesis and slow development in history; in the different phases through which they have passed; in their literature, institutions, present status, character, and teachings, have set the example of a very different strain. No doubt a desperate and often unreasonable antipathy to Christianity inspires most of the extravagant and vague eulogies bestowed on heathen ethics and religion, but that ought to make the judicious advocate of Christianity not less but more anxious to be fair and equitable. The hoary and venerable errors inwoven in ethnic religion and philosophy are all the more effectively exposed when there is quick and cordial recognition of the few strands of truth they contain. And, even if our duty required of us an absolute and unqualified condemnation, the difficult task of weaning the heathen mind from systems under which it has been molded, and by whose idioms of thought and conception its very texture has been saturated and colored for centuries, would seem to suggest the need of an intelligent and sympathetic in-

sight and of discrimination, delicacy, and fairness in our method of treating them rather than a spirit of supercilious pity, impatience, or contempt.

Speaking of Buddhism, for example, in whose teachings countless millions of mankind have sought consolation and guidance in life and final escape from the interminable chain of births and deaths and strange transmigratory experiences in which human existence is believed by it to be held, the Bishop of Colombo says: "The important literature in which this system is embodied, its earnest moral tone and the immense numbers of those who have professed it give it a strong claim on men's attention."* He points out that before Islam arose and when Greeks and Romans, Jews and Christians, were few in numbers it was the religion of the majority of mankind; that "more men have owned the Buddha than have owned as yet any other teacher," and he remarks, "The spectacle of human multitudes is still an impressive and moving spectacle, often a pathetic one." Nor is it conceivable that these millions of human beings have submitted to the yoke of Buddhism and sought to follow its holy eightfold path of *right belief, right aim, right speech, right-conduct, right livelihood, right endeavor, right recollectedness, and full-souled meditation,* whose goal is the external calm of annihilation, without some measure of moral elevation and inward spiritual repose.† " Happy is the solitude of him who is full of joy, who has learnt the truth, who sees (the truth). Happy is the freedom from malice in this world, self-restraint toward all things that have life. Happy is freedom from lust in this world, getting beyond all desires and the putting away of that pride which comes from the thought, 'I am.' This truly is the highest happiness."‡ Such are the words which the *Vinaya Pitaka* ascribes to the sage of the forest. "Gazing forth

---

* *Buddhism, Primitive and Present,* by the Right Rev. Reginald S. Copleston, D.D., p. 1. † *Ibid.,* p. 43. ‡ *Ibid.,* p. 38.

like the Sage of Lucretius from the serene heights of wisdom over the varied world of life, but radiating forth, unlike the sage, rays of kind feeling and love in every direction; calm amid storms, because withdrawn into a trance of dreamless unconsciousness; undisturbed, because allowing no external object to gain any hold on sense or emotion, or even thought; owing nothing and wanting nothing; resolute, fearless, firm as a pillar; in utter isolation from all other beings, except by feeling kindly to them all; such is the ideal 'conqueror' of Buddhism. The last point of vantage by which existence could lay hold of him is gone; he cannot continue to exist."* Neither the man who conceived this noble ideal nor the people who have respected it for so many centuries can justly be considered "men hopelessly benighted," either morally or intellectually. As the learned author of *Buddhism, Primitive and Present*, justly remarks: "No one can claim for either Old or New Testament the exclusive communication to man of the theory of disinterested kindness and the law of love. The same Holy Spirit who wrote our Scriptures *gave to some of the Buddhist teachers no despicable measure of insight into these truths.*"

2. But though we do not allow ourselves to lose sight of the redeeming features of heathen cults, it is nevertheless necessary to look at them steadily and impartially, not as they appear in the occasional glimpses of truth and flashes of fine moral sentiment to be found on the pages of their sacred books, nor yet as rehabilitated by the philosophic and poetic genius of their most enlightened native and most enamored European apologists and exponents, in their well-meant efforts to eliminate their uglier features or hide them from criticism. We must contemplate them in their everyday and stay-at-home aspect and attire, and in their practical tendencies and actual effects on the lives and morals of

---

* *Buddhism, Primitive and Present*, p. 99.

their votaries. The visitor to the shrines of Hindu gods in the various temples of the holy city Benares and of other cities in India may or may not feel an unconquerable sensation of moral disgust as he looks upon the spectacles of filth, obscenity, and shame that everywhere meet his eyes. He may or may not see "in popular Hinduism the worship of the incarnation of the worst vices of mankind." He may or not deplore the repulsively suggestive carvings which adorn the idol cars in the public streets and thoroughfares, the hideous symbols of passion worshiped in every Sivite temple, or the band of Nautch girls attached thereto for purposes unmentionably vile. All this and much more may or may not seem to him to be more than a mere difference of national taste. But when the traveler in India pauses to contemplate the effect of caste on Hindu society as a whole, the insuperable stumbling-block it offers to the intellectual, moral, and social improvement of the people, the millstone-like pressure with which it weighs upon, crushes, and grinds the inferior classes ; when he considers the position of isolation and ignorance and often of hopeless infamy to which it consigns womanhood from the earliest years of infancy to mature age—when he finds her branded with diabolic levity as "a necessary evil," lampooned in reputable literature as "faithless, dangerous, impure;" when he thinks of twenty millions of Hindu widows—many of them mere children—subject to "degradation of all kinds," and made "the instruments of hateful impurity," as Pundita Ramabai Sarasvati has shown in her book, *The High Caste Hindu Woman*—when he looks steadily at these facts he finds it difficult to deny the breadth and power of the curse with which Hinduism burdens and oppresses human life.*

Of Buddhism, though at first a revolt against Brahmanism and undoubtedly in its earlier stages an evangel of peace,

---
* "No wonder," said Mr. B. B. Najarkar in an address at the Parliament of Religions, in Chicago, " poor, forlorn, and persecuted widows often drown themselves in an adjacent pool or well, or make a quietus of their lives by draining the poison cup."

kindness, unselfishness, and good will, a not much higher estimate can be formed as it anywhere exists to-day. Indeed, it is inconceivable to the Western mind that its fundamental doctrine—the weary interminableness of transmigration—can at any time have been other than the weight of a perpetual nightmare on the energies of the human spirit. "The view of the soul underlying this idea is that there is no permanent independent soul existing in or with the body, and migrating from one body to another. The self or personality has no permanent reality; it is the result of a combination of faculties and characters. No one of these elements is a person or soul or self. Death is the breaking up of this combination. But there is a force by which these elements on which life depends *tend to recombine* (*karma*), a fatal attraction (*upadana*) by which these elements of life cling together and recombine. So this force (*karma*) remains a kind of desire for new life and animates with desire to recombine those severed elements of life. This recombination may become a man, a demon, a deity, or a dog."

The tears a man has shed over his fathers amount to more water than all the oceans. Everyone has been everyone's father, mother, son, etc. The blood certain ascetics shed when slaughtered as oxen, goats, birds, dogs, exceeds all the waters of all the seas. The bones of one individual in the course of an age (*kalpa*) make a great mountain. A *kalpa* is so long that if a solid mountain were lightly brushed with a silk handkerchief once in a thousand years, it would be worn away long before a single *kalpa* was exhausted. Yet the beings born again as men are only as a nailful of dust to the whole earth." What is there in such teaching to illumine life, to elevate sentiment, or inspire men with hope and high moral aims?

"I have climbed," says the Rev. T. Mosscrop, Wesleyan missionary in Ceylon, "through the chilly night up the steeps of Adam's Peak to the sacred footprint, seventy-five hundred feet above the sea, and as the first rays of the sun have come over the eastern hills I have heard the great bell toll and seen the people gather for service, such as is repeated continually in the Buddhist temples throughout the land. The priest begins to chant the Three Refuges of Buddhism :

> Buddham saranan gachchami,
> Dharman saranan gachchami,
> Sangham saranan gachchami.
>
> I take refuge in Buddha,
> I take refuge in the Law,
> I take refuge in the Priesthood.

And you hear the thin piping of the little child, the shrill treble of the Singhalese woman, the deep bass of the strong man in his prime, and the husky tremor of the old man nearing death blend in these promises of refuge. And we are particularly anxious to know what it is to take refuge not in the law or the priesthoood, but in the Supreme Person, and we find that Buddha has passed into Nirvana, the state and place of passionless bliss and eternal calm ; that he can hear no prayer, and send down no help. And we are reminded of the colossal images of Buddha found throughout the land, near to the ways and woes of men, the face impassive with dreamless sleep, the ear heavy that it cannot hear, the arm shortened into the lap, indicative of meditation—shortened that it cannot save ; and the Christian heart recoiling from the illusive hopes of Buddhism, centers itself once again on the living, the reigning Christ, and sings:

> Other refuge have I none,
> Hangs my helpless soul on Thee.

And tested thus, the witchery, the glamour of popular, philosophic, poetic Buddhism go, for it is found wanting in the simplest elements of the Christian hope. As a matter of fact, Buddhism does not satisfy the people, for the bed rock on which they rest in life's crisis hours is demonism."

3. Another consideration to which a true missionary policy and an adequate preparation for missionary work must have regard is the material to be handled. This, of course, differs widely among different races. And the circumstances affecting the diversity, many and varied as they are, are all of them worthy of careful study, such as race, religion, historical antecedents, present political conditions, degree of civilization reached, extent and character of previous acquaintance with Christianity. In the nature of things the work of Calvert, Hunt, and others in Fiji, of Williams in Erromanga, of Paton in the New Hebrides, of Gilmore among the Mongols, of Moffat and Livingstone, of Bishops Hannington and Taylor among the semisavage tribes of Bechuanaland and of Eastern, Western, and Central Africa, required very different methods from those of the missionary who undertakes to evangelize the Japanese or the Chinaman, or turn the philosophic Hindu from his idols and his sensuous worship of four thousand years to serve the living God.

The missionary of to-day in Ceylon finds the Buddhist of that island under alert and able leadership. And with the wariness and caution taught by the past reverses of his cult and a sense of equality if not of superiority to any rival faith, born of its present triumph, he is much less susceptible to Christian argument and appeal than he was twenty years ago, before the present remarkable resurgence of Singhalese heathenism began. On the other hand, while diplomacy has secured for the missionary in China a protection from official interference and a freedom of access to the people he never enjoyed before, it has seemed only to intensify the antipathy and hate of the educated, the wealthy, and the ruling classes, and made them more difficult of approach.

In India the presence of Mohammedanism, with its unsavory past record, its political ambitions, treasonable temper, and love of rule, its lofty pride, fierce fanaticism, and sullen distrust of everything not Mohammedan, makes Hindus the more ready to listen with respect to Christian teaching. And yet here, where caste is supreme, pronounced, all-pervasive, inveterate, the problem which confronts the missionary is the most complex and difficult to be met with anywhere. The three classes which invite his attention and labors offer about an equal amount of difficulty and discouragement to his undertaking. There is the upper stratum of native society—the educated high-caste Hindu numbering perhaps a million and a half. He accepts the advantage of a good secular and religious training offered him in the various missionary schools and colleges, but rarely—practically never—thinks it worth his while to forego the pride and privileges of caste for the hopes and honors of Christian discipleship. There is the pariah class, numbering perhaps seventy millions—an outcast and degraded people. Addicted mostly to devil worship, they are miserably ignorant and pitiably poor, sharing nothing without stint, except perhaps the contempt of the classes above them. These are an easy prey to missionary influence and appeal, but their moral worth when secured is not great, and the motives of their attachment are not always above suspicion. There is the average-caste Hindu, numbering between one hundred and eighty and one hundred and ninety millions. He is typically not a townsman, fond of activity and excitement, but a villager, loving quiet and repose, with a strain of the recluse in his temperament—a man of monotonous mood, of sluggish intellectual movement, of imperturbable temper. His motto is *festina lente*. He dislikes hurry, abbreviated processes, and precipitancy. He loves to approach his subject by a flank movement or by a circuitous route from the rear. He is a pantheist, but expresses his faith not in the language of metaphysics, but in the vaguer speech of poetry. "God," he says, "is in everything—in me, in the tiger, in the cow, in the crocodile." He is a philosopher, or the product of a philosophy; he is a fatalist, a stoic. He takes no note of time except as his past misfortunes remind him that there have been times in his life when he must have been trying to cut the threads of fate and dodge the decrees of destiny. He is a deeply religious man, "a convinced devotee" of his ancestral gods. "He revels in myths and regulates his life by omens." His notable experiences are sorrows, not joys. His red-letter dates are days of disaster. With him life, thought, speech, action, have no decisive moral complexion except that given them by their obvious external consequences. There is no sin in actions and purposes that succeed. There is no virtue in what miscarries and breaks down, no matter what its motive. A lie is not a lamentable thing if it is believed and is clever enough to escape detection and exposure. Truth is a crime if undiplomatically spoken and inexpediently maintained. He is a believer in transmigration, and is convinced that there is no escape from the track he has drawn for himself in some previous state of being. Work among such people needs a deep conviction of its necessity, firm faith in its ultimate success, a comprehensive and sympathetic knowledge of the type of mind to be dealt with, delicacy and tact in dealing with it and an unwearied patience in waiting for the result. For, as an experienced missionary observes, "A man cannot shed the assumptions of a lifetime, with centuries at the back of that, in an hour, as a snake would shed its skin." *

4. But if a missionary policy suited to the times needs to adjust itself to the diversified temperament and varying condition of the ethnic mind, it must keep equally in view the one aim of all missionary effort, which is primarily and chiefly not to educate nor to civilize, but to evangelize and save the people. Slowly missionary organizations of every

---

* Rev. Henry Haigh, Missionary in Madras.

denomination are waking up to the fact that the time and money heretofore expended on education other than the elementary training of the children of avowed converts are worse than wasted, inasmuch as such education actually furnishes aid and comfort to the enemy and puts into his hand a weapon which is often used with deadly effect against Christianity itself. Writing from the Government House, Calcutta, a well-known member of the British House of Commons, a leading Baptist in the city of Liverpool, and a generous supporter of Christian missions, the Right Hon. W. S. Caine, says: "It is a melancholy fact that, although the powerful and wealthy missionary organization of India has borne a large share in the Western education of the natives, the number of young men educated by them who become Christians is almost an imperceptible fraction. The work which missionaries are doing in the way of education is beyond praise, viewed as education work simply; but, so far as turning the young men they educate into Christians is concerned, their failure is complete and unmistakable.

"I have seen no better college in India than the vigorous institution founded at Lahore by the American Presbyterian Mission; a college so popular that it contains more students than its government rival. Its staff consists of five graduates of universities, with able assistants. Its professors teach mental and moral philosophy, English literature, chemistry, logic, higher mathematics, physics, Persian, Sanskrit, and Arabic. There are one hundred and thirty students, all working up to the university, sixty-five of whom are already undergraduates. Nearly all these youths come in from a fine school in Lahore city connected with the same mission. These students are literally soaked in evangelical truths for years. The state of their minds toward religion is aptly suggested in a paragragh of the interesting report of the college, which says, 'One of the brightest and most promising of the students said not long ago—voicing, no doubt, the sentiments of his class-fellows—"We do not believe in Hinduism; we have no religion now, we are looking for a religion."'"

Mr. Caine quotes from the last annual report of the Baptist Missionary Society the following words: "It cannot be too often repeated that the one supreme need of the heathen world is a personal knowledge and acceptance of Jesus Christ and his salvation. The great aim of our brethren the missionaries is to *Christianize* by means of the fearless, loving proclamation of the blessed Gospel of the grace of God," and then remarks: "It may shock some of those who subscribe to its funds to know that this object is being partly attained by the employment of unconverted Hindu or Mohammedan teachers in many of their day schools, and that this is rendered inevitable by the impossibility of filling the posts from the native churches themselves. . . .

"Only the other day, at Madras, a whole college struck work because it was rumored that one of the students was going to be baptized. How many converts have been made at the London Missionary Society's [Congregational] College at Benares? I doubt greatly if there has been one... A college education in India, even when conducted by missionaries, only appears to loosen faith in all religions and destroy the moral restraint which comes from faith of any kind."*

Other careful observers who have traveled extensively in India and made a thorough study of the educational work of its missionary organizations bear a similar witness. "What becomes of the Indian alumni of the college or university?" asks Bishop Hurst, of the Methodist Episcopal Church, and answers, "Of the many who finish the curriculum but a small fraction are Christian or have any positive Christian sympathy."† After exhibiting by cold and impartially

---
* W. S. Caine's *Letters from India*, No. ix.   † *Indika*, p. 386.

selected statistics the startling inefficiency and failure of the educational policy of his own and other denominations in India Mr. Caine proceeds to say: "I am quite sure that if the whole energy and income of missionary societies in India were concentrated on work whose sole object was conversion to a living faith in Christ, the results would be far different;" and he concludes with the stimulating conviction that "there never was a heathen nation more ripe for Christianity than India."*

5. Finally a policy of advance and triumph must make larger and freer concession to the intellectual idiosyncrasies and social usages and customs of heathen peoples. The fatal temptation of the Christian Church in every age has been to unduly magnify the outward and nonessential features of religion while failing to give sufficient prominence to truths that are the very salt of life, and to virtues that are the essence of the soul's abiding strength and glory. And this mistake, which has hampered her onward movement in so-called Christian countries, has been equally adverse to her success among the heathen. She has defeated her own purpose and retarded the triumph for which she has unceasingly prayed and sighed by seeming to demand more in sacrifice and suffering than she had to offer in life and love, in peace and joy and consolation.

The grand achievement of the Church of the twentieth century will be to distinguish with a breadth and clearness

---

* Caine's *Letters*. On the other hand, it is clear from opinions and testimonies elicited a few years ago by the Foreign Missions Committee of the Church of Scotland from various individuals, either now or at one time in high official station in India, that the educational work of the various denominational missions is highly valued by the government. Sir William Muir, principal of the University of Edinburgh, formerly secretary to the government of India, hesitated not to say "that it would be a calamity for India if missionary schools were withdrawn." Sir William Wilson Hunter, M.A. LL.D.; Sir Charles U. Aitchison, at one time lieutenant governor of the Punjab; Lord Dufferin, for some years viceroy of India; Sir Henry Ramsay, and several others express similar convictions. It may be observed, however, that no one, no matter what may be his views as to the educational policy of missionary boards, committees, etc., really doubts the immense secular and civil advantages of education. The question is, Is this the kind of work which, in view of the experience of the past, offers the prospect of largest spiritual returns for the money, time, and energy of the Christian Church?

Missionaries of the Twentieth Century 215

hitherto unknown between the soul and the body; between the essential life and the mere livery of religion, and to find out a way of making the heathen happy and exemplary Christians, while leaving them practically unchanged in their national characteristics of thought, of speech, of manner, of social and domestic usage—making them Christians, in a word, without unmaking them as Chinamen, Hindus, Japanese, Africans.

That this possibility has dawned on thoughtful minds and is slowly shaping itself into a practical policy is clear from the words of a scholarly Wesleyan missionary in India. After pointing out that, though "the first preachers of Christianity began with the simple proclamation of the Gospel to the individual, they had soon to pass on to an enlarged study and exposition of the principles of the life and law of Christ in their relation to societies and communities," he says: "In a country like India the new religion has to determine the attitude it shall adopt and the relation in which it shall stand to the long-established customs, tastes, and tendencies, the manifold characteristics, intellectual, æsthetic, moral, and religious, of an ancient civilized people. Among a race like the Fijians, of primitive fashions and passions, with customs and ideas in a perpetual flux, the task of adjustment may be an easy one. We may send to them our English nineteenth century Christianity, not only in its essential power, but in all its modes and expressions, and imprint it entire on that plastic material. So that in the religious life of Fiji to-day we might almost find repeated the religious life of English village Methodism, the same forms of worship, the same institutions, doctrines, sentiments. But when we picture to ourselves a Christianized India we cannot imagine it as a congeries of millions of units who shall all have docilely imbibed the doctrines, adopted the practices, taken the stamp of the various types of Christianity—Methodist, Anglican, Presbyterian, etc.—that we bring to them from the West. It would be a crude and hasty assumption indeed to suppose it is either desirable or possible that British Methodists or British Methodism should be reproduced unchanged in the churches we are planting in India. Sober thought recognizes that just as the English Christian is a product of the operation of divine grace upon that strongly marked type of character which we call English, so the Indian Christian of the India that is to be will be a new product, formed by the operation of the same divine grace upon very different material. And as our English forms of worship, expressions of doctrine, systems of Church government and organization, methods of work, have developed under the guidance of the Holy Spirit, in adaptation to our English character and life, so it must be expected that in India, when our religion is no longer exotic, but naturalized there, worship, organizations, types of thought, of character, of activity, will come into existence which will be strange to us, but will be in harmony with the deep-seated idiosyncrasies of that Eastern people."*

The principle of concession is a true and valuable one. But, if so, why not incorporate it broadly and at once into the practical methods of missionary work in India and elsewhere, and so, by restoring in some measure, for example, the original poverty-stricken aspect of religion's representatives, make it more attractive and intelligible to the oriental mind? "A Hindu has no sympathy with a missionary, however godly and earnest a man he may be, who lives in a good bungalow, eats the sacred cow, drives his dogcart, and is in all respects a 'Burra Sahib.' Every teacher from whom he has in time past received religious inspiration is associated in his mind with asceticism, self-renunciation, poverty, and apostolic simplicity. Christ, who had not where to lay his head; John the Baptist, in camels' hair,

---

* "How is Christianity to be Acclimatized in India?" Rev. W. H. Findlay, in *Methodist Times*.

eating locusts and honey; Paul, working with his own hands; the Jesuit preacher, in Brahman dress with his begging bowl, and the barefooted Salvation Army captain—these they can understand." Has not modern Christianity sufficient of the spirit of heroic self-effacement—enough of the genius of accommodation and self-adjustment to circumstances—to capture India by approaching her in forms she has always instinctively and warmly welcomed? in forms of lowliness, self-denial, abstemiousness, dependence, bare of foot, poor in purse and garment, but rich in faith, in courage, in kindliness and love? Shall she to-day, with such splendid prizes within her grasp as India, China, Japan, fail to make good her ancient boast of "becoming all things to all men, that she may by all means save some?" Has the Francis Xavier, Robert de Nobile, Wiliam Carey, and Henry Martyn type of missionary become hopelessly obsolete? of whom a reputable historian says: "They renounced all riches, dignities, honors, friends, and kindred; they desired to have nothing of this world; they scarcely took the necessaries of life; attention to the body, even when needful, was irksome to them. . . . *They were given as an example for all religions.* Their footsteps remaining still bear witness that they were right, holy, and perfect men who, waging war so stoutly, trod the world under their feet;" and concerning whom a recent writer declares that "they have left their mark on India as no other missionaries have ever done, and their disciples form to-day nearly two thirds of the Christian population of India."

CHAPTER X
The Itinerant and Settled Pastorates Compared and Contrasted

Their voice was soon heard in the wildest and most barbarous corners of the land, in the dens of London, or in the long galleries where, in the pauses of his labor, the Cornish miner listens to the sobbing of the sea.—*Anon.*

And that voice was a jubilatic one—it proclaimed among our hills and valleys the great, soul-saving elementary truths of Christianity, with the demonstration of the Spirit and power. Such men, with such elements of moral force, could not but succeed. Their success is not a mystery. The only problem of their history is that a class of men so unique, so uniformly heroic in spirit, and gigantic in energy, so persistent against all odds, and so calmly and confidently self-conscious of success, and even of great historical destinies, should be found among us, and should year after year continue to prosecute their unparalleled labors by the most simple machinery, and with scarcely any appreciable means of support. . . . The men we have been commemorating wrought out into an energetic and historical reality what the logic of the philosopher and the sagacity of the statesman would have pronounced impracticable to human nature. Down to the date at which we now, with truest admiration, take our leave of them most of them denied themselves the enjoyments of domestic life and remained single, that they might the more utterly consecrate themselves to their labors.—*Stevens,* " Memorials of Methodism."

1. The Itinerant Ministry not an Institution of Modern Origin.

THE itinerant pastorate is an institution distinctive of ecumenical Methodism. To cursory students of Church history it has doubtless seemed a new and modern device compared with the system of the settled pastorate, with its high antiquity, its almost universal adoption, and the magnificent array of saintly, scholarly, and even illustrious names that adorn the annals of its history. So far, however, from being a recent and novel type of the Christian pastorate, it is in reality very old. It is a reversion not only to the primitive and original order, but to a type recurring more than once during the Middle Ages, and though at present efforts are being made within some of the older, larger, and more influential of the denominations of which it is a leading characteristic to discredit and supplant it, it is doubtful whether the world will ever be able to dispense with the itinerating evangelist—the peddler of salvation. A wandering ministry answers a stronger instinct in human nature than the settled pastorate, and satisfies profounder needs of the soul. Man is by nature a rambling stone—a tramp, a vagabond. Without his migration from side to side of the broad stage of the world—a propensity which modern civilization seems rather to strengthen than to discourage—and the consequent displacement of large populations to which this wandering instinct has led in Asia and Europe in ancient times; in America, Australasia, and Africa in more recent times, the whole romance of history would be lost and the progress of the race seriously impeded if not brought to a standstill.* He is a wanderer in search of good until the restless spirit within him is satisfied and tranquillized by the chief good ; and when he has found for himself the greatest of all blessings he is then apt to become an itinerant in the interests of its announcement and diffusion. The vexed question as to the relative age of Episcopacy and Presbyterianism as ecclesiastical *régimes* is, in some of its phases at least, an open one, and is likely to be interminable; but there is not and cannot be any dispute as to the relative antiquity of the itinerant ministry and the settled pastorate in the mind of anyone acquainted with the New Testament Scriptures and the history of the apostolic and subapostolic Church. Nor can it be disputed that this was the style of organization that most commended itself to

---

* The rejuvenescence of a decaying civilization by the introduction of fresh blood into the veins of deteriorated peoples is perhaps nowhere better illustrated than in Sheppard's *Fall of Rome and Rise of the Nationalities*, but the inborn passion of the wanderer was as characteristic of the dawn of civilization as of its later stages. See Gen. x, xi ; also Sayce's *Patriarchal Palestine*, and *Higher Criticism and Verdict of the Monuments*.

the leaders of all the most potent and most popular religious movements of the mediæval Church, notably that of St. Francis d'Assisi and his Brothers Minor,* and that of St. Dominic in Italy, and the later propaganda of Wyclif and his poor friars in England.

2. Founder of the Methodist Itinerancy.

The annals of Christianity, however, nowhere display a consecration to the service of God and humanity more unreserved, more comprehensive, or more complete than is found in the record of the labors and travels of the founder of Methodism. Temporary inconvenience, occasional privation and hardship, exposure to criticism, persecution, and mortal peril, have often been incurred for the sake of some desirable worldly object. Some have found it easy to go through a little dirt to great dignity, or "wade through slaughter to a throne." But the man who calmly braved the fury of the mob at Wednesbury, Walsall, and Bolton; who traveled thousands of miles over rough roads in all kinds of weather for half a century; who rose every morning at four to break the "bread of life" to hungry souls an hour later; who during his early labors was never sure of either board or shelter; whose incessant toils and anxieties brought him neither wealth, fame, power, nor promotion, could not be actuated by any but the highest conceivable motives. The aim he set before his preachers was the object that absorbed his own soul. In the conclusion of his twelve rules of a helper he says: "Observe, it is not your business to preach so many times, and to take care merely of this or that society, but to save as many souls as you can, to bring as many sinners as you possibly can to repentance, and with all your power to build them up in that holiness without which they cannot see the Lord."

Wesley's whole life was one ceaseless self-repression, one

---
* Paul Sabatier's *Life of St. Francis d'Assisi*.

powerful and victorious effort of self-mastery. At times this spirit of self-obliteration assumes a form at once pathetic and sublime; as when, after returning to the fine old Northumbrian town of Newcastle-on-Tyne, he records in his Journal: "Certainly, if I did not believe there was another world, I should spend all my summers here, as I know no place in Great Britain comparable to it for pleasantness. But I seek another country, and therefore am content to be a wanderer upon earth." At other times the element of comedy predominates. During one of his earliest visits to Cornwall the people omitted to invite him and his companion in toil and travel to a meal. Finding that the bushes by the wayside yielded a plentiful supply of ripe blackberries, he records his heartfelt thankfulness to God that the needs of the body are met in this way by the free bounty of nature. On another occasion he and his faithful henchman and helper, Nelson, are obliged to sleep on the floor for nearly a month. Nelson, extemporizing a pillow for his own weary head of the great quarto volume of *Burkitt's Notes*, folds his own greatcoat for Wesley to rest his head on. An hour before the time for rising Wesley, on turning over, finds his companion already awake, and clapping him on the side, remarks in that vein of irrepressible humor which always characterized him, "Brother Nelson, let us be of good cheer; I have one whole side yet."

3. Itinerancy Defensible on the Plea of Past Utility and of High and Ancient Example.

To itinerancy in itself neither stigma nor special sanctity attaches. Everything depends on *how* a man does his wandering; from what *motives;* with what *objects* in view. All the great poets, philosophers, and historians of the ancient world traveled extensively. It was an essential part of the profession of poet, philosopher, historian, to see strange lands and scenes and peoples, and know foreign customs and opinions. And when the apostle Paul in the course of his missionary journeys reached Athens they took him for one of those knowledge-seeking pilgrims to whom it was their wont to give the strikingly appropriate though somewhat contemptuous name of *spermologoi*—pickers-up of stray seeds of truth, gatherers of scraps of news, and odds and ends of information. And so they said with ill-disguised contempt: "What will this babbler, or rather this *spermologos*—this dealer in ill-digested scraps of philosophy—say to us?" They took him for a hungry, migratory bird from some far-off, famine-stricken region, who had alighted among the better-fed barnyard fowl of the "city of the gods," to snatch from the once famous floors of the Lyceum, the Porch, or the Groves of the Academy a mouthful of the choicest grain of Greek philosophy. They had, however, entirely mistaken the spirit and purpose of his mission, as they discovered later. He had come not to ask them for anything except it were—like Antonius in the Roman Forum with the warm eulogy of Cæsar on his lips—"to lend him their ears," that he might tell them of "the God that made the world and all things therein, he, being Lord of heaven and earth, dwelleth not in temples made with hands; neither is he served by men's hands, as though he needed anything, seeing he himself giveth to all life, and breath, and all things." In other words, the apostle, like every true Methodist preacher, itinerated not to impoverish but to enrich the world by making known to it "the unsearchable riches of Christ," and bringing to those who believed the sovereign joy of a present and personal salvation.

This lofty purpose of his wandering mission brings the self-denying itinerant into intimate affinity and fellowship with the noblest and most beneficent souls of history. Many years ago, as the present writer was informed, during a summer tour in Wales, a man selling ornamental trinkets and cheap jewelry stood under the deep shadow of the ruins of an old Welsh castle. He was a thoroughly educated man, a gentleman in bearing, breeding, manner, and speech. As the crowd of tourists passed over the bridge that connects the railway depot with the ancient ruins of the castle and with the old town of Conway they were attracted and charmed by the spontaneous eloquence of the peddler's speech. "I am a vagabond," he said, "and belong to the noble and ancient race of vagabonds. I am not ashamed either of the name or the calling of a vagabond, for this same element of vagabondism enters into the nature and function of all noblest things. There is your beautiful Welsh river wandering through meadow, wood, and wheat field, fertilizing the farms and adorning the landscape and dispensing a thousand blessings to man and bird and beast as it hurries to the sea. Down from the central hills of the land the graceful wanderer flows, and you call it the 'Wye,' which is a corruption of the ancient Roman word *Vaga*—the wanderer—the beautiful vagabond. The Father of the faithful," he continued, "was all his days a wanderer, 'seeking a better country—that is, a heavenly.' Jehovah himself is 'a stranger in the land, and a wayfarer who turneth aside to tarry for a night.' 'And Jesus went about all Galilee, teaching in their synagogues, and preaching the Gospel of the kingdom.' And I, like the greatest religious reformer and evangelist of the last century, 'seek another country,' and therefore am content to be a wanderer among men." *

---

* When this anecdote was published by the author in a contribution to a well-known religious weekly, having an extensive circulation in New England, a former editor of that paper, who has since gone home to God, full of years and honors, challenged the narrative's originality and charged the writer with plagiarism. The accuser wrote the editor to say that the article in which the story appeared was taken *bodily* from the Rev. Paxton Hood's *Peerage of Poverty*. It is a curious illustration of the haste and hazard of nearly all such charges that when, after considerable search in a large public library the author secured for the first time a sight of Hood's book, he found that his own version of the story and Hood's were so entirely different, except in a few general features, that it was not possible for either of them to have been a copy of the other. Hood's version, which is contained in a dozen lines on the first page of his book, omits some of the most interesting details, and places the scene of the incident in a different part of Wales.

4. Develops a Noble Type of Character and a Fine Sense of Brotherhood.

One marked advantage of the itinerant fraternity as it appears to an outsider is that each member feels it incumbent on him, as sharing its peculiar honors and privileges, to preserve the type in its best form and fullest efficiency, being unwilling through lack of personal fidelity, self-control, and painstaking to allow his fair inheritance to get overgrown with brush and weeds, and become a tangled "wilderness, open to the incursions of the wild boar of the forest," to use the words of Wesley, inviting the pity or provoking the contempt of his neighbors.

It is a matter of authentic record that for vigorous faith in God, for a generous and self-sacrificing love for human souls, for warm, brotherly affection and unity among themselves, for a keen and clear spiritual insight and a sound and sober judgment, for zeal and energy, self-restraint and circumspection, for unsparing toils, and the noblest and most enduring kind of success, the early Methodist itinerants set an example that won the admiration of mankind notwithstanding the difficulties that challenged their courage and tried their souls. They were not without the capability of appreciating the happier circumstances of fellow-laborers in other fields. Amid the hardships and privations to which they were constantly exposed tempting visions of a condition very different from their own occasionally floated before their eyes. "To rise early, read and pray a few hours, take breakfast, have family worship, and then pass on from house to house, from appointment to appointment, as our custom was, we found to be laborious, wearing, and tiresome work; but the Lord was with us, and gave us to see scores of sinners con-

---

The present writer gave the story as it was told him during a vacation spent in the principality, and Paxton Hood evidently got his information from a similar source, namely, the floating folklore of the country. It is only fair to say that when the author pointed this out and proposed to his accuser to place his own version and Hood's before competent literary arbiters, and let them decide, he had the candor to confess himself, for once, mistaken. "My criticism," he said, "is logically dead."

verted to God; and their songs of praise cheered us in the glorious work." The writer of these words records that on a certain occasion "he was nearly two hours passing through a snowdrift which was four or five feet deep." "I dismounted," he says, "and made my way through ahead of my horse, as far as I could without letting go of the bridle-rein; and then he would leap and wallow up to me and wait until I had again made a track. The storm was so severe that I found it difficult, at times, to catch my breath, and our path was filled as fast as we left it." *

Among other "rich and refreshing meditations" to which such scenes and situations gave rise the following dialogue is given as a specimen:

Q. Who is that up to his arms in the snow?
A. A Methodist preacher.
Q. Who is that in a snug study by his warm fire?
A. The honorable settled minister.
Q. What is the Methodist preacher doing?
A. Making his way to his appointment, where he hopes to call sinners to repentance.
Q. What is the settled minister doing?
A. Hunting his library over, selecting portions, and adding, perhaps, some of his own thoughts, and writing out a sermon to read over to the people next Sabbath.
Q. Which of them looks most like a lazy man, and which gets the most money, the most reproaches, or follows the example of Christ and the apostles nearest, in traveling, suffering, preaching, self-denyings, watchings, fastings, and winning souls to Christ?

Here my mind looked back and saw Jesus, weary, sitting on Jacob's well, Paul tossing on the rolling waves and shipwrecked on Miletus, and John on the desolate isle of Patmos. And my soul cried out, in the midst of the tempest, "O, Lord, permit me to wear out in thy service."†

---
* Stevens's *Memorials of Methodism*, p. 413.   † Stevens's *Memorials of Methodism*.

There was from the start a feeling of brotherhood, a bond of fellowship which in its genuineness and warmth completely obliterated all distinctions of rank or office. Hardly anything can exceed the apostolic simplicity and beauty of the scene described in the following narrative : " The next morning I started, in company with several other preachers, for Conference, which sat in Monmouth, Me. After a few hours' ride we halted in a grove and let our horses feed in the highway, while we held a prayer meeting. It was a blessed season. We then passed on, meeting with great kindness, as though the Lord had given the people a command to entertain us for his sake. On the morning before we reached Monmouth we fell in with Bishop Asbury, and brought the rear of more than a score of itinerant Methodist preachers. About ten o'clock we stopped at a tavern and called for a room. After we had rested about half an hour Asbury said, 'We must have prayers before we leave ; I will go and give notice to the landlord, and some of you must pray.' I followed him to the barroom, to learn his skill and manner. He said, 'Landlord, we are going to have prayers in our room; and if you or any of your family wish to attend, we should be happy to have you.' 'Thank you, sir,' he replied ; 'please wait until I speak not only to my family, but my neighbors.' Soon they flocked in ; we sung and prayed, and melting mercy moved our hearts. When our bill was called for we were told there was no demand against us, and were requested to call again. How blessed to hold up the light of truth in all places as we pass along through the world! " *

Such were the character and spirit of the early Methodist itinerants. The work was one and the laborers were one, and the reported advancement and triumph along many lines and on many hard-fought fields evoked a common gratitude and diffused a common joy. Troublers of Zion

---

* Stevens's *Memorials of Methodism*, p. 442.

walked out unconstrained to stay. Rivalry and personal ambition perished unwept, and envy and jealousy died without pity or regret. The men of the early Methodist ministry were men of martial mold and temper, and really enjoyed the "fight of faith" by which they proposed to "lay hold on eternal life." No words could have deeper meaning for anyone than the battle cry composed by one of their leaders had for them. Their hearts found a real power in the now familiar strain:

>Stronger than death and hell,
>   The sacred power we prove;
>And, conquerors of the world, we dwell
>   In heaven who dwell in love.

Nor has this splendid *esprit de corps*—this sense of brotherly oneness—perceptibly declined in any section of the great Methodist host since the founder of Methodism closed his eyes. To-day the stranger who goes into the Wesleyan Conference when the opening hymn is being sung—sung as it was in Wesley's days:

>And are we yet alive,
>And see each other's face?

or into any Annual Conference in this country during the opening prayer meeting, sees strong men with tears in their eyes, and hears eloquent men with tears in their voices, and finds himself in an atmosphere of brotherly sympathy and fellowship for a complete parallel to which he will probably search the Churches of all lands and times in vain.

5. Present Practical Value, an Item Worthy of Attention.

The ideal of such a relation is necessarily an exalted one, and the man who is bent on honoring it needs to school himself and his people into the proper mood for meeting its stern and inexorable requirements. One of the most trying and disrelishable things any minister has to do is to leave men, women, and young people whom he has learned to admire, esteem, and love—persons whose fellowship, sympathy, cooperation, and prayers are among the most golden and cherished of his memories, and whose names are always pleasant music in his ears. With the strength of these sacred bonds, the charm and sweetness of these memories, the Methodist pastor is probably as familiar as any. But his calling as a wanderer demands the sacrifice, in a large measure, of these relations which so often make hard duties delightful and trials and disappointments easier to bear. By the will of the appointing power one pastor leaves and another "comes after him," who may or may not be "preferred before him." He comes to fill the place his predecessor has just vacated, to seize the tools he has just dropped, and perpetuate without break or pause the hum of church life and activity. He comes to face the difficulties and hindrances his predecessor had to face, contend against the same sins and errors, attempt the solution of the same church and parish problems, and commit similar follies and mistakes. And his predecessor, with genuine brotherly feeling, uses the brief opportunity afforded him before his departure of focusing on him, as the coming man, the undivided sympathies, love, loyalty, and confidence he needs and has a right to expect. It is always felt that it is really not a question as to what is due to him who comes, or to him who goes, but as to what is due to a cause that is greater and nobler than either of them, and to which both alike owe the best that is in them. No morbid self-consciousness and self-consequentiality are permitted to blind the eyes to the grandeur of things, which, if they could be seen in their true magnitude and entire breadth and fullness, would go far to annihilate all paltry personal ambition and extravagant self-esteem. The itinerant does not dream of reversing the divine and eternal order of things, of presuming that the Church, with all her honors, offices, and varied ministries, shall be made subservient to his self-centering aims and aspirations, but heroically insists on his own self-effacement and on subordinating himself and his affairs to her sovereign claims and comprehensive scope and mission. He feels that, take what he will away from the people he has served, he is obliged to leave behind all that is most vital to their well-being—the mercy, love, patience, promise, presence, and power of God; and that under the wise guidance and sleepless care of the Almighty they are not likely to be much worse off with his erring successor than with his equally fallible self.

Nor does it need the faultless intellectual poise and trained faculty of a philosopher to perceive the progressiveness of God's purpose—to see that in spite of the death or retirement of intrepid pioneers and skillful workmen, sagacious leaders and lucid and eloquent interpreters of modern life and thought, the work of God still steadily advances; that though

> The individual withers, yet the world is more and more.

As a rule, what comes after us is better than ourselves, and the civilized world of to-day is worth, in hard cash value, but much more in moral and intellectual excellence, many such worlds as our grandfathers knew a hundred years ago. There may seem to be exceptions to this rule in a few cases of sequence. It cannot be said that every individual wave is stronger and larger than its immediate predecessor; still the tide comes steadily in. And we ought to encourage the world around us to expect not declension, but a distinct improvement on ourselves in the person of him who comes to take our place, and not imitate the unworthy jealousy for which the world has praised rather than blamed the blind old poet of the "Iliad." Like the Methodist itinerant, he was a wanderer, as every man who has had immortal things to do, or say, or sing has been since Abram's day. He was poor and physically feeble, though he was to do such great things and "to live in the mouths of a hundred generations and a thousand tribes." Blind and dependent, his wanderings were such that when he became famous neither he nor his friends could tell where he started from; his birthplace could not be ascertained. So it was said:

> Seven famous towns contend for Homer dead,
> Through which the living Homer begged his bread.

The story is that as he wandered over the sunny islands of the Ægean and the Asiatic coasts he tenderly entreated those who had known and loved him to cherish his memory above that of every other minstrel when he was away. As he had been expected with pleasure, he hoped he would be regretted when he had gone, and would be rewarded by the sympathy and praises of his friends even in the presence of other minstrels who might come that way. A set of verses pretty well authenticated is ascribed to him, in which he addresses the Delian women thus: "Farewell to you all, and remember me in time to come, and when any one of men on earth—a stranger from afar—shall inquire of you, 'O maidens, who is the sweetest of minstrels hereabout, and in whom do you most delight?' then make answer modestly, 'It is a blind man, and he lives in steep Chios.'"*

6. Drawbacks as Compared with the Settled Pastorate.

But an itinerant ministry as compared with the settled pastorate has obvious disadvantages as well as some marks of superiority. And no one sees this more clearly than those whose ecclesiastical polity subjects them to a rigid rule of periodical change of place. The agitation for a change in the itinerant law which has existed for some years in the older Methodist denominations, and the modifications of it, long ago adopted by others, like the English Primitive Methodists and the Free Church Methodists, show how impossible it is to construe the divine institution of the ministry and devise an adequate arrangement for the evangelization of the world, so as to combine in any given

---

* See Newman's *Idea of a University*.

system every desirable feature and eliminate every obvious fault, and adjust thereby the ministration of the living word to different ages and circumstances and to the varied tastes and temperaments of mankind.

Leading clergymen and many intelligent laymen in the Methodist Episcopal Church contend that, though the restriction of the pastorate to a brief term of years was serviceable and necessary so long as the denomination was distinctively evangelistic and missionary in its spirit, policy, and methods, it is impossible to maintain that feature in the present altered condition of affairs without serious injury and loss, especially in large cities, which "are becoming the great *thought* centers of the nation, forming and shaping its politics and its religious life." Says Dr. H. R. Carroll, Associate Editor of *The Independent*, in an article in *Zion's Herald*, Boston, Mass.: "A people's Church, as I like to think ours is, ought to be strongest where the people are most numerous; but I am persuaded that our work, our influence, and our power in cities fall far below the possibilities. We are losing constantly an element which we ought, for every reason, to retain; and we are losing it chiefly because of the persistence of our arbitrary rule which has served its end, and which can be modified without in the least endangering the principle on which it is based."

It is alleged that, while many pastors are removed long before their resources are exhausted, and sometimes just at the moment of their widest popularity and greatest power for good, others are stimulated by the itinerant rule to spasmodic and unhealthy exertion with a view of making the most of their brief opportunity. It is held that the rule "interferes with the fullest development of the pastorate;" that in many instances it induces indolence and moral and intellectual atrophy; that "it destroys continuity of work and dissipates energy;" engenders "a feeling of unrest among the membership" of the Methodist Episcopal churches, and a love of novelty for its own sake; renders "confidence in pastoral leadership impossible;" keeps pastors and people perpetually strangers to each other; gives no opportunity of continuous oversight over the religious life of young people and of exerting a helpful influence on family life; estranges families from the Church of their choice, and practically forces very desirable people outside the Methodist fold. It is even contended that the wandering pastorate militates against the very purpose which is the principal reason of its being namely, "the successful evangelization of the masses," because it "offers no stability in pastoral leadership at strategic points where success requires: (*a*) thorough, detailed mastery of local conditions, possible only after years of study on the ground; (*b*) confidence of the community, coming only from long acquaintance with man and work; (*c*) courage on the part of the minister to enter on a long campaign," with the prospect of having "the opportunity of pushing his carefully planned work to completion." It is argued, in a word, that "it degrades the pastorate and is the standing occasion of a humiliating exodus of Methodist ministers into other denominations." The following paragraphs, quoted by the author's permission from an article by Dr. Robert McIntyre, one of the most popular and most powerful preachers of the West, in any denomination, present the defects and disadvantages of the itinerant system from the point of view of one who has had every opportunity of knowing its strength and its weakness.* The author's apology for inserting so lengthy an extract is that it is a manifestly fair and forcible putting of the case by one whose loyalty to the polity of the Methodist Church is unquestioned:

---

* The representation above given, which the present writer is unable to indorse without qualification, contains the gist of the statements of some twenty leading Methodist ministers and laymen, published in *Zion's Herald*, August 7, 1895. In most cases I have used the *ipsissima verba* of those sharing in the symposium, and where that has not been done care has been taken in the abridgment to reflect the obvious thought of the writer.

"1. We are known," he says, "as transients, having no local habitation, therefore no local interests. Our welcome is a half-hearted one because we will not doff our sandals or set away our staff. We are pilgrims, not pillars; never knitted into but only stitched on the spiritual garment of the city, and the basting threads show through the first sermon. Any self-respecting town desires its pastors to be drenched in all its serious concerns and baptized with its peculiar spirit. It is no answer to assert that other pastors move as often as we do. They *may* stay, so are warmly greeted and helped. We *must* go, and bear 'emigravit' on our banner, so the eyes that should shine on our approach to the gates are staring with far-away ken to discern who is coming after us. Thus we get a civil nod instead of a hand-grip, and are set farthest from the fireplace and nearest the door, that our coming and going may not disturb the peace of the home people.

"2. It is unjust to the preacher. He can lay no broad plans; his successor will upset them. He dare not put that precious element, his personality, into his methods, but only into his sermons. If he has constructive capacity, or organizing talent, he does not develop it. To do so would be to overturn his predecessor's work, which done, his successor is ready to overturn his. Men strong enough to bring great enterprises to the capstone want to lay foundations themselves, or have assurance that the plan will not be changed when the structure is one story high. He will dig no well, for the next may prefer a hydrant. He plants no palms, for the one rising the near hill may delight only in terebinths. Thus between the man of action and the man of insight, 'twixt Peter and John alternating, the inconstant church comes into the condition of the perplexed lover:

> Who stood a spell on one foot first,
> And then a spell on t'other,
> And on which of 'em he felt the worst
> He couldn't have told you nuther.

"3. It is impertinence to God. If the Spirit calls a man, it is not a general but a special call; not to a nebulous but to a definite work, in a fixed time and particular place. The Spirit gives some men to the world—as Booth and Taylor; some to the nation—as Gough and Vincent; some to the city—as Brooks and Storrs. He does not say everywhere and every when to the individual—this he says to the Church; but to the preacher he says 'Now' and 'Here.' How can any man presume to lift a preacher who is palpably fitted for the place he fills? We are told that the Church has done good work under this rule. Even so. Poe wrote good poetry despite his infirmity; but it was his genius, not his bottle, that gave it birth. Not Procrustes' bed, but the penitents' bench, is the throne of Methodism.

"Our beloved Church has gone forward because of her theology, her heroism, and her hymnology. These three are the mighty team that has drawn this King's chariot round the earth, and the time limit has never been other than a drag on the wheels. Loose them and let them go! Set no metes or bounds to the Spirit's work!"

CHAPTER XI
The Popular Preacher

That he hath wondrous power of language no one denieth; he useth large words and many, and withal hath no interpreter, which for the unlearned's sake is pity; yet hath his heart warm sympathies with the commonest of his kind.—*Anon.*

Eloquence is a divine gift which to a certain point supersedes rules, and is to be used like other gifts to the glory of the Giver, and then only to be discountenanced when it forgets its place, when it throws into the shade and embarrasses the essential functions of the Christian preacher, and claims to be cultivated for its own sake, instead of being made subordinate and subservient to a higher work and to sacred objects.—*John Henry Cardinal Newman.*

1. Popular Eloquence not the Primary Qualification of the Christian Preacher.

A CAREFUL and thorough analysis of the elements usually most conducive to success in sacred oratory would probably result in surprise and disappointment. "Eloquence is a great gift, never more valuable, perhaps, than in the present day; overrated, as some quiet-minded philosophers think; but their opinion carries no conviction, for the masses will ever follow the seductive sound of 'the silver tongue.' A good gift it is, indeed, but not perfect; for it gains all the adulation and most of the prizes of life, and those who have it, seeing more perfect but more silent wisdom neglected, are apt to imagine that all the wisdom of the world flows through fluent tongues."

The charm and fascination of the orator will be found for the most part to be a gift of nature rather than an acquisition of severe moral discipline, on the one hand, or the hard-won præmium of painstaking intellectual and vocal culture, on the other. Of him, as of the poet, it may be said, *nascitur non fit*—he is born, not made. But while perhaps the majority of successful speakers are eloquent mainly by virtue of natal good fortune and inherited endowment, there are many others, and those of greatest account, very often, who acquire a wide public influence only by dint of personal labor, character, courage; by a resolution to succeed in spite of almost insuperable natural defects and difficulties. A pen-and-ink sketch by an admiring disciple of one of the greatest thinkers and most interesting personalities of his country and time—a man who, though he profoundly influenced the religious life, thought, and literature of his age, could scarcely be considered eloquent in the commonly accepted sense of the word, shows how, before the spirit and purpose of the persevering student, everything gives way: "Precisely at 11:15 A. M. in shuffles a little black Jew, without hat in hand or a scrap of paper, and strides up to a high desk, where he stands the whole of the time, resting his elbows upon it, and never once opening his eyes or looking his class in the face—the worst type of Jewish physiognomy in point of intellect, though without its cunning or sensuality; the face meaningless, pale, and sallow, with low forehead, and nothing striking but a pair of enormous black eyebrows. The figure is dressed in a dirty brown surtout, blue plush trousers, and dirty top boots. It begins to speak. The voice is loud and clear, and marches with academic stateliness and gravity, and even something of musical softness mixes with its notes. Suddenly the speaker turns to a side. It is to spit, which act is repeated every second sentence. You now see in his hands a twisted pen, which is gradually stripped of every hair, and then torn to pieces in the course of his mental workings. His feet, too, begin to turn. The left pirouettes round and round, and at the close of an emphatic period strikes violently against the wall. When he has finished his lecture you see only a mass of saliva and the rags of his pen. Neander is out of all sight the most wonderful being in the university."*

How vivid and powerful the picture is! And yet how utterly inadequate to satisfy the craving which every thoughtful student feels, to know something of the personal charm and secret of power not merely of "the most wonderful being" in a great university, but of one of the most learned and most luminous teachers of his age †—a living exemplification of his own motto—*pectus est quod facit theologum*—the heart makes the theologian.

Even in the case of the man whose sustained power and world-wide popularity for more than forty years have placed him as a star apart among the distinguished pulpit luminaries of the century now passing into the "sere and yellow leaf," and made his name a household word in all Anglo-Saxon lands, a catalogue of those qualities that most deeply impressed the popular mind affords no clew whatever to the immense, continuous, and far-reaching influence he wielded. And those who, like the present writer, went to see and hear Spurgeon for themselves were just as puzzled to account for the crowded thousands, the close attention, the warm, all-pervading enthusiasm in work and worship, and the occasional *Bochim* that transpired when the preacher's heart grew tender and his voice became tremulous with an emotion all too deep for tears. "His voice is clear and musical," says one who listened to one of the great preacher's early sermons, "his language plain, his style flowing but terse, his method lucid but orderly, his matter sound and suitable, his tone and spirit cordial, his remarks always pithy and pungent, sometimes familiar and colloquial, yet never light or coarse, much less profane. Judg-

---

* See *Life of Dr. John Cairns*.
† "Berlin has never had a more beloved teacher," says Dr. Philip Schaff. "His character and example were even more impressive than his profound learning and original genius. . . . He was one of the greatest and best men I ever knew."—*Life of Dr. Philip Schaff*, p. 34.

ing from a single sermon, we supposed that he would become a plain, faithful, forcible, and affectionate preacher of the Gospel in the form called Calvinistic, and our judgment was the more favorable because, while there was a solidity beyond his years, we detected little of the wild luxuriance naturally characteristic of very young preachers."

"The crowds which have been drawn to hear him," gravely remarks a London Quaker, "the interest excited by his ministry, and the conflicting opinions expressed in reference to his qualifications and usefulness have been altogether without a parallel in modern times. It is a remarkable sight to see this round-faced country youth thus placed in a position of such solemn and arduous responsibility, yet addressing himself to the fulfillment of its onerous duties with a gravity, self-possession, and vigor that proved him well fitted for the task he had assumed."

"His appearance in the pulpit," says another acute observer, "may be said to be interesting rather than commanding. . . . His figure is awkward, his manners are plain, his face (except when illumined with a smile) is admitted to be heavy. His voice seems to be the only personal instrument he possesses by which he is able to acquire such marvelous influence over the minds and hearts of his hearers. His voice is powerful, rich, melodious, and under perfect control. Twelve thousand have distinctly heard every sentence in the open air, and this powerful instrument carried his burning words to an audience of twenty thousand gathered in the Crystal Palace."

Before the majestic voice, dramatic gestures, melodious fluency, and pathetic earnestness of George Whitefield everything went down. His popular influence and power to enthrall a promiscuous crowd was to his contemporaries a marvel before unheard of in the history of preaching, and it has never been repeated since. Ten, twenty, on one notable occasion thirty thousand people listened breathless to his

The Popular Preacher 239

words. The colliers of Kingswood, with the tears washing their way down their coal-begrimed faces, and the less emotional multitudes assembled on Boston Common, Massachusetts; skeptical philosophers like David Hume; fastidious critics of men and manners like Horace Walpole; men of the world like the suave but insincere Lord Chesterfield; astute diplomatists like Benjamin Franklin; experienced statesmen of the type of Bolingbroke; women of birth and refinement like the devout but imperious Lady Huntingdon, were all equally powerless to resist the charms of the orator of the fields. Other men as noble in character, aim, and purpose, with better furnished minds and much weightier things to say, counted their congregations by tens where Whitefield numbered his auditors by thousands. As regards solid and suggestive thought, the little finger of Jonathan Edwards was thicker than Whitefield's loins, but Edwards never addressed the crowds that listened to the appeals of his more gifted and everywhere triumphant friend.

2. Popularity no Infallible Sign of Public Usefulness.

It would be quite unwarrantable to say that the popular mind is wholly indifferent to the charms and insensible of the worth of high moral character in those by whom its opinions and sentiments are molded in literature, in politics, and in religion, but it certainly is not as quickly responsive to or as warmly appreciative of those grand moral attributes in which personal worth mainly inheres as it is of others of more showy and more striking though less solid and less serviceable character. The public mind as a rule is too preoccupied or too hurried in its intellectual and ethical judgments to carefully distinguish between efforts which are only fitted to produce a transient impression and those which promise deeper and more enduring results. Talents which win wide attention and attract the crowd have no necessary relation to the supreme interests of morality and religion or the great problem of human well-being. If there is no necessary antagonism, there certainly is no essential affinity between distinguished intellectual oratorical or artistic powers and the intense moral enthusiasm which exclaims, "God forbid that I should glory save in the cross of our Lord Jesus Christ," and which unweariedly *labors to hasten the coming of the kingdom of God.* An incident in the life of Herr Von Gerok, renowned in his day both as poet and preacher admirably illustrates the wide chasm of difference which often yawns between genius consecrated to God and brilliant gifts which find a congenial sphere for their exercise on the lower plane of art and histrionic exhibition. Gerok was one day walking along one of the principal streets of the old German town of Stuttgart with an umbrella under his arm when the prima donna of the Stuttgart Opera troupe happened to glide softly past him on the sidewalk without that protection against the weather. Unexpectedly just at the moment the rain began to fall and Gerok invited the lady, who was evidently surprised by the shower, to share his shelter. Though entire strangers to each other, they soon disengaged themselves from the trammels of an embarrassing silence. After a remark or two about the weather the distinguished preacher said, "May I venture to ask your name?"

"It is plain to see that you never go to the opera," proudly and tartly answered the lady. "Everybody knows that I am the leading singer at the Court Theater. Now it is my turn to ask to whom I am indebted for the protection of an umbrella."

"Your question clearly proves that you never go to church," was the prompt reply, "for all religious people know that I am chief pastor of this town."

It will be admitted that whatever personal gratification preacher or prima donna might have had in their respective circles of admirers, the mere fact of a large following had in itself no particular moral value or significance in either case. The "religious people" were not necessarily pious because they admired the preacher and enjoyed his ministrations; the patrons of the Court Opera were not necessarily wicked because they surrendered themselves to the charming strains of the prima donna. A popular preacher, a crowded church, and an overflowing treasury are in themselves no more an evidence of evangelical vitality, of spiritual prosperity and power, than a popular prima donna and a crowded theater are signs of high moral enthusiasm and refined histrionic taste among theater-goers. It is well to remember this at a time when the tendency of churches is to degenerate into social clubs—associations for the promotion of literature, amateur art, histrionic culture, or military drill, as in many American Churches, whose membership, in their anxiety to loom up large in the view of the public, are tempted to rely on anti-evangelical measures and methods to replenish their treasury and attract the people.

The question as to the extent and value of the influence exerted by the Christian religion on the civilization of any particular age would be very inadequately answered by a reference to the popularity or otherwise of its ministry. The sands of the centuries are thickly bestrewn with the wreckage of gifted men who were once borne proudly forward on the crest of the wave of popular feeling. On the other hand, the reign of error and superstition has been strenuously and successfully disputed, immorality, vice, and crime have been restrained, the battle of civil and religious liberty has been fought and won, and the banner of truth and justice has been unfurled and borne forward by men of whom the world showed itself unworthy—accounting them "the filth and offscouring of all things," and consigning them to the gloom of the dungeon, the tortures of the rack, or the slow agonies of marturial fires.

16

Not in vain Confessor old
Unto us the tale is told
   Of thy day of trial.
Every age on him who strays
From its broad and beaten ways
   Pours its sevenfold vial.

Happy he whose inward ear
Angel comfortings can hear
   O'er the rabble's laughter;
And while Hatred's fagots burn
Glimpses through the smoke discern
   Of the good hereafter.

Knowing this, that never yet
Share of truth was vainly set
   In the world's wide fallow.
After hands shall sow the seed,
After hands from hill and mead
   Reap the harvests yellow.

Thus with somewhat of the seer
Must the moral pioneer
   From the future borrow;
Clothe the waste with dreams of grain,
And, on midnight's sky of rain,
   Paint the golden morrow.*

3. Antipopular Elements Inhere in the Essence of Christianity.

In the attempt to popularize the Gospel it is often forgotten that antipopular elements inhere in its very essence; that these unacceptable ingredients are among its most prominent and most essential characteristics, are vital to its aim and purpose, and can neither be suppressed, slurred over, nor apologized for without flagrant dereliction of duty and betrayal of sacred trust. Whether it be the people of Nineveh, of Jerusalem and Judah, or of this modern time who are recalled to duty, a faithful and unreserved announcement of the divine message is imperatively required. "Preach the preaching that I bid thee;" " Stand in the court of the Lord's house, and speak unto the cities of Judah, which come to worship in the Lord's house, all the words that I command thee to speak unto them; diminish not a

---

*Whittier's *Barclay of Ury*.

word" (Jer. xxvi, 2). "I came," said the Peacemaker, "not to send peace on earth, but a sword;" "Behold I send you forth as lambs among wolves;" "Ye shall be hated of all men for my name's sake;" "Whosoever shall not receive you, nor hear your words, when ye depart out of that house or city, shake off the dust of your feet (Matt. x, 14.) "We know and are verily persuaded," wrote Calvin, "that what we preach is the eternal truth of God. It is our wish, and a very natural one, that our ministry might prove beneficial and salutary to the world, but the measure of success is for God to give, not for us to demand. If this is what we have deserved at the hands of men whom we have struggled to benefit, to be loaded with calumny and stung with ingratitude, that men should abandon success in despair and hurry along with the current to utter destruction, then this is my voice (I utter words worthy of the Christian man, and let all who are willing to take their stand by this holy profession subscribe to the response), 'Ply your fagots.' But we warn you that even in death we shall become the conquerors; not simply because we shall find, even through the fagots, a sure passage to that upper and better life, but because our blood will germinate like precious seed and propagate that eternal truth of God which is now so scornfully rejected by the world."*

It is safe to say that no occupant of the modern pulpit will be long embarrassed by the popular admiration who unsparingly declares the whole counsel of God and denounces sin in the concrete as well as in the abstract, in the individual life as well as in the temper, manners, and general conduct of society. A gifted young American preacher in a prohibition State—a man of genial spirit, many personal attractions, and remarkable aptitude for public address and leadership, whose following was large and influential, and whose capacious church was crowded

---
* *Necessity of the Reformation.*

Sabbath after Sabbath with people of many different denominations drawn from every section of a community of seventy thousand people—was struck with the total disregard of the statutory restrictions against the sale of liquor in the community, and resolved to urge the enforcement of the prohibitory law by the mayor of the city. He accordingly preached a sermon on the subject to a crowded audience, which created quite a sensation. He interviewed the mayor—one of the most capable, most public-spirited, and most exemplary chief magistrates that ever honored the office in that city or any other—presented his demand and was courteously listened to. The mayor at once took action, with the result entirely unlooked for, either by the mayor or the minister, that among a dozen other persons a leading member of the popular preacher's own fold was fined forty dollars for illicit sale as a wholesale druggist. When reminded of the statement authoritatively formulated and announced to the world by the official leaders of his own church—" The liquor traffic is so pernicious in all its bearings, so inimical to the interests of honest trade, so repugnant to the moral sense, so injurious to the peace and order of society, so hurtful to the home, to the Church, and to the body politic, and so utterly antagonistic to all that is precious in life, that the only proper attitude toward it for Christians is that of relentless hostility. It can never be legalized without sin "—and asked why he did not enforce the law of the Discipline in his church against those who had been publicly convicted of its violation, as he had very properly insisted the mayor should do in regard to the law of the State in the municipality, he replied, with a politic and worldly prudence worthy of a Machiavelli (though himself the most sincere and honest of men), " If anyone cares to carry the Discipline to such extreme lengths and create trouble for himself, let him do it. I will not commit myself to any such foolish step."

The Demosthenes of the pulpit, though a roaring lion for a sensation, is not always to be relied on for the steady and self-sacrificing prosecution of the work of practical reform. Yet he is apt to look down calmly and compassionately from the lofty and serene heights on which his "gifts, graces," and prudent policy have placed him on the martyrs to piety, conviction, and high-minded Christian principle fighting on the plain below him and wonder why God should have given men such noble souls, such effective thinking faculties, such lofty faith and courage, and so little tact and worldly wisdom to take care of them and turn them to popular account and pecuniary advantage. In his sovereign self-complacency he forgets that (to quote the words of Wordsworth, which the much-maligned Frederic W. Robertson, of Brighton, used to cite with passionate satisfaction):

> One single self-approving hour outweighs
> Whole years of stupid starers and of loud huzzas;
> And more true joy Marcellus, exiled, feels
> Than Cæsar with a senate at his heels.

The fact is, the popularity for which so many noble-minded and godly young ministers unwisely hunger and thirst is totally incompatible with a continuously faithful administration of the word of life. "Will ye also go away?" said Christ with evident surprise and pain to the last rapidly diminishing remnant of a crowd who but a few hours before had wished to take him and crown him as their king. "Hosanna! Blessed is he who cometh in the name of the Lord," is the popular cry to-day; to-morrow the same voices shout themselves hoarse with the strangely different demand, "Crucify him, crucify him." "The disciple is not above his master, nor the servant above his lord. . . . If they have called the master of the house Beelzebub, how much more shall they call them of his household" (Matt. x, 24, 26). "Ye received me as an angel of God, even as Christ Jesus," are the words in which the apostle recalls the warmth of welcome with which he had at first been met by a people to whom he is subsequently impelled to address the uncomplimentary salutation, "O foolish Galatians, who hath bewitched you?"

Not with wreaths of bay, nor coronets of gold, but with crowns of thorns, has the world too frequently rewarded its faithful ministers and teachers whose feet at first were beautiful upon the mountains to the fickle multitude to whom they published salvation and seemed for the moment to "bring glad tidings of good things."

4. Christianity; Nevertheless a Religion for the People.

And yet the religion of Jesus is manifestly fitted and intended to be a religion of the people. And on the part of the people there are not wanting signs of a tacit acknowledgment of its claims in that regard. Its simple announcements, "God so loved the world," etc., "God would have all men to be saved," etc., "If any man thirst, let him come unto me, and drink," have influenced popular thought and feeling in regard to its essential character, scope, and purpose and relation to the race as a whole more deeply than all the creeds, theologies, and theories of the atonement of Christendom put together, whether Augustinian or Pelagian, Calvinistic, Arminian, or Socinian. And if the Christian preacher has no liberty to alter the substance and tenor of the divine message or tone down its solemn admonitions against sin, there is at least promised and pledged to him a heavenly power sufficient to clothe its very terrors with an attractive sublimity and grandeur and make its sternest claim acceptable to thoughtful and worthy souls. On the hard wayside, on the rocky ledge, and among the thorns much of the precious seed he sows will be sure to fall, but sufficient will drop on the more promising soil of " good and honest hearts" to reward his toil, bringing forth thirty, sixty, and even a hundredfold. "He that goeth forth and weepeth, bearing precious seed, shall doubtless come again with rejoicing, bringing his sheaves with him." "Even the dark and solemn theme of corruption," says Dr. Shedd, "expounded by one who has been instructed out of the written revelation and the thronging, bursting consciousness of his own soul—even this sorrowful and abstractly repellent theme, when enunciated in a genuinely biblical manner, fascinates the natural man himself like the serpent's eye. . . . And still more is this true of that other and antithetic doctrine of the divine mercy in the blood of the God-man. This string may be struck with the plectrum year after year, century after century, and its vibration is ever resonant and thrilling, yet sweet and æolian." *

The people will never endure the doom of unforgiven sin and of sinners announced by one who has never felt the incidence of the penalty in his own soul, and the pangs and bitter questionings of an awakened and troubled conscience. But to one who like Paul has been impelled to cry, "O wretched man that I am! who shall deliver me out of the body of this death?" or who like Bunyan preaches to others what he himself "has smartingly felt," or like Charles G. Finney knows by bitter personal experience the intolerable weight of the soul's unlifted load, or like Spurgeon has been driven by the storm of the mind to seek shelter in the harbor of divine mercy at the first opportunity, "the poor, the maimed, the lame, the blind," will come as to a feast prepared, and many will be led to abandon the error of their ways. The Christian Gospel in and of itself has never been unpopular and never will be in its proper constituency. And those who preach it with wisdom, tenderness, earnestness, and power will never want an audience. But he who conveys his message to the people as men carry a dead man to the grave—gently, quietly, solemnly, decorously, and with as little stir as possible—ought not to be surprised if he and his few friends are largely left to bury the corpse alone.

---

* *Homiletics and Pastoral Theology*, p. 33.

248 Ecce Clerus

5. Elements of Power.

The elements of a real power and a serviceable popularity in the pulpit are not beyond the reach of any man who is truly called of God to preach and is willing to submit to the inexorable law of spiritual elevation and achievement. The noblest efforts of the human soul in any department of activity—in art, science, handicraft, philosophy, poetry, eloquence—are always responses to the appeals of things higher and grander than itself. In painting, sculpture, music, literature, there is no upward movement without the tacit recognition of an ideal. And if in all the higher realms of human endeavor a dominating ideal is essential to a true and sustained inspiration, can it be less so in religion, the highest realm of all? The man who by his word would lift men above their ordinary plane of thought, purpose, and attainment must himself be lifted by the word of God. Power over others comes by obedience to the best and truest in oneself. "Rule thyself, thou rulest all," was the favorite maxim of the Greeks. Shepherds of the people in the noble sense that Agamemnon was one ('Αγαμέμνονα ποιμένα λαῶν) are few; but when they appear the best and bravest are willing to obey them. The great orators of Christian history—the Chrysostoms, Athanasiuses, Augustines, Savonarolas, Calvins, Bossuets, Massillons, Wesleys, Whitefields, Beechers, Spurgeons, Simpsons, Durbins, Finneys—the men who nobly succeeded where others signally failed, have been men mighty in the word of God and richly invested with his Spirit's power. They drank like men athirst at the fountain of divine inspiration. They had a whole-souled faith in God's revealed will, and being themselves fully convinced that the Gospel they preached was able to make men "wise unto salvation," they bore that conviction in upon other minds. They loved, studied, understood, wept, prayed over, and preached the everlasting word. And what in other hands was feeble became in theirs "a hammer to break the rock in pieces" (Jer. xxiii, 29). Here, as in other things, the secret of great achievement is the man that wields the *tool*. "Show me," demanded Omar, "the sword with which you have fought so many battles and slain so many thousands of infidels." Amrou unsheathed his scimitar, and to the caliph's ejaculation of surprise and contempt at its common appearance made reply, "Alas! the sword itself without the arm of its master is neither sharper nor more weighty than the sword of Farezdak the poet." *

Dr. Shedd has the authority of the brightest eras in the history of the Christian pulpit for saying, "If sacred eloquence is to maintain its past commanding position in human history, and is to exert a paramount influence upon human destiny, it must breathe in and breathe out from every pore and particle the living afflatus of inspiration. By this breath of life it must live. If the utterances of the pulpit are to be fresh, spiritual, and commanding, the sacred orator must be an exegete. Every discourse must be the elongation of a text."†

The word of God calls for faith—faith in the lofty things of God. And faith in the revealed word, particularly in Him who is himself the eternal Word—the embodiment of all our best ideals, the fulfillment of our highest hopes—gives the sublimity and charm of personal holiness, the courage of conviction, and the accent and emphasis of authority. It begets, too, a sense of utter dependence on God and of utter independence of mammon, the great enslaver and corrupter of gifted and ingenuous souls in every age, and never more than in the present. It puts the preacher near the popular heart—the great weary soul of humanity, with its doubts and fears, sins and sorrows, its craving for affection,

---
* Mills's *History of Mohammedanism*, p. 73. Farezdak was a poet famous for his fine description of a sword, but not equally famous for his use of one. (Pocock's note in *Carmen Tograi*, p. 184.)
† *Homiletics and Pastoral Theology*.

sympathy, and fellowship. It gives him the infinite human yearning that made Lord Shaftesbury so popular with the poor of London, leading him to begrudge himself even the victory over death and the glorious rewards of eternity so long as there were human wrongs to redress and sorrows and miseries to relieve, and forcing from him the pathetic murmur, in his last moments, "How can I die and leave all this unrelieved misery behind?"

CHAPTER XII
The Minister in Authority

Do ye, as elders of the Church, adorn with discipline the bride of Christ—and by the bride of Christ I mean the whole assembly of the Church—in moral purity; for if she be found pure by the bridegroom King, she herself will attain the height of honor, and ye, as guests at the marriage feast, will gain great delights; but if she be found to have sinned, she herself will be cast out, and ye will suffer punishment because, it may be, the sin has happened through your neglect.—*Clementine Epist. Clem. ad Jacob.*

1. No Divinely Authorized Form of Ecclesiastical Polity.

BY his able and scholarly discussion of the organization of the early Christian Churches the Bampton lecturer of 1880 created something akin to a sensation among Roman Catholic and Anglican Churchmen. Employing a method of investigation "which deals with the facts of history by processes analogous to those which have been applied with surpassing success to the phenomena of the physical world, and which have there vindicated their accuracy as methods of research by proving to be methods of discovery,"* he found it necessary to cross-plow an old and well-trodden path, and disturb one of the most fundamental and most familiar of Catholic traditions—the hoary and venerable figment of the divine origin and the unbroken succession from apostolic times of the order and polity of the so-called Catholic episcopate. It was a bold thing for a clergyman of the English National Church and the occupant of an important position in her oldest university to question what almost all her most distinguished theologians and Church historians had regarded as an unassailable article of faith.† But the

---
* Hatch's *Organization of the Early Christian Churches*, p.2.
† Dr. Lightfoot, late Bishop of Durham, is a marked exception to the general rule. See his essay "Christian Ministry" in his Commentary on the Epistle to the Philippians.

claims of truth are ever paramount with candid and cultured minds. With the calm dignity of conviction and the scholarly confidence which is conscious of being sustained by indisputable facts Dr. Hatch affirms his position at the outset, and by an almost overwhelming array of proof drawn from sources mainly contemporaneous with the facts attested proceeds to make it good. "But when," says he "we descend from poetry to fact, from the dreams of inspired and saintly dreamers to the life of incident and circumstance which history records and in which we ordinarily dwell, then, if the evidence shows, as I believe it to show, that not only did the elements of the Christian societies exist, but that also the forces which welded them together and gave them shape are adequately explained by existing forces of human society, the argument from analogy becomes so strong that, in the absence of positive proof to the contrary, it is impossible to resist the inference that in the divine economy which governs human life, as it governs the courses of the stars, by the fewest causes and the simplest means, the Christian societies and the confederation of those societies which we commonly speak of in a single phrase as 'the Visible Church of Christ' were formed without any special interposition of that mysterious and extraordinary action of the divine volition which, for want of a better term, we speak of as 'supernatural.'" Defining his position further, he says, "It may be—nor is it a derogation from its grandeur to say that it *was*—out of antecedent, and, if you will, lower forms, out of existing elements of human institutions by the action of existing forces of human society, swayed as you will by the breathing of the divine breath, controlled as you will by the Providence which holds in its hand the wayward wills of men no less than the courses of the stars, but still, out of elements and by the action of forces analogous to those which have resulted in other institutions of society and other forms of government, came into being that widest and strongest and most enduring of institutions which bears the sacred name of the Holy Catholic Church. The divinity which clings to it is the divinity of order. It takes its place in that infinite series of phenomena of which we ourselves are a part. It is not outside the universe of law, but within it. It is divine as the solar system is divine, because both the one and the other are expressions and results of those vast laws of the divine economy by which the physical and the moral world alike move their movement and live their life."*

2. Early Christian Leaders Indifferent as to Names, Titles, and Specific Forms of Ecclesiastical Authority.

But though the unprejudiced reader feels himself obliged to acknowledge the force of an argument remarkable for its cogency and clearness, he is at the same time unable to suppress a sense of something lacking. He cannot understand why from first to last no reference whatever is made to the distinctive Christian doctrine of authority as stated by Christ and propounded and exemplified by his apostles, all the more as the omission is a fatal one and vitiates the author's whole conclusion. It may be urged that Dr. Hatch is not concerned with the *spirit* and *method* of ecclesiastical authority, but only with the genesis and growth of its historical *forms* and *institutions*. But the former is really the vital and all-important question, compared with which the latter is of little practical account. And it was hardly to be anticipated that a religion whose leading characteristic is its intense inwardness and spirituality would assign an undue importance to external forms—to matters of polity and order, terminology and title. Christianity is never an innovator for innovation's sake. Its mission is one not of destruction or supersession, but of conservation and fulfillment. In its work of renewal and reformation, whether of the individual man, of society, of morals, politics, or methods of govern-

---

* Hatch's *Organization of the Early Christian Churches*, pp. 18, 19.

ment, it proceeds from within outward, not from the outside inward. And it was surely no more wonderful that the visible body of Christ in the world should adopt the names, forms, and functions of approved contemporary magistracies and governments for its various organizations and institutions, as Dr. Hatch insists was the case, than it was that men whose rule of life was "not to be conformed to this world," but "transformed by the renewal of their minds," should yet live as denizens of earth and express the new and divine life within them—their faith, hope, love ; their peace, joy, and consolation, not in some celestial tongue, but in the terms of a world they had professedly abandoned and renounced as being destitute of sympathy with their peculiar aims and a total stranger to their sublime experiences, hopes, and aspirations. Having made its adherents in all their ruling ideas, principles, pursuits, and purposes citizens of heaven,* Christianity is no more concerned as to the particular name or nature of the earthly authority they may choose to institute and obey, whether in Church or State, than it is concerned about the skies under which they live, the clothes they wear, or the architectural style and character of the homes they inhabit.

The early Christian communities manifested no anxiety to find hints in the words of Jesus as to the particular form of ecclesiastical government they should establish.

Though he twice used the word "Church" (ἐκκλησία, *assembly*) as a fitting designation for the gathering of his people, the Christian congregations in Palestine for a long time retained the old Jewish nomenclature for their assemblies and called them synagogues (συναγωγαί). And it remained for the extra-Palestinian communities—Greek, Roman, and Hellenist—to whom Christ himself had no personal mission, to give currency, supremacy, and a fixed significance to the word *ecclesia*.

---

* ἡμῶν γὰρ τὸ πολίτευμα ἐν οὐρανοῖς ὑπάρχει (Phil. iii, 20).

Again, Christ called his followers disciples (μαθηταί); but that authoritative and strikingly significant and appropriate designation was soon to be completely superseded by a nickname—an originally meaningless though now universally accepted and honored epithet. Not from the lips of Christ, but from an unfriendly and scornful Syrian community; not from the land of its *birth*, but from the wider world of its *destiny*, was the Christian Church to receive the name by which its members were to be everywhere known to the end of time. The rabbins of the Palestinian schools, probably hoping to confine a hated sect within an abominated province and preserve Judea and Jerusalem from the stain and scandal of the new religious movement, named the companions of the Lord *Nazarenes* or *Galileans*, but these provincial designations, inaccurate in their application and narrow in their scope, were quietly allowed to drop. The scurrilous wits of the Syrian metropolis made a luckier hit; they called the objects of their scorn and contempt *Christians* (Χριστιανοί),* and the mud stain struck deep and became indelible. The opprobrious epithet, exalted and transfigured in the light of history and by the lapse of centuries, remains. Nor is at all likely that religious people would be any wiser, purer, more exemplary, or more happy if known as *disciples* or by other more frequent epithets of the apostolic age, such as believers (οἱ πιστοί), brethren (οἱ ἀδελφοί), saints (οἱ ἅγιοι), names far more definitely and happily indicative of their calling, character, and relations —rather than as Christians. In the same way it was a matter of absolute indifference to the apostles whether the leaders of local Christian communities, in their day, were called presbyters or bishops.† The same standard of qualification,

---

* Acts xi, 26. In only two other places does the word "Christian" occur in the New Testament (Acts xxvi, 28 and 1 Pet. iv, 16), and in each place it seems to be used as a term of opprobrium. In the thirteen epistles of St. Paul it does not occur once, and yet it must have been familiar to him as a nickname, for it is his traveling companion, Luke, who first calls attention to its use at Antioch.

† This is clear from such passages as 1 Tim. iii, 1–5; v. i, 17. Tit. i, 5–8.

character, and conduct applied to both. The terms are interchangeable. The duties and functions were the same.

3. The New Testament Doctrine of Authority.

But if the Founder of the Christian Church and his apostles left its organization and government in an inchoate and indeterminate condition—to be molded by time and by local needs and circumstances under the controlling hand of Providence, the example of secular governments, the current sentiment of the age, and the growing experience of godly men—they have not been similarly indifferent as to the spirit and manner in which the place of authority is to be occupied, its responsibilities sustained, and its duties and functions discharged. Here, where their teaching was foreseen to be vital to the purity, peace, and well-being of the Church in every land and age, their statements are full, clear, definite, and decisive. That teaching may be briefly summarized as follows :

1. They show that the faculty for spiritual government is a gift of the Holy Spirit, not bestowed by him indiscriminately and at random on every aspirant to place and power, but distributed like the gifts of teaching, prophesying, miracle-working, healing, knowledge and interpretation of tongues to whomsoever he will.* "Blessed art thou, Simon Bar-jona," said Jesus, warmly, in recognizing Peter's primacy in the apostolate, "*for flesh and blood hath not revealed it* (the Messiahship and divinity of the Christ) *unto thee, but my Father which is in heaven.* And I also say unto thee, that thou art Peter, and upon this rock ($\pi\acute{\epsilon}\tau\rho\alpha$) I will build my Church.†

2. The essential qualifications for the exercise of authority in the Church are personal goodness, an unblemished reputation, spiritual insight and sagacity, the possession in a special degree of virtues common, in varying measure, to all

---
* 1 Cor. xii, 11, 28; Eph. iv, 11. † Matt. xvi, 17.

the members of the Christian brotherhood—"the wisdom of the serpent and the harmlessness of the dove." Upon these leading requisites special stress is laid in the injunction given by the apostles to the Church when selection is to be made of the members of the first Christian diaconate. "But, brethren, look ye out from among you seven men of *good report, full of the Spirit and of wisdom*, whom we may appoint over this business."* So indispensable, indeed, are these marks of fitness for the functions of the spiritual rectorate held to be that when the first of the apostles—the holder of the kingdom's keys—yields to motives and impulses below the lofty plane of Christian rectitude, and blindly stumbles on a policy of compromise with the spirit of prejudice and error, his authority is at once challenged and set aside and his fault publicly rebuked by one whose spiritual vision is clearer and more accurate than his own. †

3. The power of authority is a responsibility imposed by God only on those by whom it is unsought, unexpected, and usually undesired. The attitude of our Lord toward mistaken aspirants is typical, and was meant to be extended to all similar cases in all time. To the mother of James and John, craving priority and distinction in the administration of the kingdom for her two sons, his answer was: "Ye know not what ye ask. . . . To sit on my right hand, and on my left, is not mine to give, but it is for them for whom it hath been prepared by my Father."‡ It was the special sin and condemnation of Diotrephes (thought by some to have been a bishop) that "he loved to have the preeminence,"§ and the indelible brand of infamy on the memory of Simon Magus is that he was willing to purchase the gift of God with money as many have in vain attempted to do since his day.

4. The ends for which authority in the Church exists are purely and exclusively altruistic. The whole spirit and

---
* Acts vi. 3.   † Gal. ii. 11.   ‡ Matt. xx. 22, 23.   § 3 John 9.

aim of Christianity are a rebuke of the one crying sin of worldly power, namely, its selfishness displayed in varying but congenial forms, as pride, self-will, self-importance, self-seeking, disregard of the rights of the poor, the weak, the disinherited, the defenseless. Jesus came to make a nobler and tenderer heart beat beneath the vestments and insignia of authority. He called attention to the moral grandeur of self-denial and self-effacement.* He spoke of the beauty of social modesty, of the blessedness of humblest service, of the indisputable primacy and preeminence of those who, though entitled to sit among the first and greatest, are yet content to take the lowest places.† For him the Christian spirit is willing to rule only for the sake of the service it can render. Commenting on the bold request of "the mother of the sons of Zebedee" which had stirred the indignation of their ten fellow-apostles, he said: "Ye know that the rulers of the Gentiles lord it over them, and their great ones exercise authority over them. Not so is it among you: but whosoever would become great among you shall be your servant ($\delta\iota\acute{a}\kappa o\nu o\varsigma$); and whosoever would be first among you shall be your bondslave ($\delta o\tilde{\upsilon}\lambda o\varsigma$): even as the Son of man came not to be ministered unto, but to minister, and to give his life a ransom for many."‡

There was no enormity the apostle Peter was more anxious the elders of the Churches of the Dispersion should avoid than that of *over*-ruling God's heritage.§ Nor was there any personal virtue of which the apostle Paul was more sensitively jealous than of his absolute disinterestedness in the service of the Church. "But I call God for a witness upon my soul, that to spare you I forbare to come unto Corinth. Not that we have lordship over your

---

* Matt. xxiii, 12. † Luke xiv, 9.
‡ Matt. xx, 25-28. In these striking words Christ completely ignores the incident that gave rise to them as an abnormity and contradiction powerless to interrupt the operation of the kingdom's law. It is as if he had said, "This is the order now instituted and existing among you, and never to be changed, namely, ' Whosoever would become great among you,'" etc. § Pet. ii.

faith, but are helpers of your joy."* Expressing near the close of the same epistle his joyful readiness to spend and be spent for the souls of his Corinthian friends, he asks: "Did I take advantage of you by any one of them whom I have sent unto you? I exhorted Titus, and I sent the brother with him. Did Titus take any advantage of you? Walked we not in the same spirit? in the same steps?" and then closes with an avowal of his disinclination to "deal sharply" with the Corinthian delinquents, but rather to use "the authority which the Lord gave" him "for building up and not for casting down."†

It is clear that if the leaders of the Church in succeeding times had kept these obvious facts and principles steadily in sight, her dominion and influence in the world would have been far more widely extended than they are to-day, and her record through the ages would have been very different. Instead of staining her annals with scenes of unseemly contention, of barbaric pomp, of diabolic intrigue and ruthless despotism; with tales of blood and slaughter, of marturial fires, of fiendish torture, imprisonment, and exile of the innocent and the just, her story might have been an unbroken recital of aggressive enterprise, of moral and spiritual conquests won by wise and beneficent government, exemplary citizenship, saintly sufferings, generous sacrifice, and heroic toil. "The light of the moon" in her cloudless sky might have been "as the light of the sun," and the light of her sun might have been "sevenfold."

4. Forms of the Embodiment of Authority in Apostolic and Sub-apostolic Times.

There is hardly anything more interesting in the life of the early Church than the determined effort on the part of the apostles to secure permanent recognition of the lofty ideal of authority the Lord had set before them, in spite of

---

* 2 Cor. i, 23, 24.   † 2 Cor. xii, 17, 18; xiii, 10.

the painful consciousness which they appear to have shared in common, and which they make no attempt to conceal, of the utter hopelessness of the struggle in their own age at least and for some time after.* Content to intrust the Churches they had labored and suffered to found to the most general and vaguest outline of a system of ministry, authority, and government, as if purposely providing liberty and scope for different ages and diverse peoples and varying sets of circumstances to adapt it and mold it into definite shape to meet their own specific needs,† they never weary of placing in bold and striking relief the leading moral and spiritual features of the Christian rectorate,‡ laying special emphasis on the intrinsic blessedness of ministering §—the honor of an oversight which always and essentially means moral exemplification and spiritual leadership, personal primacy in all the gifts and graces of the Spirit, and the virtues of a self-denying, aggressive, and all-victorious faith. The orders instituted and the titles chosen plainly disclose the underlying motive and the controlling aim and purpose. The nomenclature is old and familiar, but it acquires a new and deeper meaning as applied to persons, offices, functions, solemnly set apart to the glory of God in the relief of man's temporal need

---

* 2 Thess. ii, 2. Whatever interpretation may be put upon the "mystery of iniquity" and "man of sin," it clearly refers to an authority in the Christian Church opposed in spirit and purpose to the authority of God. The apostle's admonitory words in parting with the Ephesian elders are full of vivid foreboding (Acts xx, 29 ; see also 2 Tim. iv, 3 ; Tit. i, 11 ; 2 Pet. ii, 1 ; Jude ; 3 John 9).

† "The whole condition of the Churches was plastic; apostles and prophets are placed side by side with teachers, powers, helps, governments (1 Cor. xii, 28). Whatever actual offices may have existed, they are regarded by St. Paul rather according to the general effect which they in common with others might produce upon the life of the Church as permanent orders. Out of them all emerge in the time of the pastoral epistles the two offices of deacons and presbyters. Later on (perhaps some thirty or forty years after) we find the episcopal office rising to preeminence above the presbyterate. . . . It is sufficient to note that the episcopate, like the other offices, was due not to any formal appointment which it would be impious to alter, but to providential necessity, and that a similar necessity has constantly changed its form. . . . The Church . . . is not bound to any one type, but has power to adapt its institutions to the needs of mankind and its own position in the world."—*The World as the Subject of Redemption*, Freemantle, p. 112. See also Hatch's *Organization of the Early Christian Churches*, lecture 1, and Lightfoot's *Christian Ministry*.

‡ 2 Tim. iv, 1-5 ; ii, 22 ; Tit. i, 6 ; 1 Tim. iii, 1-13 ; 1 Pet. v, 1-3.

§ Paul's favorite words are "minister" and "ministering."

and the edification and wardship of his soul. Pagan communities amid which the early Christian Churches were planted had been familiar, for example, with the name and office of deacon (διάκονος) long before the word was whispered or the institution dreamed of among the obscure little groups of Christians, but never before had it been employed to connote and cover so much of moral wealth and worth and such keen and tender sympathy with human distress and suffering; and never before had it required such a rare combination of ethical and intellectual qualities to fit men for its delicate functions. Similarly men had long been accustomed to intrust their municipal, state, and religious affairs to presbyters (οἱ πρεσβύτεροι), as in the case of the Jews; to men having the well-seasoned experience of age, or to gifted minds capable of wise and safe counsels at an earlier period of life (οἱ γερούσιοι), as in the case of the Greeks; to senators, as with the Romans; to aldermen, as with the Saxons; but they never dreamed of demanding that the years which gave the position its specific character and distinctive title should carry into the office such a blending of mature wisdom and goodness as the early Church required of her chosen counselors and rulers. The word *episcopos*, used interchangeably with *presbyteros*,[*] and referring always in the apostolic writings to the same ministerial rank and order, though in a slightly different aspect, was a common designation of a well-known and honored civil functionary—an officer of administration and finance, an overseer of a temple, a dispenser of charitable funds—but it never suggested the all-providing goodness and watchful care of God as it did when it came to be applied to the presbyter who was chosen from among his brethren as almoner alike of God's spiritual and temporal bounty, distributing in almost every town and village

---

[*] The admissions of both mediæval and modern writers of almost all schools of theological opinion have practically removed this from the list of disputed questions.—*Hatch's Organization of the Early Christian Churches*, p. 39.

the thank-offering of the Church to relieve the necessities of widows, orphans, and the poor—presiding as God's representative at the great altar (θυσιαστήριον) of human need, while at the same time dispensing the word of truth and wisdom for the comfort, quickening, and upbuilding of men's souls. "The glory of a bishop," says St. Jerome, in one of his epistles, "is to relieve the poverty of the poor." And many of them acquitted themselves so praiseworthily in this delicate and difficult function that their memories were cherished with gratitude and affection long after they had passed away. The epitaph of one represents him as saying, "My solicitude was this: to clothe the naked who came to me, to freely bestow upon the poor whatever the circling year did yield."* Of St. Tetricus of Dijon an inscription records, "Thou wast the food of the destitute, wast a guardian of widows, didst assume the care of minors, wast altogether a shepherd in every duty."† Of a bishop of Gaeta another inscription says, "Courteous to strangers, he bestowed his very self upon the indigent; those he satisfied with pleasing talk, these with generous aid."‡

"O Eligus," the bereaved people are represented as exclaiming at the funeral of another, "thou delight of the poor, thou strength of the frail, thou protector, and only less than divine comforter of the needy, who after thee will give liberal alms as thou hast done? or who will be our defender, good shepherd, as thou hast been?"§

"It was as becoming thus," says Dr. Hatch, "the center around which the vast and growing system of Christian charity revolved that his function [the presiding presbyter's] of

* Hæc mihi cura fuit nudos vestire petentes. Fundere pauperibus quidquid concesserat annus.—*De Rossi's Bulletino di Archeologia Christiana*, p. 55.

† Esca in opum, tutor viduarum, cura minorum, Omnibus officiis omnia pastor eras.—*Le Blant's Inscriptions Chrétiennes de la Gaule.*

‡ Hospitibus gratus se ipsum donavit egenis. Illosque eloquio hos satiavit ope.—*Mommsen's Inscriptiones Regni Neopolitani.*

§ "O Eligi, dulcedo tu pauperum, fortitudo debilium, protector et impar egentium consolator; quis post te eleemosynam sicut tu dabit largam: vel quis nostri erit protector sicut, tu bone pastor?"—*Vita S. Elig.*, vol. ii, p. 25.

administration overshadowed his function as presbyter, and the name of the latter fell gradually into disuse."* The apostles had deemed the exercise of "prayer and the ministry of the word" the noblest part of the service of God, and they definitely determined to give themselves exclusively to this. But it requires a strong and vivid faith and an intensely spiritual imagination to perceive the superior glory of spiritual service, and this faith and this refined imaginative faculty have not always been shared in an eminent or even in an equal degree by those called to the ministry of salvation. A preference for limited authority and prominence early took the place of the older and wiser preference for unlimited spiritual influence and power; and a desire to rule men supplanted the far nobler longing to save, illumine, console, and edify them. "The gift of ruling, like Aaron's rod, seemed to swallow up the other gifts."

5. Abuse of Power.

It is very evident that between the simple form of presbyteral and episcopal rule in apostolic and subapostolic times and the highly organized ecclesiastical monarchies with which the Church later became familiar there is only the remotest resemblance. In fact, scarcely anything remains to identify them but the name. The careful student of early Church history is, even now, at a loss to account for the complete change which, in a brief period of less than forty years, was effected from the joint and coordinate control of presbyters under the presidency and leadership of a *primus inter pares* in the apostolic age to a widely established episcopal *régime* in the opening years of the second century. Even the earliest post-apostolic writing, the letter of Clement, Bishop of Rome † (circa, A. D. 90), to the disorderly Corin-

---

* *Organization of the Early Christian Churches.*
† Clem. *Rom. ad Corinthios.* Gebhardt and Harnack, Patrum Apostolicorum Opera.

thian Church, though expressly dealing with the question of discipline and government, makes no mention of or allusion to an episcopate in that Church. Clement appeals to the entire body of believers, and asks them to restore their *presbyters* just as the apostle Paul had earlier appealed to the same Church as a whole, insisting on their maintaining and enforcing the principles of a wholesome Christian discipline.

The spirit of assumption once encouraged grew apace. For its early triumphs and rapid spread it was largely indebted to Ignatius of Antioch, whose deep, almost seraphic devotion and lofty ideal of official character and duty make him at once the most imperious and most impressive personality of his age.* It is not difficult to conceive how very different must have been the character and tone of the Christian ministry in more than half of modern Christendom, and how very different must have been the entire current of ecclesiastical history if the Syrian bishop had been permitted to die a natural death among his beloved fellow-presbyters and people in the goodly city of the Orontes instead of having the opportunity of posing as an exultant candidate for marturial honors in the metropolis of the empire. It is certain that few events of the first five centuries exerted a profounder influence on the fortunes of the Church than the martyrdom of St. Ignatius. His letters addressed to various churches on his way to Rome (and there is no need to doubt the authenticity of the shorter Greek recension) contain the deadly germs of more than half the practical as distinct from the speculative, of more than half the internal as distinct from the external, evils from which the Church has suffered. But for these effusions and their unwarrantable episcopal pretensions and claims the world would probably never have heard of the

---

* In his letter to Polycarp the martyr Bishop of Antioch styles himself 'Ιγνάτιος ὁ καὶ Θεοφόρος.

apostolic origin and divine authority of the episcopate. To make room for the bishop of the Ignatian letters the mystical body of Christ—the Bride of the Lamb—has been ruthlessly deprived, one by one, of her most distinctive rights and privileges. Fascinated and stimulated by the totally anti-apostolic and antichristian conception of a bishop who takes the place of God and of Christ in the Church, the ministry of brothers among their brethren—their equals—slowly developed into a hierarchy, overshadowing the Church and arrogating to itself a large part of the common inheritance of the people of God. The "liberty of prophesying," which was shared, as is clear from the Acts of the Apostles and from the epistles of St. Paul, by the whole membership of the Church, irrespective of sex, was restrained. The right to baptize, to administer the sacrament of the Lord's Supper, to actively participate in the discipline of the Christian community, was taken away, and finally it was assumed that the bishop, whom heaven had invested with the power of the apostles in the bestowment of spiritual gifts, was the sole and exclusive channel through whom the Spirit of God was pleased to descend into the souls "either of individual Christians at baptism or confirmation, or of church officers at ordination.*

The whole conception of the Christian Church and ministry underwent radical and essential change, though not without protest, and at length the foundations were laid for

---

* "Little by little those members of the Christian Churches who did not hold office were excluded from the performance of almost all ecclesiastical functions. At first a layman might not preach if a bishop were present, and then not if any church officer were present, and finally not at all. At first a layman brought his own gifts to the altar and communicated there; and then he could only—unless he were an emperor—stand outside the dais upon which the officers stood; and finally, in the East, he might not even see the celebration of 'the mysteries.' . . . By the force of changing circumstances and by the growth of new conceptions the original difference of rank and order became a difference of spiritual power; and a mediæval theologian writing of the same officer whom Justin Martyr describes simply as a president, offering prayers and thanksgiving in which the congregation take their part by the utterance of the solemn Amen! says that 'the orders of the heavenly host, although they enjoy beatitude and want nothing to the sum of felicity, still revere the glory of a priest, wonder at his dignity, yield to him in privilege, honor his power.'"—*Hatch's Organisation of the Early Christian Churches*, p. 128.

the oppressive, ruthless, and wasteful tyranny of the mediæval papacy; and pretexts were provided for the less excusable attempts to force the consciences of men and exercise lordship over God's heritage in later and more enlightened times. The love of power is an essentially earthly passion, and ever resorts to earthly means to obtain its objects. With the extension of the Church's spiritual dominion there has grown the tendency to grasp the sword of temporal power.* A prelate's hold of heaven may be illusory and unreal, and if only he can securely retain the honors, emoluments, pomp, and prestige of office, he is usually content to let the rest go. Not so with his earthly authority and prerogative. He leaves no means unemployed to make these as real and effective as possible. If he cannot save men's souls from error by acts of kindness and arguments of truth and love, he can at least starve, torture, mutilate, imprison, exile, or burn their bodies. And to this his last argument he has not hesitated to resort. He has never scrupled, either as Catholic or Protestant, Arian or Orthodox, Calvinist or Quaker, to use force to coerce the soul where he could do so under legal forms and with impunity. H. T. Buckle, author of the *History of Civilization*, held that genuine religious beliefs that firmly grip men's souls necessarily impel them to persecute in one way or another those who do not share their convictions. And certainly intense faith, unaccompanied by an intenser benevolence of heart, and armed with power to enforce its peculiar dogmas, has uniformly played this rôle. The inconsiderateness, harshness, and cruelty which so often mark the footsteps of authority in the annals of the Church present the most violent contrast to the proverbial

---

* Even so sagacious and careful an historian as Ranke sees some excuse for this. "There was," he says, speaking of the empire of Henry III of Germany, "a principle inherent in the ecclesiastical constitution which opposed itself to a secular influence so widely extended, and this would inevitably make itself felt should the Church become strong enough to bring it into effectual action. There is also, as it appears to me, an inconsistency in the fact that the pope should exercise on all sides the supreme spiritual power and yet remain himself subjected to the emperor."—*History of the Popes*, vol. 1, p. 20, Bohn's edition.

"meekness and gentleness of Christ." The honest fisherman who stood at the head of the apostolate coveted nothing more than the defensive armor of a clear head, a pure heart, and a good conscience, and contented himself with exhorting those over whom he had any influence to be similarly provided.* Later Peters, claiming direct spiritual descent from him of Capernaum, have been less single-minded, presenting startling proof how far divergence from an original type may proceed without attracting special attention or awakening in those most immediately concerned the remotest consciousness of the ever-widening gulf of difference. The apostle John can only complain to his well-beloved Gaius of the malicious prating and high-handed despotism in the Church of Diotrephes, but Cardinal Richelieu puts St. Cyran, the friend of his youth, and the most glorious of contemporary saints, whom he can neither cajole nor terrify, in prison, while he himself spends a considerable portion of his time with the dissolute grandees of the court at the comedy in the Royal Theater.† St. Paul in writing to Timothy complains that "Alexander the coppersmith" did him "much evil." What would he have said could he have been told that in the very city where he wrote, after more than fourteen centuries of active Christian effort to convert the world to God, an Alexander claiming to be shepherd of the universal fold would be guilty many times over of nearly all the sins and crimes condemned in the Decalogue?‡ Polycarp, "the blessed and apostolic presbyter,"

---

* 1 Pet. iii, 14, 15.

† The famous John of Werth was a fellow-captive with the Abbot of St. Cyran in their common prison of Vincennes. Brought from his confinement to witness the sumptuous representation of Richelieu's comedy of "Miriamne" before the king and court, he was invited to express his opinion of the spectacle. He replied that it was magnificent, but what astonished him most was to find in "the most Christian kingdom the bishops at the comedy and the saints in prison."—*R. Lodge's Richelieu*, p. 20.

‡ See Roscoe's *Life of Leo X*. Gibbon, in his *Antiquities of the House of Brunswick*, speaks of Pope Alexander VI as "the Tiberius of Christian Rome," and of his bastard daughter Lucretia as the offspring of "a sanguinary and incestuous race." See Roscoe's Dis., on the character of Lucretia Borgia. "The great object of Alexander through his whole life," says Ranke, "was to gratify his inclination for pleasure, his ambition, and his love of ease." In attempting to poison another he took his own life.

as Irenæus names him, is satisfied to rebuke the arch-heretic Marcion as the firstborn of Satan (πρωτότοκος τοῦ Σατανᾶ) in the public streets of Rome, but Calvin, with the civil power of Geneva behind him, sends Servetus to the flames. The man whose name has conferred the greatest moral and intellectual splendor on the historic see of Alexandria submits to be driven from his people by a popular heretical presbyter of his own diocese and favorite of the imperial court. Archbishop Laud, on the other hand, puts the refractory Puritan clergy of his time to all kinds of pains, penalties, and embarrassments,* citing them before the high commission, scolding and suspending them, expelling them from their cures for "Gospel-preaching," and giving them certain indelible marks of his affection for their souls in sundry mutilations of the organs of the face.† Chrysostom dies in exile, exulting in the presence of the Comforter. Cardinal Wolsey, parasite, tool, and attorney of a lustful and imperious king, dies brokenhearted, bewailing his fidelity to an unworthy master and his infidelity to God.‡ Leo I resists, with hands uplifted in devout deprecation, the rage of the barbarian Attila § and his hordes, as Raphael has nobly pictured him; a later and more martial wearer of the pallium, scorning the ethereal and ghostly weapon of Leo, keeps the proud scion of the House of Hapsburg, Henry IV, shivering in his penitential shirt at the gate of Matilda's impregnable fortress of Canossa through cold days and frosty nights, piteously imploring the forgiveness of his sins and the gift of his hereditary crown.‖ The first of the Gregories, with true Christlike compassion for sheep outside the fold, " scattered abroad

---

*" The great obstacle in his way was the Puritanism of nine tenths of the English people, and on Puritanism he made war without mercy."—*Green's History of the English People*, vol. iii, p. 158.
† Green's *History of England*, vol. iii, p. 167.
‡ *Ibid.*, vol. ii, p. 150.
§ Sheppard, *Fall of Rome and Rise of the Nationalities*.
‖ Stephen's essays, *Hildebrand*.

without a shepherd," sends Augustine with forty companions to evangelize the paganism of Britain.* More than a thousand years after a degenerate and unworthy occupant of the same ecclesiastical throne gloats, with a satisfaction worthy of the devil himself, over the blood and misery of massacred Christians—men, women, and helpless little children. When his shameless correspondent, Catherine de' Medici, jubilantly informed the pope of the slaughter, in cold blood, of seventy thousand Huguenots on the fatal 20th of August, 1572, the heartless hireling thought it a fit occasion for a stately exhibition of public rejoicing. "Innocent III went in solemn procession to render thanks for the victory vouchsafed over his enemies, and struck medals in honor of the deed," says the historian White,† and then asks, "Has that medal been yet thrown out of the collection of the Vatican and broken to pieces by the hangman's ax?" The apostolic rule demands of the *episcopos* "a spirit and attitude of gentleness unto all men, aptness to teach, and patience,"‡ but when Paul IV asked Caraffa, the founder of the Order of the Theatins, "what remedy could be devised" for the doctrinal disputes to which the Reformation had given rise in Italy, Spain, Germany, and other countries, the fierce and gloomy cardinal replied with a proposition which justly entitles him to the unenviable distinction of having been the inventor of the most ruthless engine of spiritual tyranny and oppression known to history. The manuscript life of this man who, armed with the papal bull, published July 21, 1542, gave all his time, energy, and fortune to efforts "to suppress and uproot the errors that have found place in the Christian community, permitting no vestige of them to remain," gives the following rules as drawn up by Caraffa himself, and as being "the best he could devise for promoting the end in view:"

---

* Green's *History of the English People*, vol. i, p. 40.
† White's *History of France*, p. 276.   ‡ 2 Tim. ii, 24; 1 Tim. iii, 3.

"First. When the faith is in question there must be no delay, but at the slightest suspicion rigorous measures must be resorted to with all speed.

"Secondly. No consideration to be shown to any prince or prelate, however high his station.

"Thirdly. Extreme severity is rather to be exercised against those who attempt to shield themselves under the protection of any potentate; only he who makes plenary confession shall be treated with gentleness and fatherly compassion.

"Fourthly. No man must debase himself by showing toleration toward heretics of any kind, above all toward Calvinists."*

The terror spread like a plague. The rancor of contending factions aided the sinister designs of the inquisitors, and men of differing views became each other's bloodthirsty accusers before the dread tribunal. "I tore myself from all those false pretensions," said the learned and renowned Peter Martyr Vermigli, "and saved my life from the danger impending." "Scarcely is it possible," mournfully exclaims Antonio dei Pagliarici, "to be a Christian and die quietly in one's bed." Not inaptly does the historian of his order † describe the melancholy pause of Bernardino Ochino on reaching the summit of Mount Bernard: "When, looking once more back on his beautiful Italy, he recalls the honors he had received there; the countless multitudes by whom he had been eagerly received and respectfully listened to, and who afterward conducted him with reverential admiration to his abode; certainly no man loses so much as an orator in losing his country; yet was he leaving it, and that when far advanced in years. Up to this moment he had retained the seal of his order; this he now resigned to his companion and then turned his steps toward Geneva." Even books were subjected to careful and thorough examination as be-

---

* Ranke's *History of the Popes*, vol. i, p. 159. † Boverio's *Annali*, vol. i, p. 438.

ing suspected of teaching pestilent heresy. "In the year 1543 Caraffa decreed that no book, whether new or old, and whatever its contents, should for the future be printed without permission from the inquisitors. Booksellers were enjoined to send in a catalogue of their stock and to sell nothing without their assent. The officers of customs also received orders to deliver no package, whether of printed books or manuscripts, to its address without first laying them before the Inquisition."*

And this relentless, sleepless, deathless spirit of ecclesiastical despotism is the only one which remains unalterably pagan—the same *after* Christian baptism and the assumption of the Christian name as before. The traditional Peter learns nothing. Theology is a mummy in his keeping. History and its facts and lessons are an impertinence. Historical criticism and investigation of his pretensions make no more impression on him than is made by the flying sparks of the anvil on the blacksmith's dog lying upon the smithy floor. Science lights its torches round him only to make him the more resolutely close his eyes. Adversity and misfortune leave him unsubdued, unmollified. To the claims of advancing truth and freedom he pays no heed. The most solemn and imperative moral obligations are often with him trifles to be played with. The charms of saintly heroism, purity, and devotion never seem to touch his heart. Art, literature, philosophy, music, poetry, eloquence, have often been pressed into his service only to sacrifice, after a time, their freedom, freshness, vigor, leaving his spirit unelevated, unsoftened, by their noble ministries, his purpose unchanged, his policy and methods unmodified. The Ethiopian cannot change his skin, nor the leopard his spots. Within the recollection of living men he has proclaimed himself infallible *ex cathedra*, and lost a short time after, through the sheer shortsightedness of the pro-

* Ranke's *History of the Popes*, vol. i, p. 160.

ceeding, never again to recover it, the last remnant of his temporal sovereignty. We have seen his authority openly confronted and defied on free American soil by one of the most virile, fearless, and popular of demagogues and charlatans, and after many months of apparent impotence on Peter's part we have seen the rebel and maligner subdued, reduced to silence, relegated to obscurity, and brought in an attitude of childlike penitence to plead for mercy and pardon at Peter's feet.* More recently yet we have seen him sternly deny the validity of non-Catholic ministerial orders—both those of Rome-aping Anglicans and those of more independent and uncompromising Protestant churches —and waving aside the solemn overtures and deprecations of one of the oldest and greatest of modern statesmen recently passed away amid the regrets of mourning millions of the English-speaking peoples. And later, still resolutely bent on checking the liberalizing tendencies of American Catholicism at its social, intellectual, political, and hierarchal headquarters, his mailed hand has fallen with such weight, force, and suddenness on leading dignitaries of the Catholic communion in the United States as to make them literally "tremble" beneath its blow. Even to-day eminent sons of the Church, like Gibbons, Ireland, and Keane, are not left unaware of the sharpness and sleeplessness of the sword whose hilt is at Rome, but whose point penetrates everywhere.

But still more to be deprecated is the hurtful influence exerted by the Roman see on the social and intellectual

---

* " In the first centuries, as soon as the pope had been made a temporal sovereign by the King of the Franks, almost immediately, as if Christ had stood there saying, ' My word shall not be gainsaid,' that Roman see fell into the depths of infamy." " The Roman see for a generation or two was the gift actually of bad women." "He [the present pope] is selling out the people everywhere to gain strength for his diplomatic reserves." " And to-day the present dear old holy father actually thinks that the restoration of the temporal power is the one thing that should be done for the hastening of the kingdom of God, that rotten old temporal throne that the providence of God has blasted and blighted and cursed."—Extracts from Dr. McGlynn's sermon in Cooper Union, New York. Compare Dr. McGlynn's article in *The Forum* on his visit to the pope, where a very different tone is adopted.

life and political fortunes of modern nations. Ireland is a
conspicuous case in point. Of late years no people esteeming it a privilege to share the sheltering wing of Rome has
attracted the attention of the world more than the Irish
people. Struggling to advance from their low and obscure
place in the rear of modern nations, there has been cherished in the Irish breast a laudable ambition to taste the
sweets of liberty, autonomy, and national independence.
That ambition has striven to realize itself in ways not
always fitted to secure the approval of enlightened public
sentiment. Unwise and impossible political and social
doctrines have been taught. Crude, clumsy, unworkable
political agencies have been employed. And too often
methods have been adopted whose efficiency and general
application could only be secured by the almost total disregard of every element of mercy, equity, pity, and fair
play. There was exhibited in recent years, on the intensely
tragical stage of Irish life, a good deal of the "wild justice
of revenge," as Mr. Michael Davitt was pleased to call it.
And yet that astute and ever-wakeful politician who at
present occupies the chair and exercises the authority of
the fabulous St. Peter (there is absolutely no reliable evidence of the existence of a Bishop of Rome of that name),
with a wary and wily diplomacy worthy of the age of Hildebrand, kept discreetly quiet all the time. He saw cattle
houghed and maimed, men and women slaughtered, lonely
families almost frightened to death by midnight marauders.
He saw poor peasants ejected in thousands from their miserable cabins, homesteads burned, crops destroyed, and
every form of agrarian outrage perpetrated. He saw that
social anaconda, the boycott, tighten its fatal folds and relentless grip around helpless individual families. He saw
the fierce flames of religious hate rage continuously for
several weeks with murderous effect in a great and popu-
lous city in the north of Ireland. He saw these scattered,

distracted, half-maddened sheep, occupying an ancient and important corner of the great fold over which he exercises pastoral oversight, perpetrate or suffer all these and other evils, while other children of the same race and fold stood on the far-off shores of the American continent violently gesticulating their sympathy with the things perpetrated, or their marked and menacing disapproval of the things their co-religionists suffered. He who presides over the Church of

> The milk-white hind, unspotted and unchanged,

witnessed all this and kept silent—that is, he silently sanctioned it all.

Then suddenly, "like a thunderbolt out of a clear sky," the papal rescript fell into the crowded camp of the Irish nationalists. At first they were startled and surprised at this adverse and unexpected turn of affairs. There was a moment's pause, and then the low, deep growl of discontent, varied now and then by the shrill shriek of defiance. Observing this refractory and insubmissive spirit in large portions of her flock both in America and in Ireland, Rome, true to her traditional policy, slackened the screw and opened the jaws of her vise and mendaciously protested her innocence of hostile action against Irish national aspirations, or of any intention of doing what she had, nevertheless, deliberately done. "Assure the municipal authorities of Dublin," said the telegram of Archbishop Walsh at Rome to the lord mayor of the Irish capital, "that all apprehension of interference by the holy see in Irish political affairs is groundless. . . . Protest by all means at your command in the strongest terms against the action of hostile journals which insult the holy see by representing the pontiff as a political partisan, and, at the same time, make it plain that as Irishmen and Catholics you are not to be misled by any such devices of the enemies of the nationality and faith of Ireland." Such are "the winding and crooked courses" which the great English philosopher, Lord Bacon, designated "the goings of the serpent." And pity 'tis that men's perversity and blindness should provoke the God of light and wisdom to "send them such strong delusion that they should believe a lie." But believe it, after a little angry and helpless protestation, they have always done and probably always will.*

---

* Author's article in *Zion's Herald*, June 6, 1888.

CHAPTER XIII
Some Elements and Phases of Ministerial Life and Character.

Sextons and undertakers [and preachers] are the cheerfulest people in the world at home, as comedians and circus clowns are the most melancholy in their domestic circle.

Nobody supposes there is any relation between religious sympathy and those wretched "sentimental" movements of the human heart upon which it is commonly agreed that nothing better is based than society, civilization, friendship, the relation of husband and wife and of parent and child, and which many people must think were singularly overrated by the Teacher of Nazareth, whose whole life ... was full of sentiment—loving this or that young man, pardoning this or that sinner, weeping over the dead, mourning for the doomed city, blessing and perhaps kissing the little children—so that the gospels are still cried over almost as often as the last work of fiction.—*Holmes*, "Over the Teacups."

1. Past and Present.

IT is intended in this chapter to illustrate briefly, by incident and example, some of those elements and features of ministerial character which preeminently fit men for successful service in the Christian pulpit and pastorate, and win for them the esteem and gratitude of their own and later generations, marking, also, some notable instances of arrested development and degeneration of type.

The ideal pastorate, even in our partial and imperfect conception of it, has never been fully realized but once, and is never likely to be met with again. The model preacher and soul-winner of one age or country is not a standard for other ages and countries.

> The old order changeth, yielding place to new,
> And God fulfills himself in many ways.

It is impossible to conceive of any hero, reformer, martyr,

or statesman of the past being just what he was, saying just what he said, doing just what he did, outside his own age and environment. The man who has most deeply stamped the image of his moral and intellectual personality upon his age has been most profoundly influenced by it in turn; it has colored his beliefs and sentiments, determined the nature and direction of his activities, and affected appreciably his whole character. Though the essence of truth and the leading principles and obligations of morality remain unalterably the same in all times, the method of treatment and form of presentation, as determined by the taste and predilection of any particular period, are always of sufficient account to claim careful attention. He who compares the public teaching of preachers and religious writers of three, two, or even one hundred years ago, as it has come down to us in sermons and theological treatises, with that of men of power and prominence in our own time, sees at a glance the distance that has been traveled in the interval. The body of doctrine is observed to be substantially the same as regards all the leading elements and features of "the faith once delivered unto the saints," but the spirit of the olden time is dogmatic, imperious, polemical; the thought is militant and mail-clad, and the verbal dress antique, odd, and often whimsical. Even in the great ecumenical communion, which makes the proud boast of *semper eadem*, changes more aptly described in their total effect by the epithet *revolution* than by the milder word *reform* distinguish the policy and personal character of Leo X from those of Leo XIII; of Cardinals Campeggio, Pole, and Wolsey from those of Cardinals Rampolla, Manning, and Gibbons. And if within the group of Churches professedly based on the principles of the Reformation a similar comparison be made, the difference between Calvin and Godet, Luther and Schleiermacher, John Knox and Thomas Chalmers, Archbishop Whitgift and Archbishop Benson; or (narrowing the period for comparison) between

Matthew Henry and Joseph Parker, Robert Hall and Charles H. Spurgeon, John Wesley and Hugh Price Hughes, Lyman Beecher and Lyman Abbott, Bishop Asbury and Bishop Foster, is even more striking still.

The intensely spiritual tone of Richard Baxter's preaching, the exhaustively analytical method of John Owen's ministry, the epigrammatic and caustic eloquence of South, the fastidiously choice diction of Andrews, the lucidity and logical acumen of Barrow, would hardly reconcile a modern audience to their extreme prolixity and labored style of thought. Howe's noble sermon on "The Redeemer's Tears Wept over Lost Souls," which produced so powerful an impression in his day, would weary an average congregation in these hurried closing years of the nineteenth century. The massive learning and exuberant ornament of Jeremy Taylor's sermons of "The Golden Grove" would bear him down and bury him in any community—urban or rural—in our day. Stephen Charnock, Timothy Dwight, John Pearson (author of the *Exposition of the Creed*), each preached a complete system of divinity to his people;* they would travel far before finding audiences willing to be parties to a contract of that kind now. Against the steel-cold and self-consistent Calvinism of Jonathan Edwards, Charles G. Finney, quite as passionate a lover of souls and as commendable an exemplar of loyalty to God, openly rebelled, breaking down a gap in the fence of orthodoxy wide enough for the whole ministry of the Calvinistic Churches to escape from the brick fields of Pharaoh, where, as the taskmasters of a morally indefensible doctrine of God, of moral government and redemption, they had been accustomed for generations to impose on men with varying degrees of conviction the duty of making brick without straw—that is, of repenting of sins in which they were, by a divine decree, foredoomed eternally to

---

* President Dwight preached his divinity sermons to the students in the college chapel at Yale; Charnock and Pearson, in the ordinary course of their ministry.

Elements and Phases of Ministerial Life 279

perish. The Five Points of the historic synod of Dort have "folded their tents" and gone. Nobody preaches the Calvinism of Geneva now.

2. Facing Initial Difficulties.

Moral ideals and standards, however, have an authority and value of their own quite irrespective of those changes in theological belief and opinion, in times and circumstances, which so often affect the popular appreciation of them. And there are certain threads of gold present from the first in the warp and weft of noble and powerful natures, no matter what the age or social setting in which their lot is cast. A man's providential designation to usefulness and fame is usually evinced in the manner in which he meets and conquers the difficulties that obstruct his path and challenge his resolution and resources at the outset. Of the portal of the ministry, as of the "kingdom of God," it may be said, "Strait is the gate, and narrow is the way . . . and few there be [comparatively] that find it." While a few distinguished preachers have burst suddenly upon the attention of the world, the divine order for by far the larger number has been to make haste slowly, and to acquire by years of experience and successful toil the fame and power which exceptional ability wins by a single stroke of genius. The profound learning, metaphysical subtlety, and masterly facility and aptitude in debate of the young deacon of Alexandria impressed the fathers of Nicæa, and placed him at twenty-six among the foremost thinkers and teachers of the Eastern Church. At twenty-five John Calvin was not only the first theologian in Europe, but ventured at that early age to attempt through Nicholas Cop, rector of the Sorbonne, the reformation of theological science in the greatest university in Christendom, and, like the great monk of the twelfth century, St. Bernard of Clairvaux, even to offer needful though unpalatable admonitions and counsels to one of the most powerful princes of his age. Calvin's address to Francis I prefacing his *Institutiones Christianæ Religionis* is as remarkable for its sagacity and courage as for its ability and eloquence. As a boy preacher Spurgeon delighted and edified nearly a dozen small audiences in the sparsely populated villages of the English Fen Country for some time before he went to London. Before he was quite twenty he had the entire press of the great city either crying him down as a pulpit clown and theological charlatan or hailing his advent as the Chrysostom of the metropolitan pulpit. Savonarola, on the other hand, was frequently the victim of discouragement and melancholy on account of repeated failure before he suddenly acquired the fascinating and persuasive power over large audiences which marked his wonderfully successful ministry in Florence. Robert Hall did not acquire the confidence and self-possession with which he was accustomed to address large and select audiences without severe self-discipline and many humiliating failures; and even then moments of depression occasionally threatened to drive him from a calling of which he became so distinguished an ornament. Seizing the opportunity of hearing, during a visit to London, Dr. Andrew Fuller preach, he returned home so dissatisfied with his own ministry and so depressed with the precarious condition of his health that he resolved at once to resign his pulpit. But while the officials of his church were endeavoring, with small prospect of success, to bring about the withdrawal of his resignation a somewhat pompous and pedantic brother of the same denomination called on him, late in the week, whom he urged to preach on the following Sunday. The poor performance of the supply had an effect which the arguments of Hall's friends had failed to produce. On entering the minister's vestry after the morning service Hall's deacons were surprised to hear him say to the visiting preacher, "Sir, I am your debtor, unspeakably your debtor, sir," as it seemed to them the sermon was remarkable for nothing except its pedantry and emptiness. "Sir," continued Hall, "your sermon has done me good; it has broken a snare in which the devil had entangled me. I had been up to London and had heard that great man, Dr. Fuller, and was so mortified with myself that I resolved never to preach again. But, sir, I have heard you, and now, sir, I shall preach again with some comfort."

The high standard formed in his early ministry, and strenuously maintained in subsequent years, not only became an occasion of fastidious anxiety to him hardly compatible with the highest aims and motives of the ministerial calling, but also totally incapacitated him to listen with patience to public speakers of average ability. Having accompanied a brother minister to a missionary meeting where the distinguished Wesleyan orator, the Rev. Richard Watson, had spoken with characteristic power and impressiveness, he said to his friend, after hearing a sentence or two of the speaker who followed, "Let us go; this is always the way with showmen—the lions first and the monkeys after."

Two men more unlike than Robert Hall and John Bunyan it would be difficult to name in the same breath. Both were typical Englishmen. Both were men of genius. Both were distinguished as preachers and writers and masters of idiomatic English. The writings of both, by universal consent, have been assigned a place among the classics of English literature. Both did much to elevate the tone and status of the Baptist denomination in their time. But somewhere hereabouts the resemblance ends. The genius of the one was an elaborately polished gem, indebted for much of its luster to academic training and acquisition; the genius of the other was a diamond in the rough, whose light owed nothing to the lapidary of the schools. And while the works of the one lose value as they take on age, the productions of the other steadily retain their place and worth as salable wares in the intellectual market of the world. But in the circumstances of their lives the dissimilarity is even greater than in the character and product of their genius.

Probably not one in a thousand could have emerged from the severe and humiliating discipline of Bunyan's early ministry—continued without interruption for more than a dozen years—with so much to awaken admiration and so little to excite criticism or occasion regret. To most men exposure from day to day to the glances of the passing crowd on Bedford bridge—the proud scorn of one, the tender pity of another, the hideous, malignant merriment of a third, the burning, sympathetic indignation of a fourth, the cold indifference of a fifth—with his little blind daughter at his side, selling the tagged laces made within his prison walls to provide the sightless little angel and his wife and other children some scant means of subsistence—would have been hopelessly crushing. And yet with such a workman, with that old Bedford bridge and jail as scaffolding, and with such pathetic scenes and incidents as accessories, the greatest and alone immortal artist—the providence of God—was slowly and unobservedly painting one of the noblest and most imperishable frescos that adorn the stately dome of modern history, and teaching an object lesson whose significance and power two eventful centuries have not sufficed to exhaust. Of nothing particularly great or good did the opening years of John Wesley's ministry give any promise. Of the career of few men has the familiar phrase *per angusta ad augusta*—through critical and trying circumstances to a state of triumph—been more aptly descriptive. His miserable failure in Savannah—a failure due more to want of tact than to lack of talent, to viciousness of method than to defectiveness of motive—would have been fatal to the prospects of any man less nobly gifted, less evenly balanced, less cultured, less reso-

Elements and Phases of Ministerial Life 283

lute, less high-minded, and less pure. It was during some weeks of wandering among the ancient shrines and monuments of the Catholic Church in Rome and in Sicily in 1833, as he himself records, that the "irrepressible conflict" began in the mind of John Henry Newman between his religious sympathies and his intellectual convictions; between his reverence for antiquity and his reluctant recognition of the clearer and fuller light of his own times, which generated the vacillation and uncertainty that gave birth to one of the most famous though by no means most meritorious of modern hymns,

<blockquote>Lead, kindly Light, amid the encircling gloom,</blockquote>

and culminated in his secession to the Catholic communion in 1846.*

On the destiny of Joseph Ernest Renan, in whom the rationalism of Europe, and particularly of France, found for more than a generation its most scholarly exponent and apostle, the opposition of the demands of reason to the requirements of faith had a very different effect. Designated from childhood to the Catholic priesthood, his faith faltered and finally perished in the skeptical atmosphere of Paris, and, descending the steps of St. Sulspice for the last time, he deliberately disembarked from the ancient, weather-beaten "Ark of Salvation" just at the moment Newman was seeking admission to its proffered security and repose. And while, in spite of a prospect outwardly the most inviting,

---

* In his *Apologia pro Vita sua* Newman relates the circumstances under which the well-known hymn was composed and he himself first became conscious of an impulse toward Rome. He and Hurrell Froude visited Monsignore (afterward Cardinal) Wiseman at the College Inglese and were pressed to repeat their visit, when Newman said, diplomatically, "We have a work to do in England." Subsequently he fell ill of fever in Leonforte, Sicily, and was expected to die. Recovering, he set off for Palermo. Before leaving his inn he " sat down on the bed and sobbed bitterly." To the question of his attendant as to what was the matter his answer was, " I have a work to do in England." " I was aching to get home, yet for want of a vessel I was kept at Palermo for three weeks. I began to visit the churches, and they calmed my patience, though I did not attend any services. I knew nothing of the presence of the Blessed Sacrament there. At last I got off in an orange boat bound for Marseilles. We were becalmed a whole week in the Straits of Bonifacio. Then it was I wrote the lines ' Lead, kindly Light,' which have since become well known." (p. 83.)

Emerson was bidding a friendly farewell to his parishioners in the city of Boston, retiring from the "good fight of faith" before he had incurred many scars,* a young lawyer of a remote New York village, in spite of the cold shoulder accorded him by some of his brethren, and their severe criticisms of his doctrines and methods, was putting his hand more firmly to the plow he had already learned to guide in furrows deep and straight through the moral consciousness of the Gospel-loving communities of central and western New York. Returning from the New Lebanon (N. Y.) Convention, whither, with other notable Congregationalists of the time, he had gone for the purpose of confronting and exposing the supposed errors of Finney and his sympathizers, Lyman Beecher, then at the height of his influence in Boston, casually remarked to the landlord of the hotel where he stopped for dinner, "We crossed the mountains expecting to meet a company of boys, but we found them to be full-grown men."†

3. The Consciousness of Worth.

This sense of worth and of capacity which modestly asserts itself at the start is the same quality which, when subsequently challenged, unfolds itself in painstaking labor, in fidelity to duty, in acts of moral courage and scorn of threatened consequences. In the soul of the man whose masterly intellect framed the iron-clad clauses of the Nicene Creed discerning men saw the self-effacing, self-sacrificing spirit that was ready to defend the doctrines of that historic symbol in the face of repeated banishment and in the continual prospect of death. Men who had known the sincerely devout and calmly resolute spirit of Bernard, the simple monk of Citeaux, were not surprised at the manner in

---

* Hardly anything could be more beautiful than Emerson's last words to his people. See below "Minister in Age, Retirement, and Death."
† Dr. Wright's *Life of Finney*, p. 94.

which, as Abbot of Clairvaux, he swayed large councils like Sens and Vezelay, reprimanded warlike counts, and compelled attention to his counsels on the part of popes and kings.* The Hildebrand of history—self-appointed disposer of princely crowns and dominions—was the most natural evolution imaginable from the sovereign personality who, prior to his investiture with the pallium of the pontificate, had always been greater than any position he had been called to occupy, and had for years practically shaped the policy and controlled the hand of whomsoever happened nominally to hold the helm of power at Rome. Those who are accustomed to look for the presence of law in the successive stages of human development will not fail to perceive that Spurgeon's reply to his anti-Calvinistic critics at the opening of his ministry in London, † and his firm refusal to leave the post of duty for a few months in the later years of his life for a tempting pecuniary consideration which would have proved overwhelming to the weakness of most men, belong naturally to the same sublime moral category, and illustrate with equal pertinence "the final perseverance of the saints."‡ "Who are you?" demanded Mary, Queen of Scots, of John Knox, with a

---

* See J. Cotter Morrison's *Life of St. Bernard of Clairvaux.*

†"A very kind friend has told me that while I was preaching in Exeter Hall I ought to pay deference to the varied opinions of my hearers; that albeit I may be a Calvinist and a Baptist, I should recollect that there is a variety of creeds here. Now, were I to preach nothing but what pleased the whole lot of you, what on earth should I do? I preach what I believe to be true, and if the omission of a single truth that I believe would make me King of England throughout eternity, I would not leave it out. Those who do not like what I have to say have the option of leaving it. They come here, I suppose to please themselves, and if the truth does not please them, they can leave it."
—*Sermons*, vol. 1.

‡ The Redpath Lyceum Bureau having noticed in a Boston paper a statement to the effect that Spurgeon was coming to America, inclosed the paragraph and wrote:

" Boston, Mass., June 22, 1876.

" Dear Sir: Is the above paragraph true? We have tried so long and so hard for many years to secure you that we thought it impossible, and long since gave up all hope. We are the exclusive agents of all the leading lecturers in America. We will give you *a thousand dollars in gold* for every lecture you deliver in America, and pay all your expenses to and from your home, and place you under the most popular auspices in the country. Will you come?"

To this offer Mr. Spurgeon replied in less than two weeks: " Gentlemen, I cannot imagine how such a paragraph should appear in your papers except by deliberate invention of a hard-up editor, for I never had any idea of leaving home for America for some time to come. As I said to you before, if I could come, I am not a lecturer, nor *would I receive money for preaching.*"

characteristic blending of petulance and scorn, when the great reformer urged the claims of Scotland's emancipated thought and awakened conscience to royal consideration. "I am a puir sinfu' mon," was the reply, "but, nevertheless, a vera loyal and profitable subject o' this realm o' Scotland." When one of his bitterest clerical opponents charged John Wesley with "stabbing the Church to her very vitals" he retorted: "Do I or you do this? Let anyone who has read her liturgy, articles, and homilies judge. . . . You desire that I should disown the Church. But I choose to stay in the Church, were it only to reprove those who betray her with a kiss."* The writer remembers passing through a small English hamlet where stands a neat little church in which the founder of Methodism publicly rebuked the wealthiest and most influential man in all the region. The magnate in question had yielded to a fit of unseasonable merriment, laughing immoderately like a rude boy during the sermon. The preacher paused, looked at the offender for a moment with an expression of pain and disgust, and said, "I regard the sneer of a mortal no more than the laugh of a monkey."

4. The Courage of Conviction.

Sometimes this invincible courage ran risks which could hardly be justified under ordinary circumstances, but it seems seldom to have failed to accomplish its object. Of the Methodist Society in the old city of Norwich Wesley writes: "I told them in plain terms that they were the most ignorant, self-conceited, self-willed, fickle, untractable, disorderly, disjointed society that I knew in the three kingdoms. And God applied it to their hearts, so that many were profited, but I do not find that one was offended." † A similar instance of courage, also happily justified in the result, is recorded in Dr. Wright's *Life of C. G. Finney.* In a sermon

---
* *The English Church in the Eighteenth Century*, p. 180.
† Tyerman's *Life of Wesley*, vol. ii, p. 334.

on the "Signs of a Seared Conscience" the president of Oberlin is reported to have waked up the slumbering "moral sense" of his delinquent professional brethren thus : "Just consider the condition in which I found myself yesterday. I engaged a number of men to make the garden and put in my crops ; but when I went to look for my farming tools I could not find them. Brother Mahan borrowed my plow some time ago, and has forgotten to bring it back; Brother Morgan has borrowed my harrow, and I presume has it still; Brother Beecher has my spade and my hoe, and so my tools were all scattered. Where many of them are no man knows. I appeal to you, how can society exist when such a simple duty as that of returning borrowed tools ceases to rest as a burden upon the conscience? It is in such delinquencies as these that the real state of our hearts is brought to the light of day." "The effect of this appeal," says Finney's biographer, "was everywhere visible on the following day. . . . . All through the day farming implements, and tools came in from every quarter. . . . Tools came in that Finney had never owned and never heard of. Where they belonged was more than any man was ever able to tell."*

Nowhere is the holy daring born of a sense of personal worth and an unwavering confidence in God more constantly in demand than in thus proclaiming the Gospel of the grace of God, and in no department of clerical duty is its absence more enfeebling and disastrous. The venerable Dr. Newman Hall tells of a well-known English clergyman that, observing in his audience on one occasion the celebrated Wesleyan preacher, Dr. Morley Punshon, and the still more distinguished temperance orator, J. B. Gough, it occurred to him that he ought to apologize for not being better prepared. "Never mind," audibly protested a parishioner, offended at the minister's undervaluation of the intelligence of his regular hearers, "they are only worms." "Yes," said the

---
* Page 272.

preacher, making matters definitely worse by a crude and precarious speculation worthy of an amateur skolekologist, "but there is a great difference in worms." To one, newly appointed chaplain to Queen Victoria and seeking his advice as to how he ought to preach before the sovereign of England, Dr. Wilberforce, Bishop of Oxford, father of Canon Wilberforce, of Southampton, and of the present Bishop of Newcastle, said: "You will have others in the royal chapel besides the queen—members and servants of the royal household from the highest to the humblest. I would advise you to preach to her majesty with the same affectionate fidelity and earnestness as you would preach to the humblest person present, or your effort will be a failure." The man who has never felt the majesty and greatness of God in such a manner as to realize the littleness and feebleness of man lacks one of the most elementary and most vital qualifications for the ambassadorship of the cross. "You have imitated David in his sin, imitate him in his repentance," was the firm insistence of St. Ambrose as he interdicted the Emperor Theodosius from entering the Church after his merciless massacre of the citizens of Antioch. "He has done his duty, now let us do ours," was the reply of Louis XIV to one who suggested that the speech of Bourdaloue, the court preacher, had been unbecomingly plain and pungent. "Isaiah is very bold" can only be said of the prophet who has seen "the Lord seated upon a throne, high and lifted up," with "his train filling the temple."

5. The Sense of Humor, Pathos, and Romance.

No less essential than the heroic qualities just described and quite as truly a gift of God is the readiness to recognize the claims of the minor and more equivocal phases of human nature—the wit and sparkle, the humor, pathos, and romance, the depth and tenderness, of the soul—items which are all duly sampled and sanctioned in the greatest and divinest of books. The author of *Over the Teacups* sees in the words, "Thou art Peter [*petros*], and upon this rock [*petra*] will I build my Church," the playful humor that delights in punning, and though when he suggests this a "teacup" warns him against stepping with sandaled feet upon holy ground, the case is still a clear one.* "Go ye and tell that fox," etc., is a flash of sarcasm razorlike in its keenness, and irony is obvious in the words, "Full well do ye reject the commandment of God, that ye may keep your tradition" (Mark vii, 9). If in the writings of any author noted for pregnant and pithy sayings, from Solomon to Sydney Smith, the words concerning the symbol of political subjection— the penny bearing the image and superscription of Cæsar— had been found, "Render to Cæsar the things that are Cæsar's, and to God the things that are God's," they would have been in everybody's mouth as a precious scintillation of superlative wit. And as for the romance of emotion, Peter's tears in the twilight outside the Hall of Judgment, and Paul's parting with the Ephesian elders on the Milesian shore, to say nothing of the scene at the grave of Lazarus, or that at the entering in of Nain, or that in the descent of Olivet, when "he beheld the city, and wept over it," are examples of pathos unsurpassed in any other literature.

In such scenes and situations a minister's life abounds. In the pulpit and among his people he plays on a harp "of divers tones," and he himself is a harp in turn, played upon, whether he will or no, by artists or amateurs of varying purpose, character, and capacity. Hamlet, with his suspicions aroused, may protest against being played upon like a flute, but Hamlet *off* guard leaves the gateway of the soul open to influences and impressions from without like the rest of us. No other professional man touches so many aspects of existence and elicits so many latent feelings of the soul as the Christian minister. No other man's plum-

---
* Page 61.

met goes so deep down into the ocean of human life. While the physician, the lawyer, the statesman, the philanthropist, the philosopher, the novelist, the poet, are not obliged to concern themselves with anything more than surface phenomena, he is often overboard in troubled waters—fathoms deep. A close and sympathetic student of life and of the soul in all their variety of mood, motive, susceptibility, and experience, his vocation broadens him beyond the limits of his sect or creed, and his wide contact with life, in its manifoldness and complexity, convinces him that there are more things in heaven and earth than are dreamt of in any man's philosophy. He finds that there are heads as long and level, wits as quick and nimble, hearts as pure and tender, and lives as noble and exemplary, as his own, even if self-esteem permit his concession to go no farther; that the human soul is deeper and richer than he had imagined, and is capable of a fuller and more varied expression than he had ever thought of, and that the neglected chord, touched carelessly and at random, it may be by the wayside, often vibrates with a response of surprising brilliance, fullness, and power. Dr. Jobson, at one time president of the Wesleyan Conference, during an official visit to Ireland was astonished to hear the fervid eloquence of gratitude and benediction which flowed from the lips of a poor Irish woman to whom in a preoccupied moment he had thrown a penny. "May your honor live," she said, "until every hair of your head is grown into a mold candle to light your honor to glory."

It was in a typical Scotch home, redolent of theological lore and disquisition, that the laugh was turned on Dr. Punshon, when, on being asked after dinner to take an apple, he replied, "No, thank you, I do not care for apples;" thus provoking the happy sally, "Then ye sho'd ha' ben in Paradis' and ther' wad' na ha' been a Fa'." Like lightning itself the flash of genius comes, unheralded, and from unexpected quarters. It is often surprising to what an extent the beastliest vices leave the mental faculties unhampered and unclouded, suggesting the necessity of treating every creature bearing the image of God, regardless of character or condition, with respect and consideration.

Ian Maclaren, in his *Auld Lang Syne*, has not overdrawn in the person of Posty, the whisky-loving village letter carrier of Drumtochty, that painfully interesting character, the pious drunkard—black sheep of almost every fold and burden of every faithful pastor's heart:

"'Sit down, Posty, sit down. I am very glad to see you.' 'Thank ye, sir,' said Posty, in his dryest voice, anticipating exactly what Cunningham was after, and fixing that unhappy man with a stony stare which brought the perspiration to his forehead. 'There is one thing, however, that I wanted to say to you, and, Posty, you will understand that it is a—little difficult—in fact, to mention,' and Cunningham fumbled with some Greek proofs. 'What's yir wull, sir?' inquired Posty, keeping Cunningham under his relentless eye. 'Well, it's simply,' and then Cunningham detected a new flavor in the atmosphere, and concluded that Posty had been given into his hands, 'that—there's a very strong smell of spirits in the room.' 'A' noticed that masel', sir, the meenut a' cam in, but a' didna like to say onything aboot it,' and Posty regarded Cunningham with an expression of sympathetic toleration. 'You don't mean to say,' and Cunningham was much agitated, 'that you think—' 'Dinna pit yersel' aboot, sir,' said Posty, in a consoling voice, 'or suppose a' wud say a word ootside this room. Na, na, there's times a'm the better o' gless mysel', and it's no possible ye could trachle through the Greek withoot a bit tonic; but ye're safe wi' me,' said Posty, departing at the right moment."

But it is not in their lighter moods and more propitious circumstances that the clergyman obtains the broadest and clearest glimpses into the life and character of his people. The deepest and truest sympathy and warmest sense of brotherhood come more through broken hearts than brilliant repartee, and souls are closer drawn together by communion in sorrows than by fellowship in joys. "All sorrows are sisters," says Sabatier. "A secret intelligence establishes itself between troubled hearts, however diverse their griefs. Suffering is the true cement of love. For men to love each other truly they must shed tears together."* "Whom the Lord loveth he chasteneth." And the moral worth and beauty that are pleasing to God also attract the admiration of men. The rarest and choicest spirits in a minister's circle of friends and acquaintances are often the uncomplaining martyrs of affliction, bereavement, ill fortune, and narrow circumstances, just as it is the crushed plant that yields the aroma. "Prosperity," says Lord Bacon, "is the blessing of the Old Testament, adversity is the blessing of the New, which carrieth the greater benediction and the clearer revelation of God's favor. Yet even in the Old Testament, if you listen to David's harp, you shall hear as many hearselike airs as carols; and the pencil of the Holy Ghost hath labored more in describing the afflictions of Job than the felicities of Solomon."† No faithful pastor needs to be warned against hearing with "a disdainful smile"

> The short and simple annals of the poor.

Nor do his observation and experience confirm the impression that "penury" tends to chill and "repress their noble rage,"

> And freeze the genial current of the soul.

Travelers in Europe often comment on the deeper and steadier piety of the Swedish, Norwegian, and Muscovite peasantry, and their greater loyalty to their religious leaders and instructors amid the poverty and hardship of their earthly lot, as compared with the more favored dwellers in

---

* *Life of St. Francis d'Assisi,* p. 25.
† Essays, *Adversity.*

the sunnier and richer lands of southern Europe, such as France, Spain, and Italy, strongly reminding one of Tennyson's lines ascribing to the one the characteristics of fickleness and love of change, and to the other the attributes of firmness and fidelity:

> Swallow, swallow, swallow flying south,
> Dark and true and tender is the north.

The periods reputed golden in the history of every religious movement are those early days when pastors and their people were drawn or driven into intimate and heartfelt fellowship with each other either by a community of faith, love, hope, and aggressive spiritual purpose in the one case or by hardships, perils, poverty, and persecution in the other. No page in the history of Scotland is richer in ideal characters, in noble thought and feeling, heroic behavior, and romantic incident than that which chronicles the story of the Solemn League and Covenant. The Quakers of to-day, with all their increased wealth and refinement, do not appeal to the deeper religious sentiment and compel the moral admiration of mankind as did their fathers in the troubled days of George Fox * and William Penn. Puritan and Pilgrim, honorably distinguished in the early half of the seventeenth century for their intense religious earnestness, keen spiritual vision, and cherished sense of the presence of the Eternal, were early shorn of their moral strength and grandeur by careless coquetting with the

---

* As Fox stood gazing earnestly upon the people of Lancaster they cried out in wonder, "Look at his eyes;" yet those keen and piercing eyes, as his latest biographer, Hodgkin, notes, "shed tears of sympathy with the sorrowful, and there was something in his face which little children loved." "The wrathful constable who forbade him to speak at Devonshire House meeting was instantly quieted by his words and the gentle touch of his hand, and left him respectfully alone. The red-skinned hunters in Delaware, very vaguely understanding the drift of his discourse, sat soberly listening with stately courtesy."

"You may break in upon them," says Professor Masson, author of *John Milton and His Times*, speaking of the early Quakers, "hoot at them, roar at them, drag them about; the meeting, if it is of any size, essentially still goes on till all the component individuals are murdered. Throw them out at the doors in twos and threes, and they but reenter at the windows and quietly resume their places. Pull their meeting house down, and they reassemble next day most punctually amid the broken walls and rafters. Shovel sand or earth down upon them, and they still sit, a sight to see, musing immovably among the rubbish."

charms of the Philistinian Delilah. From their colony of Hernhutt amid the forests of Lusatia the Moravians a century and a half ago sent their missionaries to the ends of the earth, revived the dying fires of religion in many Christian countries, and supplied materials for one of the noblest and most fascinating chapters in the history of Christian missions. And Methodism, whose founder always confessed to have lit his torch at the hearthstone of the Moravians, presented in its journals, biographies, and ecclesiastical chronicles a gallery of characters quite unique in its variety and interest before it began to forget the days of deep emotions, exalted aims and ideals, incessant spiritual conflict with the devil, and generous personal and pecuniary sacrifices for the sake of the sheep that are scattered abroad without a shepherd. "Sick or well, I have my daily labors to perform," pathetically wrote Asbury, the first bishop of the Methodist Church, in 1807, as he wearily pushed forward to New York. "I am hindered from that solitary, close, meditative communion with God I wish to enjoy. I move under great debility." Approaching the city, he says: "I found old Grandfather Budd *worshiping, leaning upon the top of his staff—halting, yet wrestling* like Jacob. O! we remember when Israel [the Methodist denomination in America] *was a child*, but now, *how goodly are thy tents, O Jacob, and thy tabernacles, O Israel*."

"Ah! what is the toil," he elsewhere observes, "of beating over rocks, hills, mountains, deserts, five thousand miles a year!—nothing, when we reflect it is done for God, for Christ, for the Holy Spirit, the Church of God, the souls of poor sinners, the preachers of the Gospel in seven Conferences, one hundred and thirty thousand members, and one or two millions who congregate with us in the solemn worship of God—O, it is nothing!" Making every allowance for difference of times and circumstances, it would perhaps be difficult, if not quite impossible, to duplicate the inimitable pathos of the following incident anywhere in the wider world of present-day Methodism. Accompanied in his tour through New England in 1807 by a preacher named Joseph Crawford, as the travelers approached New York city it was necessary for them to bid each other farewell. "He came over the ferry with me," says Asbury. "When about to part he turned away his face and wept. Ah! I am not made for such scenes! I felt exquisite pain." "It is a tendency of minds of a superior order," remarks Dr. Stevens, the Methodist historian, "to conceal the intensity of their emotions, but at times the heart reveals itself in spite of the head, and the strong man armed is found to carry under his cuirass of strength the sensitive affections of the child." The truth is, in natures deeply religious the Holy Spirit gives every susceptibility, faculty, and affection its proper place and function, and finds for each a legitimate channel of expression. The natural enemy to this liberty of the soul is material prosperity, with its ever-multiplying cares and the worldly absorption to which it ordinarily leads. These tend to dry up the fountain of holy emotion and harden the feelings. Luxury and ease vulgarize the mind by excluding its deepest and purest experiences. With a few notable exceptions men who acquire property grow temporarily rich and spiritually and eternally poor by a law almost as steadfast and invariable as that which governs the movements of the stars or the ebb and flow of the tides of the ocean; and

> Ill fares the land, to hastening ills a prey,
> Where wealth accumulates, and men decay.

CHAPTER XIV
Ministerial Health and Hygiene

'Εχομεν δὲ τὸν θησαυρὸν τοῦτον ἐν ὀστρακίνοις σκεύεσιν.—*St. Paul.*

1. Importance of Attention to Hygiene.

THOUGH it does not fall within the scope of the author's purpose to discuss, at any length, the general question of physical health and exercise, such a task being rendered wholly needless by the existence of many works on the subject of acknowledged merit and wide renown, yet since bodily vigor and well-developed physical powers are nowhere of greater value or more absolute necessity than in the labor-loving and honored guild with which these pages are concerned, some reference to clerical hygiene may fairly claim a place here.

It has often been maintained by distinguished medical experts that brain-workers as a class enjoy advantages favorable to the cultivation of physical strength and endurance and to the extension of the limited term of life that are not shared to the same extent by other men. "I have ascertained," says an eminent physician,* "the longevity of five hundred of the greatest men in history. The list includes a large proportion of the most eminent names in all departments of thought and activity. The average of these was 64.20." Others, like Dr. Madden, have made similar investigations, with the result of showing a yet longer average term of life of hard mental toilers.

But even still more important than the question of longevity as depending on the physical condition is the question as to quality and tone of life, and the value of its moral and

---
* Dr. George M. Beard, of New York.

intellectual products as influenced by the state of bodily health. "I compare the life of the intellectual," says Hamerton, " to a long wedge of gold—the thin end of it begins at birth, and the depth and value of it go on indefinitely increasing till at last comes Death . . . who stops the auriferous processes. O, the mystery of the nameless ones who have died when the wedge was thin and looked so poor and light ! O, the happiness of the fortunate old man whose thoughts went deeper and deeper like a wall that runs out into the sea ! " We may freely admit with the same writer that "a life without suffering would be like a picture without shade ; " that "the pets of nature who do not know what suffering is, and cannot realize it, have always a certain rawness, like foolish landsmen who laugh at the terrors of the ocean, because they have neither experience enough to know what those terrors are nor brains enough to imagine them;"* yet it cannot be denied that the close union and sympathy existing between the material and spiritual parts of our nature make an afflicted and feeble *body* a hindrance and burden to the *soul*, and therefore the minister who would offer the noblest possible service to his age must keep "the earthen vessel" as sound and strong as possible for the sake of the precious spiritual treasure it contains.

2. Influence of Health on Character and Temperament.

It has not been sufficiently noted that apart altogether from the character which is the gradual and growing result through life of education, of social environment, personal habits, occupation, reading, study, and the like, each individual has a *natural* character which is conferred exclusively by physical temperament, and the healthy or morbid manifestations of which are determined largely by the state of bodily health. This subtle and potent factor of temperament is more or less present in all mental and moral action, and though it may

* *The Intellectual Life.*

be modified, controlled, improved, by the presiding mind, it can never be entirely suppressed or even materially changed. "Did not daily experience bear out the conclusion that the manifestations of mind are influenced by different states of the body in general and of the brain in particular; did we not constantly see the effect of various bodily changes—of the irritation of disease, of the influence of medicine, of returning health, of advancing age, and of a thousand other causes acting only on the organ—it would be very simple *a priori* reasoning that if the brain be the manifesting organ, which all admit, these manifestations must take a tinge from the medium through which they pass; just as water, a simple element, takes its character from the soil through which it has passed; or the air becomes impregnated with the aroma of flowers or with the various noxious exhalations; or as the rapidity of a current is influenced by the nature of its banks, the declivity of the country through which it passes, the obstacles it encounters, and a thousand other circumstances, permanent or accidental."*

3. The Inner World of Thought and Feeling Acted on by the Outer World.

So far, therefore, as the expression of thought, feeling, and purpose is influenced by physical temperament it is placed under the control of physical laws. At this point we stand, as moral and intelligent beings, in living contact with the outer world and occupy common ground with the rest of the animal creation. We are subject to physical *stimuli* from within and from without, as well as influenced by moral motives. All the raw material of knowledge as well as those appeals that test, exercise, develop, and strengthen the moral principles come to us from that cosmic panorama which, with its thousand objects, animate and inanimate, is ever moving before our wakeful senses, but beyond whose sensuous rep-

---

* Newnham's *Reciprocal Influence of Body and Mind*, p. 108.

resentations we are powerless to penetrate, and our utter ignorance of whose substratum we conceal by calling it the *material world*. "The whole mass of what may be called human knowledge (that is, of those objects and facts respecting which the mind has clear, perfect, and satisfactory perceptions) is limited to the evidence of the senses, and even the purest branch of it, *geometrical and mathematical truth*, rests ultimately on material ideas, on forms and qualities suggested by impressions made on the organs of sensation. The moment we dismiss these palpable guides to what is real and true we get within the confines of uncertainty. The regions of abstraction may be delightful, but they are a land of shadows filled by forms without substance and appearances destitute of actual existence. The honest though humiliating fact is that, laying aside those truths which are revealed to us by God in his own sacred word, we have no perfect knowledge here below of anything that lies beyond the limits of matter. All the attainments and all the powers which distinguish the most humble from the loftiest mind, the result of scientific research and the deepest knowledge of the facts, the combinations of genius, and the creations of fancy are originally derived through the medium of the senses, and *depend on the more or less perfect and delicate conformation and condition of the material part of our frame* . . . the fountain from which they spring and the channel through which they flow."*

With this view of man's intellectual constitution and relation to the world of ideas the advocate of the transcendental philosophy can hardly be expected to agree. Yet it is always likely to be a popular view, inasmuch as it offers an explanation of the genesis of human knowledge and of the nature of mental phenomena more in harmony with unsophisticated common sense, and more acceptable to the average mind than any other. And if this doctrine of man's rela-

---

* Warner's *The Anti-Materialist*.

tion, as an intelligent being, to the material universe has any truth in it, it is difficult to overrate the importance of maintaining in a sound and healthy condition that department of his bodily nature—the nervous system—which forms the borderland or meeting place between the moral and the physical, spirit and matter, heaven and earth. So far from being a point of second or third rate consequence, the gravest moral problems are really involved for the individual in the question of personal health and hygiene, and for the state and municipality in the wider question of public sanitation. The human body and soul are joined together by the Creator in an indissoluble partnership and a mutual interdependence essential to the integrity and completeness of our nature, and the farther our civilization advances the more complete this interdependence becomes. "Under our fashion of living the body seems to require greater and greater attention from the mind, and the increasing mental strain assumed under our restless, hurrying life makes a greater and greater demand on the vitality of the body."[*] "The very object of this letter," says Philip Hamerton in his delightful treatise, *The Intellectual Life*, is to recommend for intelligent purposes the careful preservation of the senses in the freshness of their perfection; and this is altogether incompatible with every species of excess. If you are to see clearly all your life, you must not sacrifice eyesight by overstraining it; and the same law of moderation is the condition of preserving every other faculty. I want you to know the exquisite taste of common dry bread; to enjoy the perfume of a larchwood at a distance; to feel delight when a sea wave dashes over you. I want your eye to be so sensitive that it shall discern the faintest tones of a gray cloud, and yet so strong that it shall bear to gaze on a white one in the dazzling glory of sunshine. I would have your hearing sharp enough to detect the music of the spheres if it were but au-

---

[*] E. Checkley's *Method of Physical Training*, p. 30.

dible, and yet your nervous system robust enough to endure the shock of the guns on an ironclad. To have and keep these powers we need a firmness of self-government that is rare."

Physical life lived according to this code would be literally a continual eating, drinking, and breathing of vitality in its purest form from the fountain of universal life, in harmony with that ancient doctrine of the "breath of life" that was breathed into man at the beginning when "he became a living soul"—a doctrine, by the way, which modern materialistic science * has labored in vain to supersede or discredit. "The most probable view," says that eminent English physician, Sir Benjamin Ward Richardson, "is that we actually feed on the vital force that endows us with mere motion; breathe it in the atmosphere in which the force once set in motion can continue to be set free; that we are, in fact, subdued fires burning passively in that invisible envelope, which itself will not burn, but will let us burn with it."

4. Health and Longevity Largely within the Limits of Individual Control.

To many strong and well persons health and longevity seem to be so much questions of heredity and original constitution, and therefore matters so little within the limits of individual control, that they feel justified in dismissing all serious thought in regard to them as far as they are personally concerned. And the fact that, while every member of the race is inevitably exposed to certain general conditions of life on the globe which are inimical to perfect bodily health, there is yet an astonishing hereditary *wealth of individual life in certain families, gives some color of truth to this assumption.* " It may be laid down as a general rule,"

---

* See "Physiological Consideration of Life-Force," by W. Xavier Sudduth, M.D., D.D.S., in *The American System of Dentistry*, edited by F. F. Litch, M.D., vol. i, p. 512.

says Dr. Richardson, "that certain external conditions of life tend to level the duration of all lives. Still, some persons escape conditions which others do not escape. Why? To this question I can see but one answer, but it is an answer which is every day yielded by experience and observation. It is that those who escape longest the freedom of external conditions telling against life possess an equal balance of good working organs of the body, not one of which is specially inclined to take on any form of disease of a particular kind, such as tubercle or cancer. The whole body, therefore, continues to work in all its parts in harmonious order of function, and by the steadiness of functional work the continuous life is maintained. Life, in short, is maintained by equality of perfection in every organ. And this is what is really meant by a good constitution, whenever that term is correctly applied. The frame of the body which offers this goodness of constitution may be small; strangely enough it may even be indifferently developed, and yet, by evenly distributed soundness of organic parts, it may continue in action longer than a larger and more finely developed frame which, pierced in one vital organ by disease, succumbs beneath a single organic failure." *

This hereditary physical sanity and wealth of life, then, is no mere accident. It is the cumulative result of wise self-government, of regular habits, of careful observance of great hygienic principles, extending back through many generations; for in this way the just providence of God visits the wisdom and virtue of "the fathers upon the children unto the third and fourth generation." "I have of late years," says the distinguished authority above quoted, "carefully noticed the relationship of family longevity to what may be called family individuality, and the fact I have arrived at is that, though individual vitality may run through a line of persons connected by blood relationship,

---

* *Ministry of Health*, p. 159.

it is not universal in that series, *but belongs only to particular members of it who by their own personal care or good fortune conserve the vital endowment that has descended to them.* What is more, I have observed that the prolonged vitality shown by individuals is not necessarily connected with any great beauty of form or muscular power, or even power of physical endurance. It is connected rather with facility of constitution to take rest, to accept anxiety with serenity, annoyance without passion, and success or pleasure without excitement or overweening gratification." *

5. Moral Value to the Minister of Sound Bodily Health.

He, therefore, who would at once acknowledge his debt of gratitude to a noble ancestry from whom he has inherited that rarest and most precious of all earthly possessions—perfect sanity of body and mind—and discharge his responsibility to those who in future ages may "spring from his loins," will see clearly that the supreme object to be kept in sight in all athletic exercise and hygienic methods is not the temporary and abnormal development of certain organs and functions of the body, but the promotion and preservation of a condition of sound general health. And this, which is a matter of incalculable importance to men in all professions and pursuits, is especially so to the clergyman of this busy and exacting age. His physical condition affects his work in its quality and tone for good or evil at every point—in the pulpit, in the study, by the bedside of the sick, in the home made sad by temporal misfortune or desolate by death, among the select circle of friends at a marriage ceremony, or in the ordinary social gatherings of his people. In all these spheres a superabundant physical vitality, supporting and stimulating an alert, cheerful, carefully cultivated mind, acts like sunshine on all around him, while a timid, retiring manner or a morbid and melancholy

---
* *Ministry of Health*, p. 170.

temperament—usually the result of overstrained and depressed nerves—irritates and repels the inconsiderate, and awakens feelings of pain or pity in gentler and kindlier souls. The present writer has few more painful recollections than that of hearing one of the most excellent of men—an able preacher, a devout and successful pastor, deservedly high in the esteem and appreciation of his people—ask at the weekly prayer meeting, in reference to some words which he feared might have given offense, to be forgiven and excused for uttering them, on the ground that they were spoken in a moment of excessive nervous excitability. He has since been obliged to retire from the work he so much loved.

It is altogether inexcusable, at this late day, when everything relating to the moral, social, industrial, and sanitary well-being of the people is eagerly discussed, when the royal road to health and happiness is neither hard to find nor difficult to follow, that any man should be so far behind his age as to imperil health, moral reputation, and professional efficiency by obvious hygienic error. And yet not a few men who begin their ministerial career with a fair amount of bodily vigor, with brilliant intellectual gifts and well-trained powers, with high moral ideals and purposes, and with the confidence and good will, withal, of a large circle of admiring friends, become by overwork and worry, or by neglect of the simplest laws of health, the victims of physical decay, the prey of various nervous maladies, of fits of melancholy and mental depression, of misgivings and miseries, doubts, and fears—of a species of mental and moral decrepitude, in a word, almost more to be dreaded than the "seven last plagues"—long before their sun has reached the meridian!

6. Notable Instances of Early Physical Breakdown.

From the days of the apostle Paul, whose thorn in the flesh—whatever it may have been—became as the angel of Satan sent to humiliate and harass him, down to the latest young clergyman of promise who died within the first decade of a brilliant and powerful ministry because he imagined he could not spare the time or take the trouble to "learn to breathe"—having been breathing very well all his life—there are few things more painful to contemplate than the early impairment or untimely termination of the work of great and serviceable souls. "Perhaps I might have lasted longer had I leaned my back against a tree," was the pathetic exclamation as he lay dying, a little over fifty years of age, of one of the most devoted and most successful of the men for whose fruitful labors and far-reaching influence for good the world is indebted to the astute ecclesiastical statesmanship and organizing genius of the founder of Methodism. And yet no one who reads with discrimination the interesting record of the herculean labors of that most saintly and most unselfish man can fail to see that it was not so much occasional rest that was needed as a little more careful observance of the obvious limits of human endurance and of the inviolable laws of health. Admire as we may the lofty aims, the self-consuming zeal, the splendid success, of Xavier in the Orient, one cannot but regret that the fine spiritual instinct that led to a complete surrender of "his heart to the Purifier and his will to him who governs the universe" did not prevent him from imagining that verminous bodily filth was an essential element of Christian humility and self-mortification. As Sir James Stephens observes, Xavier's faith "bade him look on this fair world as on some dungeon unvisited by the breath of heaven. . . . At her voice he starved and lacerated his body, and rivaled the meanest lazar in filth and wretchedness."* He perished on the shore of Siam even more a martyr to dirt and disease than to his zeal for the salvation of the heathen, great as that was. Nor with all one's reverence for the extraordinary abilities and exalted character of the man who "by his labors as a translator placed

---

* *Ignatius Loyola and his Associates.*

portions of the Scriptures within the reach of all who could read over one fourth of the habitable globe," can one's calm and discriminating judgment approve of Henry Martyn's prodigal expenditure of strength amid the perils of a climate for which, at the outset, his friends thought his frail frame totally unsuited.* And who can listen to the cry of David Brainerd as he kneels in his solitary hut amid the primeval forests that flanked the Susquehanna and Delaware Rivers in his day—" O, that I were a flame of fire in the Lord's service;" "O, that I were pure spirit, that I might be active for God"—without feeling that it is the aspiration of one whose zeal o'erleaps the limits of nature, and that the style of self-sacrifice to which it leads, though morally grand, is physically considered only a thinly disguised suicide? There is an expressible and yet characteristic pathos in Brainerd's last words, when, at the early age of twenty-eight, worn out by sickness, solitude, morbid introspection, and frequent exposure to midnight damps by sleeping in trees or by a fire of pine logs in the open forest, he exclaimed, just before closing his eyes on all mortal scenes at the house of Jonathan Edwards, in Northampton, "Why tarry the wheels of his chariot? Why is his chariot so long in coming?" The sword of the soul was sharp and cut its way, untimely, through the too slender scabbard. Hooker's *Ecclesiastical Polity* will probably be read for its sublime thought, its calm and dignified argument, and not least for its melodious and majestic English as long as the delay of judgment fires permits the existence of a record, and yet the gifted author died at forty-seven, leaving his work unfinished—a sacrifice to excessive toil, domestic worry, and want of bodily care.†

* It is a curious illustration how quickly and deeply noble natures become inoculated with the spirit of moral heroism that it was Martyn's hearing, while a student at Cambridge, Charles Simeon speak of the great good accomplished by William Carey in India that decided his remarkable career and pathetic fate.

†"Bent by the influence of sedentary and meditative habits, of quiet and retiring manners, discolored in complexion, and worn and marked in feature from the hard mental toil which he had expended in his great work," is in substance Walton's description of Hooker's personal appearance.

Bunyan had hardly become known as a popular writer and powerful preacher to the thoughtful religious public of his day when a cold caught during a journey on horseback in the rain, between Reading and London, brought his labors to a premature conclusion. Though the great dreamer's enforced confinement in that foul pigsty of a prison, which some curious official whim had perched on a pier of the bridge across the sleepy Ouse at Bedford, gave him an opportunity of producing one of the few imperishable gems of literature, the England of his day paid dearly for those years of hardship and physical wear and waste in the shortening of one of the noblest and most exemplary of lives.

The frail and sickly Baxter would undoubtedly have been a healthier man and probably a longer liver—though as it was he reached his seventy-sixth year—if in place of poring incessantly over the yellow pages of the schoolmen of which he was inordinately fond, and producing copy for the printers by the yard, he had oftener walked abroad and sought more frequent communion with that wholesome genius of the universe of which Wordsworth has given so fine a description in his well-known poem composed on the beautiful banks of the Wye :

> For I have learned
> To look on nature, not as in the hour
> Of thoughtless youth, but hearing oftentimes
> The still sad music of humanity,
> Not harsh, nor grating, though of ample power
> To chasten and subdue.   And I have felt
> A spirit which disturbs me with the joy
> Of elevated thoughts ; a sense sublime
> Of something far more deeply interfused,
> Whose dwelling is the light of setting suns,
> And the round ocean, and the living air,
> And the blue sky, and in the mind of man :
> A motion and a spirit that impels
> All thinking things, all objects of all thought,
> And rolls through all things.

One cannot help recognizing the moral heroism of George Whitefield when a few weeks before the sudden termination of his wonderfully successful ministry in the flower of his manhood he reflects, "It is the seventy-fifth day since I arrived at Rhode Island, exceeding weak in body; yet God has enabled me to preach *a hundred and seventy-five times* in public, *besides exhorting frequently* in private."* And yet our admiration does not blind us to the enormity and imprudence of this riotous expenditure of strength—this burning of the candle at both ends. If Robert Hall, whose admirers were wont to call him the "prince of preachers," had studied his body and "its needs with a tithe the masterly skill and acuteness he displayed in analyzing the nature and phenomena of the soul, and pointing out its imperative and imperishable requirements to his delighted contemporaries; and if he had striven to avoid pain with half the force of will he displayed in enduring and suppressing it, he would have served his generation no less brilliantly, but with less of physical torture and for a longer time. It is positively humiliating to find a man of Hall's imperial mold, with "a countenance," as John Foster remarked, "formed as if on purpose for the most declared manifestation of power," the helpless slave of tobacco. Of Thomas Walsh, who died at twenty-eight, one of the most accomplished Hebrew scholars and ablest preachers of his day; of John Summerfield, whose pulpit eloquence and power made him famous among the people of his own denomination—the Methodists—in England, France, and America before he was twenty-seven, at which age he died; of the younger Treffry, whose masterly exposition of the eternal sonship of Christ has won for him an enduring place among the distinguished theologians of Christendom; of Frederick William Robertson, whose heroic but unavailing struggle for a few brief but brilliant years with shattered health and the burden of public duty Stopford Brooke has

---

* To form a due estimate of these exertions it is necessary to remember this sick man was a vehement and highly dramatic speaker, and often preached over an hour to a crowd of many thousands in the open air, and that his private exhortations were often as long as many sermons in our day.

made known to the world in the *Life and Letters* of the great Brighton preacher; of Alfred Cookman, whose saintly character and consecrated labors as portrayed by Ridgway have been an inspiration and a canon of good living to many young clergymen—of these and others we can only say with regret that the larger and completer fulfillment of the splendid promise they gave was prevented only by those twin conspirators which have so often been fatal to the aspirations of noble minds, overwork, inducing close sedentary habit, and inattention to the laws of health. The varied and exhausting labors of Thomas Chalmers at St. John's, Glasgow, would have broken him down at forty-three if he had not escaped in time to the chair of moral philosophy in the University of St. Andrew's. "When a specialist in diseases of the nervous system takes up the biography of that gifted man, Austin Phelps, he reads between the lines the causes of his breakdown, and feels that such a choice spirit ought to have been saved those last twenty years of pathetic exclusion from public service."* Nor can it be denied that Spurgeon might still have been living to awaken weekly in the hearts of the thousands of every land the familiar sentiment of the prophet, "How beautiful upon the mountains are the feet of him that bringeth good tidings," etc.; might still have drawn upon himself from the lips of orphan children and hoary saints and students learning under his inspiring example the divine art of " speaking the truth in love "— the benediction that greeted the patriarch of the desert— "When the eye saw me, then it blessed me; and when the ear heard me, it gave witness to me: because I delivered the poor that cried, and the fatherless, and him that had none to help him," and might still have fed and sustained the pure flame of evangelical truth and piety throughout the world if he had never entertained the foolish dream—very foolish for such a remarkable condensation and crystallization of com-

---

* George F. Streeter, in *Congregationalist*, August, 1894.

mon sense—of "smoking cigars to the glory of God;"* if he had claimed, in a word, more leisure for physical relaxation, and had observed from the first simpler and wiser rules of living.

7. **Necessity of Regular and Systematic Exercise.**

Since the physical constitution, as well as the circumstances, habits, and tastes of clergymen are necessarily varied, it is impossible to lay down hygienic laws which shall be applicable to all. There is, however, one necessity which is sovereign, absolute, universal, and that is regular and systematic exercise of some kind. A Venetian vase, made of the thinnest glass ever manufactured, has been known to exist uninjured for five hundred years with proper care, and the frail earthen vessel in which God has been pleased to deposit an invaluable heavenly treasure may be preserved in a fair measure of health and vigor for the longest period allotted by nature to the life of man with ordinary prudence, and an hour spent every day in the active use of limbs and lungs in the open air. Every Christian student and preacher needs to believe as firmly in the necessity of out-door exertion as in the articles of the Apostles' Creed. The conviction requires to be as imperious as hunger or thirst or the necessity for sleep, and potent enough to drive the victim of an overstudious and inactive disposition out of the house regardless of pressure of work, personal mood, or unpropitious weather. The "bodily exercise" (σωματικὴ γυμνασία), whose "profit" seems to be "little" when compared with the larger advantage of the "devoutness" which extends to all things and all times, is really a great investment when one considers its effect on the whole cycle of man's physical and intellectual

---

* In less than three months after Dr. G. F. Pentecost, preaching in Spurgeon's Tabernacle in Mr. Spurgeon's presence, provoked from the great Baptist pastor this strange defense of his smoking habit before his vast congregation, the writer met a boy in the street, whom he highly esteemed, with a pipe in his mouth, and on his expressing regret was told with an air of triumph that Mr. Spurgeon smoked "to the glory of God."

existence. In any case, a religion which impressively reminds us that the body is "the temple of the Holy Ghost" cannot withhold its solemn sanction from the use of timely and legitimate measures fitted to maintain that temple in good repair. "A person naturally robust, with a clear and powerful brain, could bear twelve or fourteen hours' work every day for years together, so far as the work itself is concerned, if only so large an expenditure of time left a sufficient margin for exercise and sleep. But the privation of exercise, by weakening the digestive and assimilative powers, reduces the flow of healthy, rich blood to the brain—the brain requires an enormous quantity of blood, especially when the cerebral matter is rapidly destroyed by intellectual labor—and usually brings on nervousness, the peculiar affliction of the overdriven mental laborer. This nervousness is nature's kindly warning, preserving us, if we attend to it in time, from much more serious consequences. The best preventive of it, and often the only cure, is plenty of moderate exercise."

8. Benefits Secured Amply Compensate for Cost in Time.

Perhaps the consideration that militates most powerfully against the adoption and observance of judicious rules of hygienic and health-preserving exertion is a conscientious but short-sighted begrudgment of the time required. It is difficult to believe, especially when important business is absorbing attention, that one can reap any benefit from a long walk in the open air at all proportioned to the sacrifice demanded. Influenced by this scruple, busy men of all professions use various expedients to concentrate the benefits of bodily recreation into as small a space and as convenient a form as possible. The age is preeminently one of concentration, distillation, and dispatch, and so these time-saving experiments often take the form of some violent muscular exertion which can be gone through in a few minutes. A moment's reflection, however, will convince any person of ordinary intelligence that it is impossible to secure the cooperation of nature in small, picayune economies of that kind. To no one who hesitates to pay the price she demands will she surrender the golden secret of physical health and happiness. Her processes are broad, liberal, and unhurried, and in the building up of the physique, as well as in development and growth of the mind, time is a large factor. "It is necessary," aptly remarks a recent writer, "to *live* with a study for hundreds or thousands of hours before the mind can assimilate as much of the subject as it may need, and so it is necessary to live in exercise during a thousand hours of every year to make sure of the physical benefits. Even the fresh air itself requires time to renovate our blood. The fresh air cannot be concentrated, and to breathe the prodigious quantities of it which are needed for perfect energy we must be out in it frequently and long." As John Wesley entered upon his eighty-third year he wrote, "I am never tired, neither with riding, preaching, nor traveling; one natural cause, undoubtedly, is my continual exercise and change of air."

The time-economizing theory is founded on a narrow and inadequate estimate of the cumulative and many-sided good which accrues from systematic physical exertion in the open air, and is a profound mistake. The competence of the human brain for any intellectual task, as well as the excellence and value of its products, depends on the amount of physical energy and endurance it can command. It goes without saying that the complex and curious machinery of thought works more smoothly and to better purpose in a condition of perfect health than when handicapped by the misgivings and miseries of disease. And though a man may retain his bodily vigor and keep his intellect in good working order for months together without an hour's out-door recreation, so that the time which would have been given to exercise would seem to be so much clear loss for the period designated, yet it is certain that the experiment, if extended through the labors of a lifetime, would prove disastrous. Physically, as well as morally, it is true that

> Our deeds still travel with us from afar,
> And what we have been makes us what we are.

And a body toughened and toned up by daily exposure to summer air and sunshine, and winter's storm and tempest, until it becomes a magazine of health and energy for years to come, is, as a rule, essential to the successful accomplishment of any considerable intellectual enterprise, and the periodical sacrifice of time to one's physical well-being is found in the end to be a commendable exhibition of forethought and farsightedness, and a policy every way worthy of a rational being.

9. Errors to be Shunned.

But this mistaken parsimony as to time is not the only error to be avoided. Eager and tenacious minds are apt to trail after them when they leave the study the chain of thought that absorbed and enslaved them there. It is requisite not only to acquire the power of completely disengaging the mind from the problem with which it has immediately been contending, but to allow no other involving mental labor to take its place. The respite of the brain should be as absolute and unbroken as possible. "The fatal law of the studious temperament," says a close observer of student life, "is that in exercise itself it must find some intellectual charm, so that we quit our books in the library only to go and read the infinite book of nature. We cannot go out in the country without incessantly thinking about either botany or geology or landscape painting, and it is difficult for us to find a refuge from the importunate habit of investigation.... There is no position in the world more wearisome than that of the man who is inwardly indifferent to the amusement in which he is trying to take part."

Another common mistake which claims a brief word of mention here is the prevalent habit of overclothing in summer. "The most effectual device," says Dr. Felix L. Oswald, for diminishing the benefit of outdoor exercise "in warm weather is a heavy suit of clothes. Between May and October man has to wear clothes enough to keep the flies and gnats from troubling him; a pair of linen trousers, a shirt, and light neckerchief—whatsoever is more than these is of evil. The best headdress for summer is our natural hair; the next best is a light straw hat with a perforated crown. Hats and caps as protection from the vicissitudes of the atmosphere are a comparatively recent invention. The Syrians, Greeks, Romans, Normans, and Visigoths wore helmets in war, but went uncovered in time of peace in the coldest and most stormy seasons; the Gauls and Egyptians always went bareheaded, even in battle, and a hundred years after the conquest of Egypt by Cambyses (B. C. 525) the sands of Pelusium still covered the well-preserved skulls of the native warriors, while those of the turbaned Persians had crumbled to the jawbones. The Emperor Hadrian traveled bareheaded from the icy Alps to the borders of Mesopotamia; the founders of several monastic orders interdicted all coverings for the head; during the reign of Henry VIII boys and young men generally went with the head bare, and to the preservation of this old Saxon custom Sir John Sinclair ascribes the remarkable health of the orphans of the Queen's Hospital." The human skull is naturally better protected than that of any other warm-blooded animal, so that there seems little need of adding an artificial covering; and, as Dr. Adair observes, the most neglected children, street Arabs and young gypsies, are least liable to disease chiefly because they are not guarded from the access of fresh air by too many garments. . . . The trouble is that so many of our latter-day health codes are framed by men who mistake the exigencies of their own decrepitude for the normal condition of mankind.

10. Physical Gifts and Graces Not to be Despised.

The physical gifts of God are no more to be despised and neglected than intellectual talent or moral or educational advantages. And the bearing of the whole question of hygiene and exercise on the highest ministerial efficiency and success is too obvious to need insisting on. Health, strength, cheerfulness, ample nervous energy, complete self-command, ease and grace of public attitude, even a tall, commanding form, when crowned with a duly disciplined and powerful intellect, all contribute in their way elements of force and value to the public man's position, to the pastor's success, to the preacher's message. If, as the almost forgotten author of the once popular "Night Thoughts" reminds us, "the Christian is the highest style of man," the observation ought to apply with double force and wider comprehensiveness to the Christian preacher. In body, as in intellect and character, he should seek conformity to the highest type. It has, perhaps, been too much the fashion to exalt the intellectual and the spiritual at the expense of the physical. Byron, who was physically deformed, said bitterly of men of stately stature, for example :

> Tall men are oft like houses that are tall,
> The upper rooms are furnished worst of all.

But the present writer has noted that many of the princes of platform and pulpit oratory, in all lands, whom he has been privileged to hear are men of tall and well-proportioned physique, and he does not hesitate to say that if the brightness and clearness of the lamp of mercy held forth by them were not enhanced by the majesty of their personal presence, which may be cordially conceded, they certainly were not diminished on that account.

CHAPTER XV

The Minister in Age, Retirement, and Death

> I love the doubt, the dark, the fear,
> That still surroundeth all things here.
> I love the mystery, nor seek to solve;
> Content to let the stars revolve,
> Nor ask to have their meaning clear.
> Enough for me, enough to feel;
> To let the mystic shadows steal
> Into a land whither I cannot follow;
> To see the stealthy sunlight leave
> Dewy dingle, dappled hollow;
> To watch when falls the hour of eve,
> Quiet shadows on a quiet hill;
> To watch, to wonder and be still.
> —*Alfred Austin.*

1. Retiring to the Shadows.

IN a recently published novel—*The Story of an Island in the Northern Sea*—three mystic women sit upon the rocks, which are covered with strange runic records of prehistoric ages. All of them are moved to meditation by the suggestive scene. One of them sees only the solemn endlessness of life; another, its trivial emptiness; a third, its pathetic brevity. These aspects of existence, though essentially distinct, are not so irreconcilably antithetic as to exclude the possibility of their convergence in the same individual experience. And to the man who has devoted himself for a lifetime to the study and presentation of the deeper problems of life, duty, and destiny with a view to preparing his fellow-beings for another and better state of existence they may be presumed to be as familiar as are the strings of a favorite harp to the fingers of a skilled harpist. In his own heart the aged preacher has often heard the mysterious yet meaningful echo of these strains, at one time sharp and clear, at another indistinct and faint as of sweet bells chiming, now nearer and now farther away, and he has been depressed, roused, admonished, awed, fretted, touched to tears, and soothed by them in turn. And now that he has unbuckled his fighting gear and retired to the shadows, these aspects of being are apt to haunt his solitude, presenting themselves in sterner and gloomier form than before as food for thought and meditation.

2. Premature Senility.

A few men seem never to grow old. A larger number arrive late, and then half-protestingly, at the period when, in the words of the ancient Hebrew pessimist,

> Fears shall be in the way,
> And the almond tree shall cause loathing,
> And the grasshopper shall be a burden,
> And the caperberry shall fail (or break up*);

while quite a little army show signs of age in life's high noon, for "men may grow old without having many birthdays." The deadline is a very variable landmark, and depends largely on the mental idiosyncrasies and peculiar experience of the individual. "I am not an old man, the soul never grows old," was the mild but firm protest of a venerable friend—hale, hearty, active, enthusiastic, and hopeful in all his undertakings at eighty years of age—when publicly referred to by the writer as "My old friend Mr. ———." The benign and beautiful spirit of the last of the apostles, sitting in his chair in the church at Ephesus, to which beloved friends had carried him, exhorting his "little children" ($\tau\epsilon\kappa\nu la\ \mu ov$)—the young people of the third generation—to cultivate among themselves a genuine Christian love ($\xi\rho\gamma\psi\ \kappa a\lambda\ \dot{a}\lambda\eta\theta\epsilon\iota\varphi$), is a commonplace of Church history, but it is a picture of the geniality and

---
* Compare Revised Version and Variorum Bibles.

mellowness of age compared with which Cicero's Cato (in *De Senectute*), garrulously narrating his personal reminiscences to young Lælius and Scipio, is insipidity itself.

The history of every civilized people is eloquent of examples of men who did the best work of their lives between the ages of fifty and eighty, and yet so congenital and inveterate as a habit of mind are depression and discouragement in many persons that they seem to have a certain morbid satisfaction in seeing their own sun "go down while it is yet day."

"It is in midlife especially," eloquently observes one of these prophets of "night at noonday," "that we are conscious of jaded ardor. We have lost, to begin with, the physical buoyancy of early years. The spirit, too, is fatigued. We have learned by many repulses the hardness of the battle. In his memorable portrait of Napoleon, Hazlitt speaks of the unconquerable energy that flamed in every part of the theater of war, that ran to meet danger wherever it showed itself most formidable, of the strength of purpose and self-confidence which constitute the definition of a hero or great man, attempting the utmost that is possible with the utmost of your power and without the smallest loss of time. In the mood of midlife this sounds like dreary irony. We have proved our weapons, and their edge has been turned. Our circumstances are narrow, and they will never be expanded. Men have made up their minds about us; they have seen us, measured us, and passed us by. Except they see signs and wonders they will not believe that we are more than we have seemed to them. Standing in the center, we see behind a tame and ineffectual life, and before us monotony and decay. The hope of the world is not in us, it is in the young. We accept the fact with various feelings, but we are all prone to accept it. To some natures it is a misery; they ponder on human need, and their little and slow means of diminishing it, till their thoughts beat upon the brain like an anvil, and they become fierce through hopelessness. Others ignobly acquiesce; they turn to the comforts that are left them, and forget the lofty passion with which they once looked on life. Others see the ideal in dreams, and let the world go past them. In all these cases the man becomes practically a spent force."

It is a sad and lugubrious but not uncommon strain.

3. Verdure and Sunshine on Autumn Hills.

The aged minister, however, as a rule, is anything but a morose and gloomy person. He does not sit, like the retired Achilles, sulking in his tent. Aloof from the din and dust of the battlefield, he still keeps his eye on the varying fortunes of the fight, and feels himself at home no more among the decaying remnants of his own generation than among the men who constitute the advance guard of the hour and the youth in reserve who stand ready at call to recruit the constantly decimated ranks. The Journals of John Wesley, the literary and historic value of which a distinguished English lawyer, Augustine Birrell—essayist, queen's counsel, and member of Parliament—has recently commented on, show how richly green and beautiful the hills of age may appear in the light of the declining sun, in spite of a life of incessant hardship, care, and toil. On entering his eightieth year he observes: " I find no more pain and bodily infirmities than at twenty-five. This I still impute, first, to the power of God fitting me for what he calls me to ; second, to my still traveling four or five thousand miles a year; third, to my sleeping night or day, whenever I want it;[*] fourth, to my rising at a set hour ; and, fifth, to my constant preaching, particularly in the morning [at five o'clock]." Two years later he writes, " I am as strong at eighty-one as I was at twenty-one, but abundantly more healthy, being

---

[*] Napoleon Bonaparte claimed the same power of sleeping at will.

a stranger to headache, toothache, and other bodily disorders which attended me in my youth." A year later he says, "It is now eleven years since I have felt any such thing as weariness." At eighty-five he asks, " What difference do I find by an increase of years?" and answers: "I find, first, less activity; I walk slower, particularly up hill; second, my memory is not so quick; third, I cannot read so well by candlelight. But I bless God that all my other powers of mind and body remain just as they were." A later entry, made at the opening of his eighty-eighth year, before the close of which he died, shows with what unruffled and philosophic calmness of spirit he noted and registered the growing symptoms of physical decay: "Last August I found almost a sudden change; my eyes were so dim that no glasses would help me, my strength likewise now quite forsook me and probably will not return in this world. But I feel no pain from head to foot, only it seems nature is exhausted, and, humanly speaking, will sink more and more till ' the weary springs of life stand still.' "

And the man who by a liberal but judicious expenditure of strength and energy, and a religious regard to the laws of health, offered to his generation in the fullness of man's years a notable example of physical vigor, was equally remarkable for his intellectual and religious sanity and his perfectly balanced judgment. Probably no man has better exemplified a well-known definition of culture as "the compensation of bias" than John Wesley. Though the prevailing tone of his mind was a chastened and cheerful seriousness, and the grand purpose that absorbed him, namely, the revival and dissemination of scriptural religion, intensely practical and immovably steadfast, he was not without a strong sense of the comical and diverting aspects of human life and character. He admitted as freely the claims of humor as those of devotion, and recognized as readily the religiousness of seasonable laughter as of that of

The Minister in Age, Retirement, and Death   321

seasonable tears. Not only did he supply his people with the highest order of religious literature from his own and others' pens, and for their intellectual improvement epitomize history, abridge science, expurgate Shakespeare, and write a treatise on domestic physic; he even edited a humorous novel for their use.

As was to be anticipated, this last instance of his versatility and breadth of sympathy with the varied life of humanity drew upon him the condemnation of men of more superficial culture and narrower mind. A brief dialogue with one of these, named John Easton, is recorded:

"Did you read *Vindex*, John?"
"Yes."
"Did you laugh, John?"
"No."
"Did you read *Pythias and Damon*, John?"
"Yes."
"Did you cry, John?"
"No."

The revelation of such stolid terrestriality and invincible one-sidedness in an esteemed "helper" proved too much for the man of much soul and many virtues, and, clasping his hands and raising his eyes toward heaven, he exclaimed in serio-comical vein, "O earth, earth, earth!"*

Opposed in his work at the outset by brother clergymen, and rigorously excluded from their pulpits, the evening of his laborious day witnessed a remarkable change in their attitude toward him. The incident of his meeting the scholarly Lowth at dinner in 1777 is one of rare beauty, and is equally creditable to both men. The bishop refused to sit above Wesley at table, saying, "Mr. Wesley, may I be found sitting at your feet in another world." When Wesley declined to take precedence the bishop asked him as a favor to sit above him, as he was deaf, and desired not to

---
* Wesley's Journals.

lose a sentence of Wesley's conversation. Wesley . . . fully appreciated this courtesy, and recorded in his Journal, "Dined with Lowth, Bishop of London. His whole behavior was worthy of a Christian bishop—easy, affable, courteous—and yet all his conversation spoke the dignity which was suitable to his character."* In 1782, at Exeter, Wesley dined in the episcopal palace with five other clergymen, guests of the bishop. Two years later, at Whitehaven, he "had all the Church ministers to hear him, and most of the gentry of the town."† Three years before his death he preached on invitation at St. Thomas's and St. Swithin's, in London, and remarks, "The tide is now turned, so that I have more invitations to preach in churches than I can accept." Still, till very late in life, the appearance of his small, spare, erect form in the street stirred the bad blood of certain clergymen—deservedly designated "lewd fellows of the baser sort." Meeting one of these on a sidewalk too narrow for two to pass, the unworthy "follower of the Lamb" rudely remarked, as he held the path and faced the venerable figure approaching him, "I do not step out of the path for fools." "But I do," said Wesley, instantly stepping aside.

No wonder that, exemplifying in himself such perfect serenity and composure of mind, he succeeded in inoculating those most closely associated with him with the same spirit. At his invitation Adam Clarke left the paternal roof near Coleraine, Ireland, a youth of twenty-one, with a few shillings in his pocket. On reaching Bristol his scanty assets were all gone except three halfpence. His application for a place in the famous Wesleyan School at Kingswood failed for want of room, and it seemed as if he would be left without a place of shelter for the night. Meeting Wesley, who happened to be away from Bristol when he

---

* *Life*, by Tyerman, vol. iii, p. 253.
† *The English Church in the Eighteenth Century*, p. 336.

arrived, shortly afterward, the great evangelist's hands were duly placed upon his head, and he was sent forth to a circuit comprising three or four English counties, without the meagerest special preparation for his work. For nearly fifty years he traveled over England and the Channel Islands, acquiring a steadily increasing fame as an eloquent and powerfully persuasive preacher of the Gospel, but even still more as a man of profound and extensive learning. There perhaps never was a more striking example of the power of the human spirit to conquer apparently insuperable difficulties than Dr. Adam Clarke. Yet, though sharing to the full all the opposition, obloquy, hardship, and persecution incident to the toils of a Methodist preacher in the later years of the eighteenth century, and experiencing several hairbreadth escapes from death by sickness and overwork, by violence, by accident, and by exposure to the winter's cold, he lived to be esteemed and honored as the brightest ornament of the English Methodist Church of his day, and to publish, besides many other useful and learned treatises, the most scholarly and most valuable commentary on the sacred Scriptures that up to that time had appeared.

According to one of his biographers, the learned Dr. Etheridge, Dr. Clarke's later ministry was attended occasionally not only by distinguished representatives of the nobility of England, but also by members of the reigning family such as the Dukes of Kent and Sussex—a rare thing then, but even rarer since. His presence was sought and welcomed at royal tables,* while ecclesiastical magnates like Dr. Blomfield, Bishop of London; leading learned societies

---

* Mr. Pettigrew, Secretary to the Duke of Sussex, writing to thank Dr. Clarke for a copy of Bryan Walton's famous polyglot, which he had caused to be reprinted with the dedication to Oliver Cromwell (suppressed after the return of the monarchy), said, " His royal highness commands me to say that he trusts whenever you come to London you will honor him with a visit, when he will be proud to show you his library [it contained fifteen hundred Bibles of different ages and languages], and be most happy to make the acquaintance of a man for whose talents and character he has so exalted an opinion." (*Life*, by Etheridge, p. 395.) He was the object of similar attentions from the Duke of Kent, father of the present sovereign of England. (*Vide Ibid.*, p. 396.)

of the time, such as the Antiquarian Society, Royal Irish Academy, Eclectic Society, Geological Society, Royal Asiatic Society, and American Historical Institute; and Academical Senates, like that of King's College Aberdeen, vied with each other to do him honor. And yet this man whom poverty, disease, hardship, malignant bigotry, and providential mishap had in turns seemed to begrudge the unenvied boon of an unprivileged and laborious existence sang in life's decline one of the sublimest strains in praise of living known to the prose or poetry of any language. Occupying at Portrush, Ireland, about two years before his death the same sleeping chamber with the Rev. James Everett, who became his earliest and most discriminating biographer, he rose according to his wont at four and left Everett in bed. When the latter rose an hour later he discovered on a pane of the window looking toward the sea the following beautiful words, neatly engraven with the point of a diamond: "I have enjoyed the spring of life; I have endured the toils of its summer; I have culled the fruits of its autumn; I am now passing through the rigors of its winter; and I am neither forsaken of God nor abandoned by man. I see at no great distance the dawn of a new day, the first of a spring that shall be eternal. It is advancing to meet me! I run to embrace it. Welcome, eternal spring! Hallelujah!"*

Few of its many eminent ministers have left a deeper impress on the Wesleyan denomination in England than Dr. Jabez Bunting. He is distinguished in the annals of that Church as one of the two men who during the hundred and fifty years of its history were four times elected to the high and responsible office of president of the Annual Assembly or Conference,† the eloquent Dr. Robert Newton, of international fame—a contemporary—being the other. Dr. Bunting was powerful as a preacher, but displayed the

---

* Everett's, *Life of Dr. A. Clarke*, p. 450.
† The years 1820, 1828, 1836, and 1844.

strength of an intellectual Hercules in debate. So great and almost imperial was the influence he acquired in the free counsels of his brethren that recalcitrants and enemies of the Methodist polity, on whom the measures he advised pressed severely, spoke of him as the "pope of Methodism." That he was at least capable of a far nobler style of sentiment and conduct than is implied in that odious epithet is strikingly shown in the following incident. Invited three times in successive years after his retirement from active service to preach an anniversary sermon in a certain church, he inadvertently selected on each occasion a text in which the word "curse" in some form was prominent. "Curse ye Meroz, said the angel of the Lord, curse ye bitterly the inhabitants thereof," etc. "If any man love not the Lord Jesus Christ, let him be Anathema Maranatha." "Behold, I set before you this day a blessing and a curse," etc. Notwithstanding this repeated malediction, the church sent its committee to secure him a fourth time, but on account of a prior though minor engagement he was obliged to decline. The individual appointed to this duty, however, was a man of tact and persistency, and urged, "Nay, doctor, you have three times pronounced a curse upon us, surely you will not refuse to come and bless us." "What's that?" eagerly inquired the venerable divine. The facts were repeated to him, when he smiled and said, "O yes, my brother, I'll come down and bless you before I die." He went, and from the words, "Surely blessing, I will bless thee," preached one of the richest discourses he ever delivered.* "Give my affectionate remembrance to your *great* grandfather," said Dr. Guthrie, Scotland's princeliest preacher perhaps since Thomas Chalmers, in writing to Miss Bunting, Dr. Bunting's grandchild and sister of the present able editor of the *Contemporary Review;* and the graceful compliment immensely pleased the retired veteran. "The common people hear

---
* *Sketches of Wesleyan Preachers,* p. 26.

him gladly," was a remark apologetically made by his gifted son, T. Percival Bunting, at the close of some good-natured criticisms of the preacher whose ministry the family attended in London. "And, Percival," remarked the aged orator, tartly, "the *uncommon* people ought to."

"Robert, Robert," he faintly whispered at the close of a last affecting interview, just before his death, with the son of one of his early friends, " who's won the Derby?"—the great annual horse race held on Epsom Downs, near London, in which no Methodist preacher, old or young, is supposed to have the slightest interest.*

Luther's asperities of tone and manner disappeared as he grew old, and the fountains of playfulness and of piety in his ragged but noble nature sparkled side by side in the setting sun and mingled their waters in the shadowy vale of his advancing years. "The birds," he remarks, late in life, "must fly over our heads, but why allow them to roost in our hair? Gayety and a light heart in all virtue and decorum are the best medicine for the young, or, rather, for all. I, who have passed my life in dejection and gloomy thoughts, now catch at enjoyment, come from what quarter it may, and even seek for it. Criminal pleasure, indeed, comes from Satan, but that which we find in the society of good and pious men is approved of God. . . . Solitude and melancholy are poison. They are deadly to all, but, above all, to the young." "To the gracious Lady Catherine Luther, my dear wife," he writes, with tender playfulness, "who vexes herself overmuch, grace and peace in the Lord. Dear Catherine, you should read St. John and what is said in the Catechism of the confidence to be reposed in God. Indeed, you torment yourself as though he were not almighty and could not produce new Doctors Martin by the score, if the old doctor should drown himself in the Saal." "There is one who watches over me more effectually than

---

* *Methodist Recorder*, Christmas number, 1893.

thou canst or than all the angels. He sits at the right hand of the Father Almighty. Therefore be calm."*

"There's sweet rest in heaven," remarked a lady friend to the aged "Father" Taylor, of the Boston Seamen's Bethel.

"Go there if you want to," was the barely civil reply.

"But think of the angels that will welcome you," persisted the consoler of the worn-out veteran.

"What do I want of the angels? *I prefer folks.*" And then, as if recollecting that the poet Cædmon, who once left the feast because he could not sing, had designated those supernal intelligences "the fair folks of God," thirteen centuries ago, he added, in a more conciliatory tone, "But angels are folks."

"How pleasant it must be," said another comforter, "for you to leave this worn-out tabernacle and go to a better home!" And the reply, as reasonable and religious as courageous and stubborn, was, "I'll stay while there's a bit left."

"Your *Apologia* is really a *theodicy*, professor," the present writer remarked to the venerable American patriarch of science, Professor Le Conte, of the University of California, on a recent occasion, when having started out with a defense of his own scientific position on the vexed subject of evolution against the recently published criticisms of Professor Watson, he concluded a masterly discussion with a glowingly eloquent description of the moral and spiritual future of the human race—speaking as if he had a vivid glimpse of "the good time coming," and had made up his mind to wait here, if permitted, till the "city of God" arrived.

"Mark the perfect man, and behold the upright man," observes the ancient Hebrew sage and poet, "for the end of that man is peace" (or there is a future to the man of peace, Variorum Bible). In a letter to Dr. Wright, biographer of Charles G. Finney, the Rev. Dr. James Brand, Finney's successor in the pastorate of the First Church, Oberlin, finely

---
* Sir J. Stephen's essay, "Luther and the Reformation."

exhibits the nobility of that great preacher and revivalist's character amid the lengthening shadows of the brief repose which preceded his entrance into the rest eternal. "A more genial, tender, sympathetic, childlike character," he says, "I had never met."

. . . .

"It became the frequent delight of my life to call and question him as to what ought to be done and said for the best interests of the people. He always sent me away a wiser man and with deeper longing to win men to Christ. It was unquestionably due largely to his wisdom and Christian sympathy that the people to whom he had ministered for forty years could consent to bear with a new man and a comparative novice at that in his place. . . . Like the apostle John, President Finney made love the principal theme of his old age. He could hardly refer to the love of God without weeping."*

4. The Glow of Sunset.

But not alone as samples of the spirit and manner of godly living and of graceful "slowing up" into the shadows of life's terminus has God set forth the ministers of his word, but also of the still rarer and less valued but supremely noble art of dying well. Such is the sovereign consequence of this latter lesson that young men of marked ability and promise are sacrificed in the inscrutable counsels of Providence for the sake of it. Mustered out from the ranks at the opening of the fight, they go

> Not, like the quarry-slave at night,
> Scourged to his dungeon, but, sustained and soothed
> By an unfaltering trust, approach the grave
> Like one that wraps the drapery of his couch
> About him, and lies down to pleasant dreams.†

There is a touch of the sublime in the dying struggle of Brainerd to wean his heart from his beloved Indians whose

---

* Dr. Wright's *Life of Finney*, in American Religious Leaders Series, p. 282.
† Bryant's "Thanatopsis."

salvation he had labored for with such passionate and self-consuming yearning, and, as his strength slowly wastes away, to turn his eyes toward the portals of the eternal city, looking for the coming of the "chariot." "O, if I could be raised up now, how I would preach! I have had a sight of eternity," pathetically observed the eloquent young Summerfield, obliged to lay down his weapon almost as soon as he had tested and proved its power. And how one's deepest sympathies are stirred at the thought of Robertson, of Brighton, prostrate alone for hours on the floor of his study at thirty-seven, fighting death with closed fist and clinched teeth in resolute silence and unutterable pain. "Write on my coffin lid 'Unfaithful John Smith,'" was the dying desire of him of that name, of Cudworth, Yorkshire, one of the most tireless and most triumphant winners of souls, who even in the act of doffing his armor at thirty-two fought the great adversary of God and man with one of the most powerful arguments ever wasted on a hardened and hopeless reprobate.* Only a few hours after laying the foundation stone of one of the largest churches in Liverpool, which his immense and growing popularity had made a necessity, the lifeless body of Thomas Spencer was floating in the waters of the Mersey, while a party of ministers awaiting the amiable and brilliant young preacher's company heard the boys in the street under the window relating to each other in subdued and sorrowful strains the story of his drowning in the act of bathing.†

Sometimes a modest husbandman like Richard Hooker quietly comes forth for a brief day's labor and creates a bright oasis in the desert of the world, and, leaving it green and blossoming for the delight of all subsequent generations, retires in manhood's midday to his appointed place in the great congregation of the just. Others enter into rest full of years and honors. "My strength fails me, my memory fails me, my speech fails me, but I thank God my love

---

* *Life*, by R. Treffry, Jr.   † See article in *Pulpit Analyst*.

holds out still. That rather grows than diminishes," murmured the dying John Eliot, of whom Cotton Mather, speaking of his value to the commonwealth of colonial Massachusetts, said, "The whole building trembles when such a pillar is withdrawn." Sang the poet Herbert, dying harp in hand, accompanying himself to his own almost inspired strain:

> The Sundaies of man's life,
>   Thredded together on time's string,
> Make bracelets to adorn the wife
>   Of the eternall glorious King.
> On Sunday heaven's gate stands ope;
>   Blessings are plentiful and rife,
> More plentiful than hope.*

The close affinity between melody and blessedness has never been disputed. And there was an item of serious truth as well as an element of comedy in the words of the leader of the Christmas waits' band, when the latter having played some wretched strain, in the dead of night, under the window of Moscheles's chamber, disturbing his slumbers, the distinguished composer roused his servant and told him to request the band to leave. "Tell your master," was the loud and confident reply, "he will not go to heaven if he does not like music." The saintly rector of Bemerton loved music, and on its wings his gentle spirit went smiling home to God, even as the soul of the Whitby cowherd—Cædmon—father of Anglo-Saxon poetry, is said to have done many centuries before.

"Weep not for me, but for yourselves," said Bunyan to his disconsolate friends, wife, and children; "I go to the Father of our Lord Jesus Christ, who will, no doubt, through the mediation of his blessed Son, receive me though a sinner; where I hope we ere long shall meet, to sing the new song and remain everlastingly happy, world without end. Amen." "I have not apostatized, have I?" said Finney, curiously putting his fingers to his own feeble pulse as if measuring

---
* *Life*, by Izaak Walton.

inch by inch every step of death's approach. Butler, of the *Analogy*, perhaps the brainiest man who ever sat on the English bench of bishops, displayed considerable anxiety and alarm at the near prospect of death. His chaplain, an obscure man whose name has been forgotten, was astonished at this weakness of a great soul at a critical moment, and took no trouble to conceal his disappointment. "Why, my lord, I am surprised to find your lordship express dismay," said the chaplain. "Is not Christ the Saviour?" "Yes, I know he is the Saviour," observed the dying prelate, "but how am I to know he is my Saviour?" "Why," said the chaplain, with simple-minded amazement at the bishop's oversight of one of the most familiar of promises, "he himself said, 'Him that cometh unto me, I will nowise cast out.'" "True, true," said Butler, whose acute and capacious intellect seemed to have grasped every truth except that of his own personal salvation. "How surprising it is that I never realized that before. Now I die happy." "The best of all is God is with us," murmured the expiring "founder of Methodism," raising his arm in token of final triumph. "I have loved righteousness and hated iniquity, therefore I die in exile," was the final protest of the great Hildebrand—a man of another mold and a very different mission—as he breathed his last in Salerno. To George Whitefield, to Dr. Thomas Arnold, to Dr. Chalmers, and to many others Charon's boat came suddenly and stealthily without any premonitory splash of his mystic oar. "I am a worm creeping into the glory of God," was the characteristic last sentiment of Richard Watson, the first and greatest systematic theologian of ecumenical Methodism—a man whom even Robert Hall never heard preach without a feeling of indescribable awe and admiration. Dr. Joseph Beaumont, one of the most notable of Methodist orators in the early half of the present century, died in the pulpit in the town of Hull while in the act of reading out the inspiring lines of Isaac Watts's noble hymn:

> Thee while the first archangel sings,
> He hides his face behind his wings,
> And ranks of shining thrones around
> Fall worshiping, and spread the ground.

On the broad area of God's vineyard his faithful servants have fallen one by one in every land, in every kind of holy occupation, at every moment of the night and day, at every stage of life, but not one has dropped unnoticed by the Eternal Watcher's eye. Death has no terrors for the sons of God. They come to the field of final conflict to find that the foe is gone. Within the cold shadows of mortality they come upon the open gate of life. "You may go now, boys; it is growing dark," said Dr. Adams, of the Edinburgh High School, repeating in his last wandering moments the usual formula of dismissal when the short winter's day declined into the twilight of the evening. "God sends the gloom upon the cloud," says that charming writer, Miss Fiona McLeod, "and there is rain; God sends the gloom upon the hill, and there is mist; God sends the gloom upon the sun, and there is winter. It is God, too, sends the gloom upon the soul, and there is change. The swallow knows when to lift up her wing over against the shadow that creeps out of the north; the wild swan knows when the smell of snow is behind the sun; the salmon, lone in the brown pool among the hills, hears the deep sea, and his tongue pants for salt, and his fins quiver, and he knows that his time is come, and that the sea calls. . . . How, then, shall the soul not know when the change is nigh at last? Is it a less thing than the reed, which sees the yellow birch-gold adrift on the lake, and the gown of the heather grow russet when the purple has passed into the sky, and the white bog-down wave gray and tattered where the loneroid grows dark and pungent—which sees, and knows that the breath of the Death-Weaver at the Pole is fast faring along the frozen norland peaks? It is more than a reed, it is more than a wild doe on the hills, it is more than a swallow lifting her wing against the coming of the shadow, it is more than a swan drunken with the savor of the blue wine of the waves when the green Arctic lawns are white and still. It is more than these, which has the Son of God for brother, and is clothed with light. God doth not extinguish at the dark tomb what he hath litten in the dark womb."

5. He Being Dead yet Speaketh.

Surely not. For is it not authoritatively said, "The memory of the just is blest," and "They that be wise shall shine as the brightness of the firmament, and they that turn many to righteousness as the stars forever and ever?" The Church, in spite of her defects and blemishes, embalms and faithfully hands down from age to age the names and memories of her gifted and devoted sons who have self-denyingly proclaimed the heavenly Evangel, and the influence of their life and teaching has been extended far beyond the limits of the grave. To such a double immortality has been accorded even by consent and contribution of the children of their persecutors. "Ye build," said Christ, "the sepulchers of the prophets, and your fathers killed them " (Luke xi, 47). Of John Wesley, whom, as we have seen, the authorities of the Church of his choice and last dying confession steadily excluded from her pulpits till late in life, G. H. Curteis, the Bampton lecturer for 1871, says, "He was the purest, noblest, most saintly clergyman of the eighteenth century, whose whole life was passed in the sincere and loyal effort to do good." "Frederick William Robertson," remarks a recent essayist, "has been dead more than forty years, but to us who read his sermons to-day it seems as if under the cold clods of that cemetery near the sea at Brighton a human heart must be beating still and *sending out warm, pulsing waves of light into the veins of this aging world.*" Of the illustrious John Albert Bengel, distinguished as preacher, scholar, commentator, and theologian, his friend Fresenius wrote what might *mutatis mutandis* be said of not a few studious and devoted servants of Christ since his day:

"A pillar falls; a light expires; a star which shone so brightly in the visible heaven of the Church stops its course, withdraws, and mingles with the supernal glory of the spirits made perfect.

"An angel of peace, who was as pious as he was laborious, as childlike as he was learned, as rich in spirit as he was acute in mind, as humble as he was great, as modest as he was circumspect in his walk and business of life.

"A friend of God expires, whom the Eternal Wisdom led into her chambers; to whom were opened the outgoings of that light which enlightens human minds, the powers of that word which quickens souls, the treasures of that grace which allures, leads, and saves us.

"A great spirit leaves the earth who, whether he measured the heights or sounded the depths, showed himself equally able. The most sacred of all books was his invaluable treasure. He numbered and proved even words and points. He ventured into the obscure depths of theology, and posterity will be able to judge to what extent he found footing. What to others seemed dry, to him was verdure; what appeared despised by the many, was to him the source of light and power, spirit and life.

" He was eyes to the blind, a leader to the weak, a pattern to the strong, a luminary to the learned, an ornament to the Church.

"A treasury is closed, in which the Lord of all the treasures of grace had laid up wondrous wealth of knowledge and wisdom. A teacher mighty in the Scriptures is no more. Sigh, children; your fathers fall asleep."*

---

* Quoted in Dr. Etheridge's *Life of Adam Clarke*, p. 459.

INDEX

A

Adair, Dr., on health, 314.
Adam, Dr., of Edinburgh, last words of, 332.
Addam, Jane, her University Settlement, 167, 181.
Æneas, contemplating Troy's destruction, 137.
Æonios, meaning of, 131, 143.
Age, ministerial cheerfulness in, 319–328.
Agricola, residence of, in York, 31.
Aim, definiteness of, in preaching, 98.
Aked, C. F., on the Baptists, 42.
Akers, P., 95.
Alciati, Andreas, 64.
Ambrose, St., his rebuke of Theodosius, 94.
Amos, call of, to prophetic office, 71.
Amrou, sword of, 249.
Angelico, Fra, his work in San Marco, 148.
Angelo, Michael, his frescoes on ceiling of Sistine Chapel, 148.
Anselm, parents of, 73.
Anthusa, mother of Chrysostom, 72.
Apocalypse, date of Book of, 102; fourfold apocalyyse as to last things, 133.
Apocrypha, Fourth Book of Esdras, 15.
Apologists, early Christian, 81.
Aquinas, his estimate of Chrysostom's homilies, 62.
Arius, his heresy, 26; *Thalia*, 27.
Armenia, Turkish barbarities in, 202.
Arminius, his letter to Uitenbogaert, 44; Beza's opinion of, 74; bred as a Calvinist, 64; left fatherless in boyhood, 64; educated at the expense of the Merchants' Guild at Amsterdam, 64; rejection of Calvinism, 79.
Army, Salvation, origin of, 53; leaders of, 55; achievements of, 54; its freedom from conventional restraints, 172; its drawbacks, 182; Bishop Brooks on, 179.
Arnauld, Port Royalist, 22.
Asbury, first bishop of American Methodist Episcopal Church, 226, 297.
Assizes, English, 31.
Athanasius, his training, 72; his acquaintance with Greek philosophy, 81; influence on Nicene Council, 62; banishment, 26.
Attila, 23, 268.
Augurs, Roman, their frivolity, 107.
Augustine, St., his study of Plato, 81; his influence on Western thought, 62.
Authority, spirit of, 253; despotism of, 45; Christian doctrine of, 256; qualifications for, 256; responsibility of, 257; imposed by God, 256; ends of, altruistic, 257; abuse of, deprecated, 263, 258; forms of embodiment of, in apostolic times, 259.

B

Bacon, Lord, on adversity, 292.
Baptist, his ministry, 17; his courage, 26, 94.
Barrow, Isaac, orator, 83; mathematician, 83.
Basil, eloquence of, 22; his study of Roman law, 82.
Baxter, Richard, at Kidderminster, 48, 95; a nonconformist, 48; as a pastor, 48; his neglect of health, 307.
Beard, Dr. George M., on longevity, 296.
Beaumont, Dr. Joseph, sudden death of, 331.
Bedford, county jail of, in Bunyan's day, 21, 307.
Beecher, Lyman, his family of preachers, 75; influence on Wendell Phillips, 94.
Beet, Dr. J. A., Criticism of *Last Things* of, 141.
Bengel, John Albert, Fresenius's eulogy on, 333.
Bernard, of Clairvaux, 22, 94, 285; of Cluny, 22.
Besant, Sir Walter, on Greek athletic contests, 149.
Bethlehem, St. Jerome's retreat at, 22.
Beza, Theodore, a student of law, 82; commendation of Arminius, 74.
Bible, not "The Religion of Protestants," 113.
Bigotry in modern England, 39.
Bishop, glory of a, 262; functions of a, 265.
Booth, General, 23; founder of Salvation Army, 53; on Dante's *Inferno*, 172; on misery of the masses, 74.
Booth, Mrs. Maud B., on Salvation Army, 180.
Bolingbroke, Lord, attends Whitefield's preaching, 239.
Borgia, Alexander, crimes of, 24, 267.
Bourdaloue, plainness of speech of, 288.
Boyce, Marcella, Mrs. Humphrey Ward's, 171.
Brainerd, David, among the tribes of the Delaware and Susquehanna, 68; his dying words, 98, 329.
Briggs, C. S., on sources of authority in religion, 114.
Buddhism, in Ceylon, 207; Bishop of Colombo on, 104; alertness of leaders of, 209; effects on devotees, 207; transmigrations of, 206.
Bunyan, John, his parentage, 61; experience as a soldier, 82; his popularity, 95; journey in the rain between Reading and London, 307; last words, 330; compared with Robert Hall, 281.

336　　　　　　　　　Index

Bunting, Dr. Jabez, his power in debate, 325; eminence among the Methodists, 324; popularity as a preacher, 325; his death, 330.
Burroughs, John, on observing nature, 149.
Butler, Bishop Joseph, his death, 326.
Byron, Lord, on tall men, 315.

C

Caine, Right Hon. W. S., on missions, 212, 213.
Calvin, early good fortune of, 64; relation to the Montmors, 64; a student of law, 64; as a theologian, 61; his teachers, 64; his address to Francis I, 280; at Geneva, 96; his defiance of his persecutors, 243.
Caraffa, Cardinal, founder of the Inquisition, 269; his rules, 270.
Carey, William, his versatility, 82.
Carpenter, Bishop Boyd, letter on reunion of Churches, 57.
Catechism, Gace's, 39.
Cicero, lament of, 16.
Cincinnati, its laboring class, 169.
City, modern, its character and condition, 165; Brooklyn, 168.
Civilization, Christian, beginning of, 13.
Chalmers, Dr. T., his love of mathematics, 82; failing health of, 309; sudden death of, 331.
Channing, W. E., educated as a Calvinist, 79.
Chatham, Lord, speech against oppression of American colonies, 96.
Charles II of England, clerical satellites of court of, 28.
Chicago, foreign population of, 167.
Chirol, Valentine, on missions in China, 201.
Christ, proclaimer and proclamation of God's kingdom, 88; his love of the people, 184; doctrine of person of, 106; our Exemplar, 110; his sinlessness, 110; teacher of his people, 113; only source of authority, 113; our sacrifice for sin, 116; the solution of all problems, 118; pledge of our completed manhood, 121; our Judge, 123; his sympathy, 184; his unpopularity, 245.
Christendom, great doctors of, 71.
Christianity, in its inception a simple proclamation of good news, 87; an apocalypse, 192; superior to all other religions, 105; not narrow, 108; its relation to heathenism interpretive, 192; claims of Founder of, 105; program of Founder of, 186; ethics of, 110; hindrances of, 177; antipopular elements of, 242; a religion of the people, 246; a message of power, 248; adapted to the popular need, 249; secret of its success its sociability, 184; must get back to the people, 185.
Christians, united prayer of, 191.
Christian Year, author of, 39.
Chrysostom, John, Demosthenes of Greek Christianity, 61; piety of mother of, 72; his poverty, 61; his popularity at Antioch and Byzantium, 61; laments his failure, 98; his vision, 98; his death in exile, 268.

Church, Christian, its problem, 171; method of meeting it, 174; its failure, 177; secret of success, 183, 187; early Church, 256.
Church, R. W., 124.
Clarke, Dr. A., his early poverty, 66; called to the ministry, 323; his labors, 323; his learning, 323; his praise of life, 324.
Clement VII, his love of war, 24.
Clement of Alexandria, his knowledge of heathen philosophies, 81.
Clement of Rome, his Epistle to the Corinthians, 263.
Colombo, Bishop of, 204; Buddhism in, 200.
Congress, Church of England of 1869, 31.
Constantine, Emperor, birth of, 30; residence of, in York, 30.
Conviction, a secret of oratorical power, 93.
Cookman, Alfred, early death of, 309.
Craftsman, personality of the, 146.
Cranmer, Archbishop, his martyrdom, 95.
Creed, a necessary evil, 37; early creeds, 129.
Criticism, modern, place and value of, 76.
Cromwell, court of, 28.
Cuthbert, St., his faith, 63.
Cyprian, St., 22; in exile, 27.
Cyran, St., 21, 46.
Cyril, of Alexandria, his ambition, 27; Charles Kingsley's characterization of him, 27; Milman's, 27.

D

Dead, sainted, memory of, preserved, 333.
Death, idea of, among the Greeks, 121; skeptical view of, 122; Christian view of, 123.
De Medici, Catherine, her part in the slaughter of the Huguenots, 269.
De Nobile, Robert, 217.
Denominationalism, evils for which it is responsible, 40.
De Saci, 22; as a translator of Scripture, 46.
Destiny, human, a new doctrine of, 18.
Dharmapala, on missions in India, 197.
Difficulties, ministerial, a test of character, 279.
Di Fiore, saying of, 70.
Discipline, mental, value of, 83.
Dogma, meaning of the word, 93; decline of, 75.
Doctrines, cardinal, of Christianity, indestructible, 77.
Dominic, St., his loyalty to Rome, 45.
Dort, Five Points of Synod of, 279.
Drummond, Professor, 72; on Christian Society, 186.

E

Eaglen, Robert, spiritual father of Spurgeon, 79.
Edwards, Jonathan, as a pastor, 23, and preacher, 127.
Edwin, King of Northumbria, baptism of, 30.
Education, college, in India, 212.
Eisenach, Luther at, 63.

Index

Eligus, St., eulogium on, 262.
Eliot, John, his work among the Indians, 68; last words of, 329.
Eloquence, popular estimate, 235; element of power in sacred eloquence, 246, 248.
Emerson, R. W., early predilection for the ministry, 283.
Environment, molding of, 70.
Episcopos, word used interchangeably with *presbyteros*, 261.
Episcopate, early, contrasted with ecclesiastical monarchies of later times, 263.
Eusebius of Nicomedia, 27; of Cæsarea, 27.
Euripides, lines of, 121.
Evangel, the Christian, 88; significance of term, 102; scope of, 118; theme of, 106.
Exercise, physical, necessary, 310; requires time, 311; contributes to mental vigor, 311.
Experience, our mental, a series of contrasts, 130.

F

Fairbairn, Dr. A. M., of Mansfield College, on the fate of Edward Irving, 50.
Farel, influence of, over Calvin, 74.
Farrar, Archdeacon, on Jeremy Taylor 160.
Findlay, W. H., on missions in India, 216.
Finney, Charles G., trained for the law, 82; early difficulties of, 284; fearlessness of, 286; rebels against Calvinism, 278; his geniality in age, 327; power over the legal mind, 95; dying words, 330.
Firstborn, supremacy of the divine, 108.
Fletcher, John, of Madeley, on Arminius, 64.
Frith, W. P., on painting, 151.

G

Gehenna not the Greek *Tartarus*, 130.
Gideon, 60.
Gifts, preacher's distinctive, 19; physical, not to be despised, 315.
Gladstone, 96.
God, his glory written on the soul, 193.
Gomarus, F., his persecution of Arminius at Leyden, 44.
Gore, Charles, on the virtue of considerateness, 57.
Gospel, a call to repentance, 111; not simple, 115; existed eternally in archetype and idea, 144.
Government, spiritual, a gift of the Spirit, 256; simple forms of early Church, 259.
Gregory I, 22; VII, 22.

H

Hadrian, Emperor, residence in York, 31.
Hall, Robert, on Richard Watson, 97; early timidity of, 280; lofty standard of public speaking, 281; compared with Bunyan, 281; his neglect of his health, 308.
Hall, Dr. Newman, 287.
Hamerton, P., on longevity, 297; on preservation of the senses, 300.

Hatch, Dr. E., on early Christian societies, 252, on functions of early bishops, 265.
Health, influence of, on character, 297; value of, to minister, 303; neglect of, inexcusable, 304; injured by overclothing, 314.
Hearers, various types of, 163.
Heathenism, Christian, positive, 171; to be studied, 203; its attempts at self-reform, 196; imitation of Christianity, 200; its policy of persecution, 201; its effects on the minds and morals of its devotees, 205.
Henry IV, of Germany, at Canossa, 268.
Henry, Matthew, his estimation of the value of the soul, 98.
Henry, Patrick, aiding the American Revolution, 96.
Herald, ancient, dignity and authority of, 87.
Herbert, George, died singing, 330.
Heredity, its force, 71, 301.
Hermit, Peter the, 22.
Hernhutt, Moravian colony of, 294.
Hildebrand, death of, at Salerno, 331; majesty of character of, 285.
Hindu, his character, 209.
Hinduism a curse to Hindus, 113.
Holmes, Oliver W., catholic sentiment of, 39; his view of doctrine of eternal punishment, 138.
Home, influence of, 72,
Hook, W. F., a sectarian, 36.
Hooker, Richard, words of, 77; kindness of Bishop Jewell to, 64; pupil of a puritan, 78; Master of the Temple, 82; victim of domestic worry, 306.
Horton, Dr. R. F., his complaint of ecclesiastical narrowness, 42.
Howe, John, 278; chaplain of Cromwell, 95; his resignation, 28.
Hughes, Hugh P., his eloquence, 93; on apostolic succession, 38.
Hurst, Bishop, on Indian alumni, 213.
Hygiene, importance of, to ministers, 296.

I

Ideal, its value for the preacher, 91; in sermon making, 148; its power, 151; value for style, 151.
Ideas, moral, empire of, 84.
Ignatius, martyrdom of, effect on fortunes of the Christian Church, 264; letters of, 264.
Illustration, homeliness of, 158; employed by Christ, 158; examples of abstruse, 160.
Immortality, natural, of the soul, 142.
Inferno, Dante's, 170, 172.
Innocent III, 24; offers thanks for massacre of Huguenots, 269.
Intemperance, effects of, on industry and morals, 190.
Intolerance, religious, 39.
Inquiry, rational, its functions and limits, 76.
Inquisition, terror of, 270; victims of, 270; methods of, 271.

Iona, monks of, 62.
Irving, Edward, ministry of, in London, 50; sermon before London Missionary Society, 69.
Isaiah, his birth and pedigree, 71.
Itinerancy, its antiquity, 218; Methodist, founder of, 220; answers a profound need of human nature, 219; in the Middle Ages, 219; brotherhood of, 224; trials of, contrasted with settled pastorate, 225; practical present-day value of, 227; severe discipline of, 228; drawbacks of, 230; criticism of, 231.
Itinerant, early type of, 219; a wanderer in the interests of truth, 219; self-effacement of, 228.

J

Jenkins, E., his *Devil's Chain*, 166.
Jerome, St., fondness for study, 27.
Job, Book of, rewards of religion in, 18.
Jobson, F., benediction on, 290.
Judge, Christ our, 123; his qualification for office of, 124.
Juggernaut, story of, 197.
Julius II, warlike disposition of, 24.

K

Keble, John, 23.
Ken, Bishop, as a hymnist, 23.
Kingsley, Charles, his characterization of Cyril of Alexandria, 27.
Knowledge, origin of, 299; raw material of, 298.
Knox, John, eloquence of, 22; reply of, to Mary Queen of Scots, 285; his influence on Scotland, 95.

L

Latimer, Bishop, 27.
Labor, Report of Commission of, in United States, 168; its condition in Europe, 172.
Lahore, Presbyterian College of, 212.
Last Things, controversy concerning, 127.
Laud, Archbishop, 268.
Laymen, their rights abridged, 265.
Leaders, early Christian, indifferent to titles and forms of authority, 253; comparison of, in different ages.
League, Solemn (and covenant), 293.
Le Conte, Professor, optimism of, 327.
Leo I, his spiritual power, 23; confronting Attila, 94.
Leo X, his sensualism, 24; skepticism, 101.
Leo XIII, his temporizing policy, 273; his tyranny, 272.
Liberalism, no breadth in, 54; its denials fatal to high imagination in art and religion, 55; dogmatism of, 55; leaders of, 113.
Lichfield Cathedral, 62.
Life, quality and tone of, 296; breath of, 301.
Lindisfarne, monks of, 62.
London, Moncure Conway on, 170.
London, The, Magazine, on the churches of the city, 176.

Longevity, within individual control, 301; Dr. Richardson on, 302; the cumulative result of wise self-government, 303.
Longley, Archbishop, 31.
Loyola, his support of the papacy, 45.
Luther, 22; parentage of, 63, 73; his Protestantism, 63; his domestic cheerfulness, 326.

M

Macfadyen, Mrs., of Drumtochty, 152.
McIntyre, Robert, on Methodist itinerancy, 231.
McLeod, Fiona, on the great change, 332.
McTavish, the Highland preacher, 152.
Maimonides, Moses, his funeral, 125; epitaph on his tomb, 41.
Mallalieu, Bishop, on York Minster, 29.
Mamertine, prison of the, 21.
Man, doctrine of his relation to the universe, 298.
Manhood, ministerial, its necessity, 90; its value, 90; aim of the labor of the ages, 91; Christ the pledge of our completed, 121.
Manning, Cardinal, 79.
Martyn, Henry, 306.
Martyr, Justin, 81.
Masses, condition of, 168; their salvation sought, 177; neglected by the wealthy, 179; how reached, 183.
Mather, Dr. Cotton, on Rhode Island, 49.
Mazzini, Joseph, his estimate of Christ, 13.
Melanchthon, object of excessive motherly affection, 73; his learning, 22; versatility, 82.
Methodism, British and American, 52.
Milman, Dean, on Cyril of Alexandria, 27.
Milton, John, 91.
Minerva, shield of, 147.
Minister, popularity of, often incompatible with faithfulness, 243; his varied influence for good, 26; his self-adaptability, 32; in the making, 59; should be in touch with the people, 60; his sense of pathos, 289; his study of life, 316; his theme, 105; his poverty an advantage, 61; an artist, 148; his absorption in his work, 94, 150.
Ministers, early Methodist, 294; their physique, 218; premature death of, 328; immortal, 333; past compared with present, 276.
Ministry, recruits its ranks from all grades, 59; Methodist, 66; lofty ideal of, 220; against all forms of evil, 187; its condemnation of wrong definite and specific, 187; manifest destiny of, 56.
Missionary, work of, 198, 203; preparation needed, 197; problem of, 196; policy of 203; self-denial of, 216.
Missionaries, the Irish, 62; Moravian, 68.
Missions, a century of, 194; results of, 194; schools of, 196; results of missionary education in India, China, etc., 196; heathen criticism of, 197; ancient mission to England, 198; outlook of, 199.

Monica, Neander's praise of, 72.
Moscheles, anecdote of, 330.
Mohammedanism in India, 209.
Mystery, an essential part of religion. 107; the Gospel a hidden, 107.

N

Name, the Christian, origin of, 255.
Nations, their migrations, 219.
Nature, attitude toward her, 149; use of her pregnant hints, 150.
Nautch girls in India, 206.
Neander, 22; sketch of him, 236.
Nelson, John, traveling companion of Wesley, 221.
Newcastle-on-Tyne, Wesley's fondness for it, 221.
Newman, Cardinal, his eulogy on St. Peter, 32; converted under the ministry of T. Scott, 79; travels of, in Sicily, 283; his hymn, "Lead, kindly Light," 283.
Newnham on reciprocal influence of body and mind, 298.
Newton, John, 23.
New York, city of, 169, wage-earners in, 169.

O

Ochino, Bernardino, his exile, 270.
Odyssey, poor men of the, 65, 121.
Officials, Church, their names, whence derived, 260.
Orator, "born, not made," 236; orators of Christian history, 248.
Orders, monastic, powerful when poor, 69.
Otis, James, 96.
Owen, John, one of the founders of the British and Foreign Bible Society, 38.
Owen, Dr. John, Puritan, his opinion of Bunyan, 61.

P

Pacifex Maximus, 116.
Paganini, 135.
Parker, Theodore, 55.
Pascal, Blaise, 22.
Passover, Feast of, 14.
Pastorate, ideal of, only once realized, 276.
Paul, his courage, 26; his training, 71; hope of Rabbinism, 78.
Paulinus, Bishop, 30.
People, their humor, 288; victims of competition, 172; municipal corruption, 172; militarism, 188; of the saloon, 190; salvation of, its factors, 173.
Persecution, origin of, 266; the Decian, 27.
Phelps, Austin, his physical breakdown, 309.
Philadelphia wage-earners, 168.
Philanthropy, renaissance of, 178; literature of, 178.
Philanthropies, great, their rise, 38.
Phillips, Wendell, 96.
Pilgrims, the original, their religious earnestness, 293.

Pleroma, Christ the, 124.
Polity, ecclesiastical, no authorized form of, 251.
Polycarp, his rebuke of Marcion, 39, 268.
Poor, piety of the, 292.
Popularity, no sign of public usefulness, 239; often morally enervating, 241; examples of its enfeeblement, 244.
Population, rural, its depletion, 167.
Port Royalists, 22.
Posty, in *Auld Lang Syne*, 291.
Poverty, prominent in heathen religions, 69; its place and purpose in Christianity, 68.
Poverty, Peerage of, Hood's, 223.
Power, love of, an earthly passion, 266; abuse of, 264.
Preacher, personality of, 146; secret of his power, 20; his sphere various, 21; his influence for good abiding, 28; his sense of humor, 290; his faith in God's work, 249.
Preachers, great, their memories not recalled by monuments, 28.
Preaching, essential elements in, 87; power of, 95; prime object of, 161; must be adapted to the needs of the people, 162; test of a standing or declining church, 99; in Middle Ages, 101.
Priest, supplants the preacher, 100; resisted by the reformer, 100.
Proclaimer, dispensation of, 17.
Progress, measurable, 29.
Prophesying, liberty of, restrained, 265.
Prophet, his function, 17; decay of prophetic faculty, 15.
Protestantism, its relation to freedom, 34; disruption of its unity, 35; narrowness of degenerate, 47.
Prototokos, significance of, 108.
Providence, City of, 168.
Punishment, eternal, reconcilable with God's essential love, 138.
Punning, examples of, in New Testament, 289.
Punshon, Dr. W. M., 287.

Q

Quakers, their decline, 293.

R

Ranke, Leopold von, 101.
Raphael, his picture of Leo I resisting Attila, 268.
Rattenbury, John, 37.
Redruth, Wesley at, 52.
Reformer influenced by his age, 277.
Religion, revealed, encourages independence of thought, 78; sources of, 80; the great religions encourage poverty, 69; heathen, to be studied in their home aspect, 205.
Renaissance, its relation to liberty of thought, 34.
Renan, Joseph Ernest, renounces Catholic faith, 283.
Resurrection, hope of, 121.

Retribution, future, doctrine of, 129; decline of faith in, 128; various views concerning, 127; no figment of mediæval fancy, 129; taught in New Testament, 130; no theodicy in silence, 135; causes of silence, 137.
Revelation of the sons of God, 133.
Richardson, Sir B. W., on vital force, 302.
Richelieu, Cardinal, persecutes St. Cyran, 46, 267; his statecraft, 46.
Robertson, Frederick W., confronting doubters of Brighton, 95; his feeble health, 308; his patient suffering, 329; his permanent influence, 333.
Rome, Empire of, extent of, 15; government of its provinces, 16; despotism of papal Rome, 47; diplomacy of, 47; modern instances of, 272; change of policy of, 277.
Rule, Benedictine, 22.
Rutherford, Samuel, 23.

S

Sabatier, Paul, on sympathy, 186, 292.
Sallust, his Sempronia, 17.
Salmond, Professor, his eschatology, 140.
Savonarola, eloquence of, 22; as a statesman, 82; early discouragements of, 94, 280.
Schools, theological, must be adapted to the times, 75.
Sea, Northern, story of an island in, 316.
Sectarianism, narrowing influence of, on the mind, 34.
Senility, premature, 317.
Sermon, materials of, 153; its unity, 151; power of the ideal in sermon-building, 149; structure of, 156.
Service, spiritual, glory of, undiscerned, 263.
Settlement, University, in Chicago, 181.
Severus, Emperor, residence in York, 31.
Shelley on self-sacrifice, 153.
Simpson, Bishop, 97.
Simon (Peter), his poverty, 71.
Socialism, its worth and weakness, 181; Dr. W. Robertson Smith, his expulsion from Free Church of Scotland, 44.
Spencer, Thomas, of Liverpool, 329.
Spermologos in Athens, 222.
Spinoza, cursing of, 40. Renan on, 40.
Spurgeon, his early poverty, 67; early fame, 75; conversion, 79; his power as a preacher, 97; on plainness of speech, 155; his courage, 285; self-denial, 285; Quaker's estimate of him, 238; his charm as a speaker, 238; victim of affection, 309.
Stanley, Dean, quoting Bunyan, 41.
St. Francis d'Assisi, 70, 101.
St. Chad, 62.
St. Cyran, his imprisonment in Vincennes, 46.
St. Tetricus, epitaph of, 262.
Summerfield, John, his premature death, 308, 329.
System, the nervous, the borderland between man's spiritual and material nature, 300.

T

Talmud, traditions of the, 15.
Taylor, Father, of Boston, his struggles with early poverty, 66. Dr. Bartol on, 67; in old age, 327.
Taylor, Jeremy, his *Golden Grove*, 161.
Tennyson, 160.
Theodicy, none in silence, 135.
Theodore, Archbishop, 62.
Theme, unity of, 151.
Thompson, Archbishop, 31.
Tiberius, his oppression of the Roman province, 16.
Tongue of Fire, 92.
Training, ministerial, adapted to times, 75; liberal, 77; varied and comprehensive, 80.
Treffry, Richard, Jr., early death of, 308.
Truth, Christian, often unpopular, 242.
Type, conformity to ministerial, required, 35; penalties of departure from, 42.

U

Ulphilas, Bishop, 22.
Unitarianism a half truth, 37.
Unveiling, Christianity an, 134.

V

Vaga, Latin name of Wye, 223.
Vagabond, ancient types of, 223.
Versatility, St. Paul's, 81.
Von Gerok, 240.
Vulgate, the, 22.

W

Walsh, Thomas, Hebraist, his early death, 308.
Walsh, Archbishop, 274.
War, its evils, 188; cost, 189.
Wartburg, Castle of, 63.
Watson, Richard, last words of, 331.
Watts, Isaac, 23.
Way, Christians men of the, 112.
Wesley, Charles, 23.
Wesley, John, his parents, 65; home life, 65; his High Churchmanship, 79; his self-denial, 65; his failure in Savannah, 282; his reply to his accusers, 286; his theological liberalism, 52; his courage, 286; wit, 321, 221; meeting with Bishop Lowth, 321; his popularity among Churchmen late in life, 322; his vigor in age, 319; his twelve rules, 220.
Wesley, Samuel Sebastian, dying wish of, 54.
Westcott, Bishop, quoted, 15.
Whitefield, George, 22; early life, 66; excessive labors, 307; death of, 331; his eagerness to persuade men, 98.
Whittier, John G., lines of, 194; his *Barclay of Ury*, 242.
Wilberforce, William, 96.
Wilberforce, Bishop of Oxford, his advice to a court preacher, 288.
Williams, Roger, his militant disposition, 48; founder of American Baptists, 49; his varied ecclesiastical experience, 49.
Wiseman, Cardinal, letter on Catholic Unity, 47.

Wittenberg, 63.
Witness, use of the word in St. John's Gospel, 102.
Wolsey, Cardinal, condones crimes of his master, Henry VIII, 28; dies broken-hearted, 268.
Wordsworth, William, his lines on banks of the Wye, 307.
Worms, city of, 63.
Worth, moral, consciousness of, 284.
Wren, Christopher, his memorial, 28.

Wyclif, John, 22; as a diplomatist, 82; his dying protest, 94.

Y

York, city of, England, its cathedral, 30; churches of, 31; Minster described, 29.

X

Xavier, his work in India and Japan, 68; his cultivation of vermin, 305; Sir James Stephens on, 305; death of, 305.

www.ingramcontent.com/pod-product-compliance
Lightning Source LLC
Chambersburg PA
CBHW031851220426
43663CB00006B/583